To Rosie
from Mom

S. I. HAYAKAWA, Professor of Language Arts at San Francisco State College, is the editor and founder of ETC. Born in Canada, he holds degrees from the University of Manitoba, McGill University, and the University of Wisconsin. Author of the best-selling *Language in Thought and Action,* Dr. Hayakawa edited *Language, Meaning and Maturity* and *Our Language and Our World.* He is a member of the Modern Language Association and the National Council of Teachers of English.

PREMIER BEHAVIORAL SCIENCES

designed to bring to a larger reading public, at small cost, reprints of distinguished books concerning the nature of man and his conduct

ASHLEY MONTAGU
General Editor

The Use and Misuse of LANGUAGE

edited, and with a foreword
by S. I. HAYAKAWA

selections from
ETC.: A Review of General Semantics
previously published in
LANGUAGE, MEANING AND MATURITY
and
OUR LANGUAGE AND OUR WORLD

illustrations by
William H. Schneider
and
Frank Lobdell

A Premier Book
FAWCETT PUBLICATIONS, INC., GREENWICH, CONN.
Member of American Book Publishers Council, Inc.

A Premier Book published by arrangement with Harper & Brothers

Third Premier printing, January 1964

Premier Books are published by Fawcett World Library, 67 West 44th Street, New York 36, New York.
Printed in the United States of America.

CONTENTS

THE ARTS: LOW, MIDDLE AND HIGH

HUMAN INSIGHT

FOREWORD

The essays in this book are selected from the files of the quarterly journal, *ETC.: A Review of General Semantics,* of which I have been editor since its foundation in 1943. General semantics is the study of the relations between language, thought, and behavior: between *how we talk,* therefore *how we think,* and therefore *how we act.*

How We Talk

In general semantics, when we concern ourselves with how people talk, we are not worrying about the elegance of their pronunciation or the correctness of their grammar. Basically we are concerned with the adequacy of their language as a "map" of the "territory" of experience being talked about.

Here, let us say, is a child playing in a living room. One observer says, "What a good child!" Another observer, who loves furniture better than children, says, "What an unruly child!" Neither of these statements, it will be noted, gives us a descriptive "map" of the "territory" of the child's behavior. What are the speakers talking about that they should arrive at such different perceptions? If they imagine they are talking about the child, there is immediate cause for dispute: is the child well-behaved or not? If they understand that their utterances are about the state of their own minds, that is something else again. But whether the differences in perception result in dispute, the breaking off of communications, or the further exchange of communications, the outcome depends not only on *what* the speakers said, but even more importantly on *their attitudes towards their own utterances.*

What general semanticists mean by "language habits" is the entire complex of (1) how we talk—whether our language is specific or general, descriptive or inferential or judgmental; and (2) our attitudes toward our own remarks—whether dogmatic or open-minded, rigid or flexible.

How We Think

Words, then, are more than descriptions of the territory of human experience; they are evaluations. How we think and evaluate is inextricably bound up with how we talk. The behaviorist school of psychology goes so far as to assert that *all* thought is subvocal speech. It is not necessary to go quite so far in order to concede the importance of this behaviorist observation. Certainly most of thought is a matter of talking to ourselves silently. If our spoken evaluations are hasty and ill-considered, it is likely that our unspoken ones are even more so. A man says, "I don't like fish," although there are thousands of different kinds of fish, and dozens of different ways of preparing each kind. But he still "doesn't like fish"—so he avoids clams and oysters and lobsters, which are no more related to fish than snails are related to partridges. Perhaps the reader thinks this is a trivial example, but don't all prejudices work in just this way—racial, ideological, religious, natural, occupational, or regional? Like the man who "doesn't like fish," there are the ideologically muscle-bound who "don't like the profit system" whether it manifests itself in a corner newsstand or in General Motors, or who "reject government intervention in business" no matter what kind of intervention in what kinds of business for what purpose.

Hence the unexamined key-words in our thought processes, whether "fish" or "free enterprise" or "the military mind" or "the Jews" or "creeping socialism" or "bureaucracy," can, by creating the illusion of meaning where no clear-cut meaning exists, hinder and misdirect our thought. As C. S. Peirce said:

> It is terrible to see how a single unclear idea, a single formula without meaning, lurking in a young man's head, will sometimes act like an obstruction of inert matter in an artery, hindering the nutrition of the brain, and condemning its victim to pine away in the fullness of his intellectual vigor and in the midst of intellectual plenty.

How We Act

Except for the fact that we sometimes act without thinking, it would seem obvious that how we act is determined by how we think. But even when we act without thinking, our actions are likely to follow the lines laid down by our patterns of thought, which in turn are determined by the language we use.

The intellectually naive often objectify language as if it were something "out there," to be examined independently of speakers or hearers. But language, to be language, must have meaning, and meanings are not "out there." Meanings are semantic reactions that take place *in people.* A language is therefore not just the sounds and the spellings, but more importantly the whole repertory of semantic reactions which the sounds and spellings produce in those who speak and understand the language.

Alfred Korzybski (1879-1950), the founder of general semantics, maintained that the structural assumptions implicit in language are of necessity reflected in behavior:

> A language, any language, has at its bottom certain metaphysics, which ascribe, consciously or unconsciously, some sort of structure to the world. . . .
>
> Now these structural assumptions are inside our skin when we accept a language, any language. . . .
>
> We do not realize what tremendous power the structure of an habitual language has. It is not an exaggeration to say that it enslaves us through the mechanism of semantic reactions and that the structure which a language exhibits, and impresses on us unconsciously, is automatically projected upon the world around us.

The Goals of General Semantics

Alfred Korzybski was trained as an engineer and a mathematician; he also studied mental illnesses in association with the famous Dr. William Alanson White at St. Elizabeth's Hospital in Washington, D. C. His general semantics is the result of both his scientific and psychiatric studies. The theme of his famous book, *Science and Sanity: An Introduction to Non-Aristotelian Systems and General Semantics* (1933), is that the orientations of science and the orientations that result in sanity are identical. The orientations of science (as opposed to what he called "prescientific orientations") have at their heart an awareness of the linguistic components of human thought and perception. Korzybski believed that if, through general semantics, people generally could be trained in the orientations of science in the handling of all their problems (instead of just some of them), many social and personal problems now deemed to be insoluble would prove to be soluble. There is a messianic flavor to Korzybski's writings—a fact which led to the dismissal of his views in some academic circles.

Nevertheless, a number of people have agreed with Korzybski that the insights and the training provided by general semantics are extremely useful—and these people have explored the application of semantic ideas in a variety of fields. Among those interested in general semantics in the past two decades are businessmen interested in improving communication in their companies and in improving the quality of executive training; English teachers seeking to improve the reading, writing, and thinking of their students; psychologists and psychiatrists seeking improved ways of dealing with their patients; teachers of both the physical and social sciences seeking to overcome the traditional prejudices that distort the student's understanding of modern science; political leaders and social actionists trying to get deeper insight into why people behave as they do; painters and sculptors and dancers and film-makers seeking a better understanding of nonverbal symbolic processes; teachers of the handicapped and the mentally retarded studying the failures of symbolic functioning.

It has sometimes been said that even if Freud were proved wrong in almost everything he said about the unconscious, he would still remain a tremendous figure in scientific history, because he laid open an entirely new area of inquiry in the study of human behavior. The reason that general semantics has proved useful in so many fields is that Korzybski likewise introduced into the study of human behavior an entirely new area of inquiry, namely, the role of language in shaping the content of the human psyche and the influence of that process on human problems and behavior. General semantics continues to develop, because there is no end to the study of the intricate relationships between language, thought, and action.

The present sampling of various articles from *ETC.* cover a period of fifteen years. *ETC.* was started at Illinois Institute of Technology in Chicago, and soon moved to other offices in Chicago. The editorial office was transferred to San Francisco State College in 1955 when the editor became a professor in that institution. In 1961 the business office was also transferred to San Francisco State College. Thanks are due to the many people who have kept *ETC.* going over the years: first of all, the many writers; then the business staff, Edward J. MacNeal (now of New York City) and Carol Kessler (now Mrs. Samuel Russell of Reading, Pennsylvania) to 1950, the late Jean Taylor (Mrs. David M. Burrell) to 1955, Evelyn Rochetto (Mrs. Paul Rochetto, Chicago) to 1961, and the present staff, Russell Joyner and Evna Kellum; and finally my editorial colleagues: Professor Anatol Rapoport of the University of Michigan, Professor Walter E. Stuermann of the University of Tulsa, Professor Richard Dettering of San Francisco State College, and the many others, past and present, who have shared with me the tasks of editorship.

S. I. Hayakawa

What Is Semantics?

ANATOL RAPOPORT

THERE are two suffixes in our language (and similar ones in other European languages) which suggest organized knowledge. One is the venerable, academic "ology," that reminds one of university curricula and scholarship. The other is the energetic and somewhat mysterious "ics," which has a connotative flavor of magic. Where "ology" suggests academic isolation (ichthyology, philology), "ics" suggests a method of attack on life's problems. It contains a faint throwback to the ancient dreams of the philosopher's stone and of "keys" to the riddles of the universe. Ancient words ending in "ics" are mathematics and metaphysics. Of more recent origin are economics, statistics, semantics, and cybernetics.

It is usually easy to satisfy someone's curiosity about an "ology" and quite difficult to do the same for an "ics." An "ology" can often be simply explained by translating its front part from Greek or Latin (ornithology = study of birds). But doing the same with an "ics" is nowhere as satisfactory. Mathematics comes from a Greek word for "learning," and metaphysics means "beyond physics." The same difficulty appears in translating "semantics." Semantics is derived from "meaning" or "to signify." What is wanted, however, is some information on what semanticists do.

An embryologist may do a lot of things, but looking at embryos seems a significant part of his activity, just as one would expect. By analogy, many conclude that semanticists look at or for meanings; so perhaps they have to do with dictionaries. This is not so. Dictionaries are the business of lexicographers. What, then, do semanticists do?

Who Are the Semanticists?

To answer this question, let us go to the writings of those who make frequent references to semantics or to equivalent terms which have to do with the study of meaning. We find that a number of prominent thinkers have occupied themselves with this study. In England these include Whitehead, Russell, Ogden, Richards, Ayer, and others; in Austria (later scattered, fleeing from fascism), a group of writers who called themselves the Vienna Circle, which included Carnap and Frank (now in the United States), Wittgenstein (now in England), and Neurath (deceased); the United States is represented by Charles Morris, and Poland by Korzybski (deceased) and Tarski, both of whom emigrated to the United States.

The next thing to be noted is that most of these writers have confined themselves to traditional academic work; they are for the most part professors of philosophy. But Korzybski's career was an exception. By training he was an engineer; he served as an officer in the Russian army and later as a League of Nations official. He never joined a university faculty. Rather, an educational institution of a special kind was built around him. What is most remarkable is that Korzybski's work has had *direct* impact, at least in this country, on a far wider range of people than the work of the philosopher-semanticists. For one thing, it captured the fancy of a number of keen, active men who saw the practical educational implications of semantics. One of them was Stuart Chase, who had been close to Roosevelt's "brain trust"; another was S. I. Hayakawa, a student of linguistics and professor of English. Others include Irving J. Lee, whose work was in speech; Wendell Johnson, psychologist and speech specialist; Francis P. Chisholm, another professor of English. All these men were deeply interested in how people use words and how words affect those who use them. They were able to translate some of the implications of Korzybski's work (properly referred to as *general* semantics) into the language of the college freshman, the perplexed citizen, and the teacher or mother who took her work seriously.

Two of the books written by them became booming best sellers (Chase's *Tyranny of Words* and Hayakawa's *Language in Action*). Hayakawa's book, Lee's *Language Habits in Human Affairs*, and Johnson's *People in Quandaries* became standard college texts; courses in "general semantics" cropped up in colleges and universities, and even in high schools; an International Society for General Semantics has a growing membership; and the Institute of General Semantics, founded by Korzybski, has remained a going concern after his death. The Soviets have seen fit to "expose" semantics as a new low in bourgeois philosophy,[1] and there have appeared similar blasts from the "right."

In view of this widespread interest, the workers in the field owe the general public an explanation. In the writer's opinion, such an explanation has been provided in S. I. Hayakawa's article "Semantics, General Semantics, and Related Disciplines." There the history of semantics is reviewed, and the particular contribution of Alfred Korzybski is evaluated in the perspective of that history. Yet among many semanticists there seems to be a sharp division of opinion on the relation of "semantics" to "general semantics." Many academic semanticists are inclined to dismiss Korzybski's work as unsound and to view his "lay following" as a cult. "What is good in Korzybski's work," they say, "is not new, and what is new is not good."

On the other hand, many Korzybski-ites proclaim that Korzybski's work has nothing to do with semantics. They go so far as to say that the very term "general semantics" was an unfortunate choice; that had Korzybski known what confusion would arise between semantics and general semantics he would not have used it at all. Korzybski himself has maintained that while semantics belongs to the philosophy of language and perhaps to the theory of knowledge, *general* semantics belongs to empirical science; that it is the foundation of a science of man, the basis of the first "non-aristotelian system," which has had no predecessor and which no academic semanticist has ever achieved.

Thus, there is a resistance both among the "academicians" and among the Korzybski-ites against treating as part of the same intellectual current both the semantics of Whitehead, Russell, Tarski, Carnap, etc., on the one hand and the general semantics of Korzybski on the other. The academicians continue to associate semantics with the theory of signs and symbolic logic (written in a special sign language, which, like mathematics, only specialists can read). The extreme Korzybski-ites continue to talk of general semantics in terms of "nonverbal levels," "extensional devices," "semantic reac-

[1] See, for example, B. Bykhovski, "The Morass of Modern Bourgeois Philosophy," *ETC.* VI (Autumn, 1948), 1–15; see also "A Soviet Account of Semantics," pp. 347–349 of the present volume.

tions," "colloidal level," etc., and maintain that it is a far-reaching technique of psychotherapy. For the former, semantics is really an "ology"; for the latter, general semantics is definitely an "ics," with which one can finish the sentence, "It's all a matter of . . ."

This writer thinks the academicians are partly right and the Korzybski-ites are partly right. The accusations of cultism leveled against Korzybski's followers are not altogether unfounded. In the United States there is a large floating population of "truth-seekers." Many of them lack the capacity for the strenuous intellectual effort required in a fruitful pursuit of knowledge and wisdom; others lack the power of critical evaluation, which would enable them to tell the genuine from the false. Still others cannot be comfortable until they find a panacea to believe in. These people support "movements" and cults. They are as likely to "go for" Christian Science as for technocracy, for psychoanalysis as for theosophy, for the Great Books program as for dianetics. And so inevitably one finds some of them among the adherents of general semantics. Moreover, the seminars conducted by Korzybski at the Institute of General Semantics emphasized problems of personal integration, of human relations, etc., and so attracted considerable numbers of people without sufficient background to understand the philosophical implications of Korzybski's ideas. As often happens, many of these people came out of those seminars happier than when they went in. Whether they were actually helped by general semantics or by other factors cannot be determined without sufficient controls. But they went about spreading the faith, thus giving a cultist flavor to the "movement."

The accusation of dilettantism frequently leveled at Korzybski in scientific circles has a similar basis. Korzybski's aim was to place the principles of general semantics within the grasp of everyone. His was a program of "retraining nervous systems" toward greater sanity. Such a program demanded that the discipline have a primer level. Hence Korzybski's "extensional devices," which to the casual observer appear simply as eccentric punctuation habits: unrestrained use of quotation marks, hyphens, and numerical subscripts on words. Hence the "structural differential," which to many looks like a crackpot gadget. Nor was Korzybski too careful in his use of terms, which referred to various specialized branches of science in which he gave no evidence of extensive knowledge. In his major work, *Science and Sanity,* he often refers to events on the "colloidal level," to the functions of the cerebral cortex and of the thalamus, without corroborating his statements by evidence acceptable to workers in colloid chemistry or in neurophysiology. He makes a critique of the foundations of mathematics which has not impressed many mathematicians. He speaks with assurance about the power of the physico-mathematical method in science, but his work does not contain any mathematical derivations. One can understand why his book and particularly his lectures have irritated many conscientious scientists.

On the other hand, it would be a mistake not to recognize the very great importance and especially the timeliness of Korzybski's ideas. His was not a mere rehash of academic semantics with a psychiatric angle. The Korzybski-ites are right in maintaining that general semantics is considerably more than an "ology" of meaning. But in stating their case, they persist in disavowing Korzybski's intellectual debts and continue to use the characteristic Korzybskian terminology, which irritates the prejudiced academicians.

To recognize the fruitfulness of Korzybski's ideas, one must relate his work to that of the academic semanticists (over the protests of both the academic scientists and the Korzybski-ites), and one must attempt to explain it in terms other than those coined by Korzybski. This we shall attempt to do. Let us therefore first look at "ordinary" semantics and then pass to general semantics.

BASIC PRINCIPLES OF SEMANTICS

Perhaps the most important ideas in semantics (with which modern logic is intimately interlaced) are (1) the propositional function, (2) the operational definition, (3) predictive value as the criterion of truth, (4) the theory of types.

The first and last of these are largely the work of Bertrand Russell. The second and third have a long history. They emerged with the development of modern physics and are already recognizable in the work of Ernst Mach, the exponent of the "positivist" approach to physics. Rudolf Carnap (a philosopher-logician) and P. W. Bridgman (a physicist) have stated the principles of operational definition and the predictive criterion of truth in unambiguous terms.[2]

Like most great ideas, these four principles are relatively easy to grasp. One wonders how the great thinkers of past cen-

[2] See Carnap, *Philosophy and Logical Syntax* (London, 1935); Bridgman, *The Logic of Modern Physics* (New York, 1927).

turies missed them. But evidently it is the same with great ideas as with great inventions: they seem simple only after one has been shown how.

Let us take the propositional function first. Classical logic (whose founder was Aristotle) took it for granted that all judgments could be broken up into simple propositions, that is, statements in which something (a predicate) is asserted about something (a subject). Examples are *water is wet; grass is yellow; some Greeks are rich; no animal is rational.* It was also assumed that such propositions were either "true" or "false": *water is wet* is a true proposition; *grass is yellow* a false one. Logic was a set of rules for deriving propositions from other propositions. If *some Greeks are rich* is a true proposition, and *no Spartan is rich* is another true proposition, then *some Greeks are not Spartans* must also be a true proposition.

From the days of Aristotle to the nineteenth century hardly any important innovations were made in logic. Logic was considered largely a closed system (like euclidean geometry) and was taught in Western universities in much the same way Aristotle had taught it about 350 B.C.

The notion of the propositional function, however, was an innovation. The central idea of that notion is that one can make an assertion which *grammatically* looks like a proposition (a predicate asserted about a subject) but which cannot be said to be either true or false. An example of such a function is the statement *x is green.* One cannot tell, without knowing what *x* stands for, whether the statement is true or false. If *x* is grass, it is true, but if *x* is milk, it is false. The idea of the propositional function is obviously rooted in mathematics, where statements like $x^2 - 5x+6=0$ are commonplace. It is evident that this statement is true if *x* stands for 2 or 3, but is false otherwise.

The propositional function is important in the theoretical development of logic. Just as arithmetic became algebra with the introduction of symbols to stand for variables (unknown quantities), so classical logic became symbolic logic with the introduction of the propositional function and of symbols to stand for propositions. Rules were developed for operating on propositions (like the rules of algebra which operate on variables), and logic became a branch of mathematics (or, one might say, mathematics was shown to be a branch of logic). And just as mathematics found wide application in science and technology, so symbolic logic is beginning to bear fruit in the design of computing machines, for example, and some theories of the structure of the nervous system.

But the notion of propositional function has another consequence more pertinent for this discussion. It showed that practically all our judgments are made not in terms of propositions but in terms of propositional functions! Consider the statement *grass is yellow*, which looks like a proposition. If by "grass" is meant the stuff that grows in Vermont in May the statement is false, but if one means the similar thing in California in July, then it is true! But then again it is not true if by "yellow" one means the color of ripe pumpkins.

Potentially, then, the question "What do you mean?" is pertinent at all times even when the "simplest" things are talked about, because the truth of statements depends on the meaning one assigns to the terms involved. This brings us to the second notion of semantics, the operational definition.

Again we must go back to Aristotle, because he made the first rules about definitions. According to Aristotle, a definition does two things. It places the thing defined in a class and then it tells how the thing is to be distinguished from other members of its class.

"Man is a featherless biped" is an aristotelian definition. It places man in a class of two-legged animals (bipeds) and distinguishes him from other members of that class such as birds (by the qualification featherless). Aside from the fact that plucked chickens and kangaroos are also featherless bipeds (as Norbert Wiener remarks), such definitions have even more serious pitfalls. Anything can be formally defined whether it exists or not. Furthermore, the class and the distinguishing characteristics, in terms of which aristotelian definitions are made, may be no clearer than the thing defined. If the purpose of definition is to make meaning clear, then many aristotelian definitions fail to do so. If a *xyphia* is defined as a three-legged bird, and if there are no three-legged birds, then *xyphia* is just as meaningless after having been defined as before. If *worry* is defined as a species of anxiety accompanied by hypertension, the definition is useless unless "anxiety" and "hypertension" are closer to our experience than "worry."

In contrast to the aristotelian definition by "class" and "characteristic," semanticists recommended the operational definition, which is widely used in science. An operational definition tells *what to do* to experience the thing defined.

Asked to define the coefficient of friction, a physicist says something like this: "If a block of some material is dragged horizontally over a surface, the force necessary to drag it will, within limits, be proportional to the weight of the block. Thus the ratio of the dragging force to the weight is a constant quantity. This quantity is the coefficient of friction between the two surfaces." The physicist defines the term by telling *how to proceed* and *what to observe*. The operational definition of a particular dish, for example, is a recipe.

From the operational definition to the operational meaning of truth is only a step. Carnap and others distinguish two kinds of truth. One is the formal kind, based only on logical consistency within itself or with certain propositions *assumed* to be true. Carnap prefers to call propositions which are true in this sense "valid." For example, *If all x are y, and all y are z, then all x are z* is a valid proposition, because of its internal consistency independently of what *x*, *y*, and *z* stand for. The propositions of euclidean geometry are valid with respect to the postulates and axioms chosen for that geometry. One may also choose other postulates with respect to which some propositions of euclidean geometry will not be valid. Validity, then, has nothing to do with observation or experience.

A true proposition, on the other hand, must be related to some kind of experience. No amount of formal proof is sufficient to establish that grass is green. The decisive criterion is looking and experiencing greenness. In a way, the criterion involves a prediction of an experience: "Look and you will see that it is green." This is not to say, however, that "seeing is believing" is always a sound criterion. No amount of "seeing" will establish the roundness of the earth or the inverse square law of gravitation. The criteria for these "facts" are indirect. They consist of certain experiments, the results of which are *predictable* if the roundness of the earth or the law of gravity is assumed true. If we assume that the earth is round, we can predict that departing ships will seem to sink into the horizon, and that the shadow on the moon during an eclipse will have a round edge, and that one can circumnavigate the earth.

Now we come to the fourth idea in semantics, the theory of types. It was known in antiquity that formal logic can be driven into a blind alley by a number of paradoxes. A typical one is the following. Consider the statement within this square.

> Every
> statement
> in this
> square
> is
> false.

Suppose the statement is true. Then, since it is the only statement in the square, it must be false. On the other hand, suppose it is false. Then, there must be true statements in the square. But again it is the only one; so it must be true. The example is trivial, of course, but similar paradoxes arise in mathematics and make difficulties for mathematicians. Since progress in mathematics depends on its complete internal consistency, it was necessary to re-examine the logical foundations of mathematics. One of the results of this re-examination is the theory of types. The theory rests on the principle that "a class cannot be a member of itself." That is, if you make a statement about *all* statements of a certain class, the statement you have made cannot be itself considered to be in that class. This was the principle violated in the paradox just described.

PRINCIPLES OF KORZYBSKI'S GENERAL SEMANTICS

Now let us look at Korzybski's basic principles (or the non-aristotelian postulates, as they are sometimes called), on which his "non-aristotelian system" is built: (1) the principle of non-identity, (2) the principle of non-allness, (3) the principle of self-reflexiveness.

As we shall see in a moment, logically the first principle is included in the second, so that it can be omitted. But we shall also see that, from the point of view of further development of Korzybski's system, there is a very good reason for not omitting it, and even for putting it first. However, we shall look first at the second principle. To use Korzybski's figure of speech, it says, "The map does not represent all of the territory"; that is, no matter how good a map you make, you cannot represent all of the territory in it. Translated in terms of language, it means that no matter how much you say about some "thing," "event," "quality," or what not, you cannot say *all* about it. The connection between this principle and the notion of propositional function is not hard to trace. According to the latter, *grass is green* is a propositional function, because both "grass" and "green" are variables. Grass can refer to vegetation in Vermont, Kentucky, or California. Green can range over the color of canaries, emeralds, or gall. Therefore, even such simple propositions as "grass is green," "the earth is round," etc., can be true only within limits.

Now let us go back to the first principle, which can be stated as "The map is not the territory"; that is, the word is not the thing it represents. Clearly, if the map does not even *represent* all of the territory, it cannot *be* the territory. So logically there is no need to state the principle of non-identity in addition to that of non-allness. However, the development of Korzybski's non-aristotelian postulates implies far more than relations between language and fact. His big point is that the structure of our language affects the *functioning of our nervous systems,* and this is where his work departs radically from that of the "classical" semanticists. To say "the word is not the thing it signifies" is not just to indicate the obvious. It is to draw attention to a fundamental inadequacy of human behavior and to trace this inadequacy to the interaction of nervous systems with language.

According to Korzybski (and his idea is corroborated by numerous psychological and psychiatric findings), people do behave *as if* they identified words with things. Identified does not mean "equated verbally." Practically everyone will agree that the *word* Negro is not the same as Mr. Smith, to whom the label Negro is applied. Nevertheless many people, in judging Mr. Smith, react to the label rather than to Mr. Smith. To take another example, a man may react to some situation, say a rejected application for a particular job, by labeling the situation "I am a failure." He may then react to the *label* in ways that are far removed from an effective remedy of the situation.

The orientation recommended by Korzybski to free the individual from the tyranny of words was called by him *extensional.* Roughly speaking, to be extensional is to be aware of things, facts, and operations in the way they are related in nature instead of in the way they are talked about. The extensionally oriented person differentiates better than the word-minded (intensionally oriented) one. He is aware of the basic uniqueness of "things," "events," etc., and so he is more aware of *change* than the intensionally oriented person, who mistakes the fluid, dynamic world around him for the static, rigid world of labels, "qualities," and "categories" in his head.

The extensional orientation of Korzybski is quite analogous to the "operationalism" of semantics. An operational definition is essentially an extensional definition, because it tells what to *do* (instead of what to say) to bring the thing defined within the range of experience. Likewise the criterion of predictive value in establishing truth is basically extensional. According to this criterion, statements, assertions, judgments, principles—in short, all kinds of talking—are rated much as checks are rated in our economy: they are accepted if one is reasonably sure they can be backed by currency. For an extensionally minded person, words that cannot be defined by operations, and statements that do not by implication contain predictions of experience, are like checks on nonexistent accounts.

This brings us to the third non-aristotelian postulate of self-reflexiveness. An ideal map of a territory, says Korzybski, would have to include a map of itself, if the map were part of the territory. But then it would have to include the map of the map of itself, etc., without end. This principle is illustrated on some packages, on which there is a picture of the package itself, which in turn contains another picture of itself, etc. To avoid this difficulty, the principle of non-identity is extended to the more general principle of multi-ordinality. The map is not the territory. Neither is map_2 of the map_1 itself a map_1. A map of map_2 would then be a map of the third order, etc., etc. In terms of language, this means that theoretically we may have a $language_1$ about things, a $language_2$ about $language_1$, etc. As Korzybski himself points out, this principle is an outgrowth of Russell's theory of types. It has "counterparts" in classical semantics, where logicians talk about languages of different order (meta-languages). In terms of human behavior, this suggests that one may react to the world, then react to his reaction, then to reactions of higher order, etc.

Thus, Korzybski's principles have a close relation to semantic principles. It follows that the whole Korzybskian system is an outgrowth of semantics. But the Korzybskian system goes much further. When its implications are worked out, it will be as far removed from semantics as semantics is from logic, and as logic is from grammar.

Grammar deals only with word-to-word relations. It teaches how to put words together into a sentence. It is not interested in how sentences are related to each other or how they are related to facts. Logic goes further. To a logician, sentences are assertions, and he is interested in relations between assertions (if this is true, then that is true). But for the logician words need not have any meaning except as defined by other words, and the assertions need not have any relation to the world of fact. The semanticist goes further than the logician. To him words and assertions have meaning only if they are related operationally to referents. The semanticist defines not only validity (as the logician does) but also truth. The general semanticist goes the furthest. He deals not only with words, assertions, and their referents in nature but also with their effects on human behavior. For a general semanticist, communication is not merely words in proper order properly inflected (as for the grammarian) or assertions in proper relation to each other (as for the logician) or assertions in proper relation to referents (as for the semanticist), but all these together, with the chain of "fact to nervous system to language to nervous system to action."

General semantics may indeed be considered of fundamental importance in the science of man. In Gestalt psychology, phenomenological psychology, psychiatry, and cultural anthropology, the "neurolinguistic" factors of human behavior are assuming an ever greater importance. Human experience (according to the views developed in those disciplines) consists of *selecting* certain ones out of innumerable stimuli in the environment; and human behavior consists of *organizing* experiences along certain patterns. There is strong evidence that both the selecting and the organizing patterns bear a definite relation to the structure of language and to linguistic habits.

TOWARD AN EMPIRICAL SCIENCE OF MAN

Man's evaluative mechanisms are both causes and effects of the uniquely human trait, culture. Culture rather than the number of legs is what most clearly distinguishes man from other animals and plants. Already in an earlier work (*Manhood of Humanity,* New York, 1921) Korzybski had developed the idea that whereas plants live by "binding energy," animals, in addition to being energy-binders are "space-binders," and man, besides being an energy-binder and a space-binder, is also a "time-binder." This is to say, animals, by moving about, are able to seek their necessities (food and mates) in space, while man, able to transmit experience by means of symbols, thereby interacts with his ancestors and descendants over periods of time, which other animals cannot do. Man thus has an extra-corporeal mechanism of "heredity," culture. This "heredity" can work for better or for worse. If experience transmitted to successive generations is organized into true-to-fact orientations, man can become even more a master of his environment and of himself. If, on the other hand, experience is organized into false-to-fact orientations, man becomes a slave of his neurolinguistic reactions and a menace to himself.

All existing cultures are based partly on true-to-fact orientations and partly on false-to-fact orientations. A tribe may have highly efficient fishing and canoe-building techniques, but its notions of health and disease may be organized into a body of superstition, which renders it helpless in an epidemic. Our own culture has attained a high level of true-to-fact orientation with regard to technology and hygiene, but our social organization is such that technology threatens to blast us out of existence, and a great deal of our knowledge of health (especially mental health) cannot be applied.

Korzybski examined these discrepancies in the light of language behavior. He found that this behavior has a broad range in our culture. At the one extreme is the language behavior of scientists and engineers at work. This behavior is highly effective. Its tasks are to explain the world and to learn to control it whenever possible so as to satisfy specific needs. At the other extreme is the language behavior of psychotics and of people under the spell of superstition and of demagogy. Korzybski finds that the language behavior of scientists at work is in harmony with his non-aristotelian principles: scientists at work are aware of the limitations of language; they constantly put their notions and judgments to operational tests of meaningfulness and predictive value. They are aware of different orders of abstraction. The linguistic behavior of psychotics, of rigid "believers," of demagogues and of victims of demagogy, on the other hand, violates semantic principles. These individuals confuse words with things; they mix orders of abstraction, etc. The shaman of a prescientifically oriented tribe and the demagogue of the modern national state both hold their power because people react to words as if they were facts. Both word magic and demagogy aim to channelize the reactions of people to symbols, so as to make responses automatic, uncritical, immediate (what Korzybski calls "signal reactions"). Such reactions make possible gigantic sales volumes unrelated to the quality of the product; they make for persistent hostilities among groups; they make wars inevitable.

Korzybski set for himself the task of analyzing the structure of language (ranging from the language of the insane to that of the mathematical physicist) and of relating that structure to human behavior, to a theory of culture and of history. This task was a means to an end. Korzybski's ultimate goal was to construct a program of retraining human nervous systems toward more hygienic neurolinguistic habits (i.e., toward greater sanity). A description of this program can be found in *Science and Sanity* (Lancaster, Pa., 1933) and in various books which have utilized certain aspects of the program for various educational tasks.

As already stated, Korzybski preferred to think of general semantics as an "empirical science." Perhaps this emphasis on empiricism was called forth by Korzybski's displeasure at having his work confused with the purely linguistic aspects of semantics. As we have seen, there is a great deal more to general semantics than a "theory of meaning." An impartial examination of Korzybski's actual output, however, fails to reveal anything like a systematized empirical science. Doubtless Korzybski has made extensive observations, and he must have read an enormous amount. But conclusions and conjectures based on observations stretched over a half a lifetime and on what various thinkers have written do not constitute an empirical science. This does not, of course, detract from the importance of Korzybski's work. For that matter, neither was Freud's approach to behavior and personality an empirical science. Freud's work contains brilliant conjectures, fruitful generalizations, signposts for future workers; and, in the opinion of this writer, so does the work of Korzybski.

If Korzybski cannot be said to have established an empirical science, what then has he done? He has pointed a way toward the establishment of such a science. He was a precursor of an intellectual revolution which is just now beginning and which promises to match that of the Renaissance. If Korzybski is seen in this role, then the question of his originality or erudition is not important. He might have had something of the dilettante in him. He might have pretended to have more specialized knowledge than he actually had. Great portions of his outlook might be found in the works of more modest and more meticulous workers. That is not important. He was a man of vision and an apostle. Such men are all too rare in our age of specialization.

There is evidence that his vision (an empirical science of man formulated in a structural language, like that of mathematical physics) is already in the making. An attack on the problem of constructing such a science has been launched from two directions. On the one hand, the rise of automaton technology (servomechanisms, "mechanical brains," etc.) made necessary the development of a structural theory of that technology. Norbert Wiener, a leading theoretician in this field, called the theory *cybernetics*. He has pointed out that in view of the striking analogies between the behavior of automata and the seemingly "purposeful" behavior of organisms, one might well try to apply cybernetics to a theory of behavior controlled by the homeostatic functions of the nervous system. On the other hand, the new hybrid science of mathematical biology, developed largely by Nicolas Rashevsky and his associates at the University of Chicago, has made the methods of mathematical physics available in the development of a unified theory of the living organism.

It might be noted that this work has gone on independently of Korzybski, and perhaps many workers in those fields might even resent the implication of Korzybski's intellectual paternity. But one must not confine oneself to Korzybski's intellectual progeny in estimating the influence of his ideas. One must also count his "nephews," and "cousins," yes, and even his "stepchildren," whom he has repudiated and who have repudiated him. That is to say, in our culture based on a tremendously dense communication net, it is a hopeless task to trace the ancestry or the "legitimacy" of ideas. Ideas simply diffuse through our culture. They are in the air and are often picked up unconsciously and then propagated in modified form. This is why questions of priority should not in our day be taken seriously. *Relations* between ideas, however, are important. What we have attempted here is to show, not who learned what from whom, but rather what relation some leading intellectual movements of our time have to each other.

Anatol Rapoport is author of Science and the Goals of Man *(1950),* Operational Philosophy *(1953), and* Fights, Games and Debates *(1960); member of the editorial board of* Journal of Conflict Resolution *and* Behavioral Science *and associate editor of* ETC.; *professor of mathematical biology, Mental Health Research Institute, University of Michigan.*

THE ART OF COMMUNICATION

Why Discussions Go Astray

IRVING J. LEE

THE points of breakdown in group discussions are many and varied. Much of the time they coincide with the failure of participants to understand each other. Sometimes they occur when the participants understand each other too well. Very often it is by the expression of differences of opinion and interest that ideas are clarified and solutions worked out. But whenever the controversy and conflict signalize a loss of rapport, so that the participants seem to be talking at or past rather than with each other, then the differences should be recognized as disintegrative rather than productive.

A comprehensive catalogue of such disintegrative patterns is not yet available, but the following are typical: when the argument moves from the issue to the personalities; when colloquy between factions is marked by such "ego-statements" as "You're absolutely wrong," "I've had years of experience on this," "I know what I'm talking about," etc.; when a speaker identifies himself so thoroughly with an issue that criticism of it is construed as an attack on him; when one participant fails to deal with a question or argument raised by another who continues to call attention to the failure; when inaccuracy or falsification is charged; when there are discrepancies in the assertions of "the" facts, etc. It is worth noting that these do not mean that breakdown is inevitably at hand. On occasion they are manifested with maintenance of rapport.

On the assumption that the study of the sources of conflict might throw light on the processes of understanding, patterns of disintegration were looked for in fifty discussion groups. This essay summarizes some of the preliminary findings which came from focusing attention on the character of the understanding shown by the participants of what was said.

It was realized in the early phases of the investigation that "understanding" was a many-faceted phenomenon. As a working basis, six possibilities (considered neither exclusive nor exhaustive) were isolated.

Understanding$_1$ = the following of directions. A understands$_1$ a time-table, when by following the printed instructions, he is able to board the train he wants. A understands$_1$ B when he does what B tells him to do in the way B wants it done.

Understanding$_2$ = the making of predictions. A understands$_2$ B when A is able to predict accurately what nonverbal action B will take after the utterance.

Understanding$_3$ = the giving of verbal equivalents. A understands$_3$ what B says or writes when he is able to translate the verbalization into other terms which B admits are adequate approximations. A understands$_3$ B when he is able to describe what B wants in terms admitted by or acceptable to B, whether or not A wants the same thing.

Understanding$_4$ = the agreeing on programs. A under stands$_4$ B when they will undertake any agreed upon action, whether or not there is verbal agreement.

Understanding$_5$ = the solving of problems. A understands$_5$ a situation or problem when he recognizes the steps that must be taken for its solution or resolution regardless of the facilities or his ability to take such steps.

Understanding$_6$ = the making of appropriate responses. A understands$_6$ the proprieties, customs, taboos, works of art or music, poetry, architecture, etc. when his responses to them are of a sort considered appropriate by B.

SIMPLICITY AND PROPER EVALUATION

Much of the professional concern of those interested in the improvement of "understanding" in communication centers around the means whereby a speaker or writer can "say it clearly" or "put it into plain words" so that the processes occurring in understanding$_{1,2,3}$ can be facilitated. The effort is to reduce the verbal specialization, complexity, incoherence, compression, diffuseness, vagueness, generality, and impersonality by any or all of the known devices of reduction, amplification, concretion, iteration, variation, dramatization, and visualization.

Throughout the study an effort was made to determine the

relationship between the conflicts and the degree of clarity of the statements made. The method of analysis consisted mainly of questioning the participants involved both during and after the discussion for their understanding$_3$ of what was being said. Despite the incompleteness of this procedure there is some evidence that, had the speakers been trained in the rhetorical techniques of simplification and attraction, a sharper understanding$_3$ would have resulted. As the observations continued, however, it was noticed that no matter how clearly the participants said they understood$_3$ the arguments, the points of conflict still remained and, indeed, were in many instances sharpened. It was as if this rhetorical emphasis dealt with a symptomatic or marginal matter rather than with the fundamental dislocation.

After twenty of the group discussions had been analyzed and after the sectors of controversy had been re-examined, another definition was added.

Understanding$_7$ = the making of proper evaluations.[1] A understands$_7$ B, a thing, a condition, a situation, a happening, a relationship, etc. (i.e., nonverbal phenomena), or what is said about each, when his response is to it rather than to something else; when his sizing-up of anything, any situation, etc. is free of indentification of it with anything else; when his taking account of it is not affected by assumptions of which he is unaware; when what he says about the situation, etc. fits it, that is, neither distorts, disorders, oversimplifies, overcomplicates, overgeneralizes, negates, adds to, takes from, nor artificially separates it. A understands$_7$ anything, then, when his diagnosis, at any moment, is free from identifications and when he is cognizant of the structural relationships discoverable both in what is talked about and in what is said.

The emphasis in the study of the remaining thirty group discussions was turned to a descriptive listing of the kinds of misevaluations manifested. Three of the most persistent are here set out.

THE PREVENTION OF PROJECTION

Bertrand Russell introduced the term *propositional function,* concerning which Cassius J. Keyser observed that "it is, perhaps, the weightiest term that has entered the nomen-

[1] Evaluation involves an integration of the "emotional" and "intellectual," giving an organism-as-a-whole response. This analysis of the methods of proper evaluation was based on formulations developed in Alfred Korzybski's *Science and Sanity* (2nd ed., Lancaster, Pa., 1941).

clature, in the course of a hundred years." Roughly, a *propositional function* is a statement containing one or more variables. By a variable is meant a term whose meaning or value is undetermined and to which one or more values or meanings can be assigned at will. A propositional function becomes a *proposition* when a single value is assigned to the variable.

A significant characteristic of the propositional function (e.g., "x are scarce," "Shakespeare was a great writer," "Religion is an opiate," etc.) is that such a statement is neither true nor false, but ambiguous.[2] If to x is assigned the single, more definite value "Houses for rent in 1947"[3] and we say, "Houses for rent in 1947 are scarce," the propositional function has become a one-valued true proposition. "Negroes are cowards" is to be considered a many-valued statement and therefore indeterminate. But assign to the variable "Negroes" the value "Pvt. Woodall I. Marsh of Pittsburgh, of the 92nd Div., who won the Silver Star for taking twelve wounded paratroopers out of the front line to safety, fording a raging torrent in his truck, after an officer had said it couldn't be done," and the resulting statement is a proposition, but now a false one.

A rather considerable amount of the talk in the discussions was carried on in statements containing many-valued variables *as if* they were single-valued. Much too often a permanence and a specificity were assumed in the speaking, where on closer analysis there could be found only processes and varieties, even though concealed by the terms as used. Difficulties were to be expected (and they occurred) whenever the distinction was not recognized and wherever there was confidence that single values prevailed. It should be noticed that difficulty arises not because variables are used, but only when they are presumed to be something other, i.e., identified with nonvariables.[4]

[2] For a further analysis of this along with the factors of meaninglessness here omitted, see Alfred Korzybski, *op. cit.*, pp. 135-145, and Cassius J. Keyser, *Mathematics and the Question of the Cosmic Mind* (New York, 1935), pp. 4–7.

[3] Of course, since there are varying degrees of rigor in the assigning of values, "Houses for rent" can be further located and specified.

[4] This does not say that many-valued statements ought to be eliminated from use. It does say that for maximum "understanding," participants must know the difference and not respond as if one were the same as the other. Nor is there any reason why anyone must speak at all times in the rigorous mood of propositions. It is enough, in the present context, to recognize that the lack of rigor, when unnoticed, was a persistent source of one kind of disturbance.

Some surprise was shown at the San Francisco Conference on World Security when the Polish question became a source of controversy, as both the American and the Russian delegates took for granted a nonexistent singularity in value in the variable "democratic." [5] Democratic$_1$, concerned with the protection of minority opinions, is not democratic$_2$, the Soviet notion of racial equality and Communistic dominance. It is not argued that the awareness of the semantic distinction would have dissolved the difference in interests at the conference—but in terms of our findings it is believed that the awareness might at least have exposed the source of the friction which grew out of the belief of each delegation that the other was behaving badly, since had not both agreed on the necessity of "democracy" in Poland?

The mechanism involved here can be put in focus by comparison with the simplicity-clarity doctrine. This view would locate the trouble in the word "democratic," making it the "barrier rather than the medium of understanding." Our view suggests that it might be equally cogent to note the projection-response, i.e., the assumption of a listener that he knew how the term was being used.[6]

At the heart of the projection-misevaluation is the belief that there are values or meanings *in* terms. But values and meanings are assigned to terms by a human nervous system. But so pervasive is the unexamined notion that words can have exact meanings compounded in and of themselves, in the way a tree has branches, that it is often difficult to persuade a listener that in discussion the other fellow may be assigning a value to his variables which is not at all the one the listener would assign if he were speaking.

In the thirty group discussions the projection-developed conflicts arose mainly at three points: in the exploratory phase where the effort is to locate and expose the problem to be talked about; in the search-for-solutions phase where the conflicts of interests arise; and in the formula phase where effort is directed to the search for a program of action on

[5] See the statement by Dean Virginia C. Gildersleeve in *The New York Times* (Oct. 31, 1945), 21.

[6] John Buchan, commenting upon Marshal Haig's reserve, told the story of the latter's attempt to be friendly with a solitary private by a roadside: "Well, my man, where did you start the war?" Private (pale to the teeth): "I swear to God, Sir, I never started no war." "Start" is a "basic" word, but start with value$_1$ equivalent to a place of induction, is not start with value$_2$, equivalent to causing a war to begin. This is, of course, projection and by-passing at its simplest level.

which agreement can be reached. Present findings suggest that irrelevant discords which arise because of failure to uncover the individual values assigned to variables, and because of the unconscious assumption of the participants that each knows how the variables are being used by the others, are an irritating influence on the rest of the discussion.

Obstructionists, either naïve or sophisticated, can readily tie up any discussion by insisting on the fixing of all variables. This is the age-old sophistry which insists that terms be defined once and for all. But no definition can prevent a speaker from assigning other values to the variables, either by design or accident, as the discussion continues. In fact, the investigation revealed that there is most danger of by-passing when the members of the group hold fast to the belief that since the term has been given a definition everyone will use it in just that way. But it should be clear that no matter how terms are defined, the necessity of analysis for the values being assigned in the course of the talk still exists.

STATEMENTS OF FACT AND INFERENCE

A rich source of misunderstanding[7] was the belief of many of the participants in the factuality of their assertions. It was rarely sufficiently realized that a statement of fact can be made only *after* someone observes some thing or relation. Any utterance made prior to observation or when observation is not possible involves an inference or guess. One cannot speak with more than some degree of probability about what is to happen or about what happened before records were made. Nor, because of the recalcitrance of nature and life, is it possible to be factual about a host of present perplexities. Thus, in 1947, can anyone do more than conjecture about the precise cellular functions which end in cancer?

Although in discussion people are quick to assert "the" facts on any topic, it makes more than a little difference if instead of giving statements which fit observable phenomena they give their conjectured version of what was observed. An example may make the point.

[In an Ohio State Hospital] . . . the attendant yelled at a patient to get up off the bench so the worker-patient could sweep. But the patient did not move. The attendant jumped up with an inch-wide restraining strap and began to beat the patient in the face . . . "Get the hell up!" It was a few minutes before the attendant discovered that he was strapped around the middle to the bench and could not get up.[7]

The attendant observed one thing but assumed in his response something more, i.e., a reason for the patient's immobility. His analysis of the situation added to what could be observed and must, therefore, be considered inferential.

It seems unlikely that a discussion can be carried entirely on a factual basis using only statements based on the observations of the participants or anyone else. Any argument which seeks to prove that what is true of some, must be true of many, cases, which concludes that if a program did or did not work in one place, it will or will not work in an essentially similar place, which supposes that certain effects will follow from the operation of indicated causes—such typical lines of argument have an inferential basis which calls for little explication. But if conclusions and suppositions are presented *as if* they were factual and thus necessarily certain rather than tentative and probable, then an identification is at work which must affect the decisions being reached. Furthermore, if inferential utterances are passed off by participants in a discussion as if they were factual or as if they had the same degree of probability as factual statements, then there is created an atmosphere in which the search for understanding$_{4,7}$ on the issue tends to be subordinated to the vigor of the contending speakers, with the issue decided by attrition rather than by the adequacy of the assertions.

DEFINITION-THINKING

Pete Hatsuoko had been born in this country, though one of his parents had been born in Japan. He went to the public schools and received a degree from the State University. He had never been to Japan. He could not read or write Japanese. He knew only a few Japanese phrases used in family small talk. After his induction into the Army, he was assigned to the Infantry. The orientation program included talks on the nature of the enemy. The captain in charge thought Pete should give one of the talks on "The Japanese Mentality." Pete tried in all candor to explain that he knew practically nothing about Japanese life and culture, that

[7] Albert Q. Maisel, "The Shame of Our Mental Hospitals," *Life* (May 6, 1946), 105.

both his and his father's education had been received in this country. "But you're a Japanese," argued the Captain, "and you know about the Japanese. You prepare the talk." Pete did—from notes after he had read an Army handbook and a half-dozen popular magazine articles.

The evaluation of the two men may be analyzed as the prototype of a pattern which occurred frequently in the discussions. In a sense communication between them stopped when the conversation began. The issue was faced on quite different grounds by each. Pete oriented his thinking about facts. He talked in terms of them. He was, as far as is known, making statements which could have been verified or at least investigated. The Captain, on the other hand, seemed preoccupied with associations stirred up inside his nervous system by an accident of phrasing. The verbal classification "Japanese" received his attention so that Pete's talking was neglected. It was as if the label Japanese served as a stimulus pushing off the Captain's thinking in a direction removed from the situation. The direction can be plotted by his definition: "A Japanese is a person who knows about the Japanese. It follows, therefore, that Pete Hatsuoko is a person who knows about the Japanese. It follows, therefore, that Pete Hatsuoko can give the talk. Other factors in the situation need not be considered."

The Captain's misevaluation can be viewed as a response to his private verbal definition as if it were something more. The point being made is not that there is anything sinister in the Captain's private conjuring up of images. It is enough to note that the behavior which resulted was of a kind very different from that which would have taken account of the outside phenomena. Furthermore, decisions made on the basis of verbal associations, no matter how elaborate, are not the same as nor commensurate with those derived from consideration of facts. The point, in short, is this: evaluations based on the private elaboration of verbal formulae are not the same as nor should they be equated with evaluations based on verifiable descriptions or observations.[8]

[8] An approach to (but not the same as) this distinction may be seen in the somewhat neglected insight of William James that most of the civilized languages except English have two words for knowledge, e.g., *savoir* and *connaître, wissen* and *kennen,* or *knowledge-about* and *knowledge-of-acquaintance.* The latter is derived from direct experience of fact and situation; the former arises from reflection and abstract (i.e., verbal) thinking.

What is important here is not the particular dodging of the issue by the Captain, but that this is a type of reaction which is in evidence in a very wide variety of human situations. Two examples are given.

According to a popular account, George Westinghouse designed a train brake operated by compressed air. After it was patented he struggled to convince railroad men of his invention's value. Cornelius Vanderbilt of the New York Central is said to have replied: "Do you mean to tell me with a straight face that a moving train can be stopped with wind?"

The mechanism of the misunderstanding$_7$ may be generalized thus:

1. The issue was presented by reference to something nonverbal and observable.

2. The reply was oriented by a verbal definition. "What is wind? Something less solid than iron. A nonmassive thing like wind cannot stop an iron train. Therefore the proposal is to be dismissed." Our discussion experience suggests that the misunderstanding$_7$ would move directly to overt conflict were the conclusion to be personalized by some such assertion by Vanderbilt as, "Westinghouse, you're a fool."

That this sort of generalized verbalistic orientation to situations is not without its significance in human affairs is, perhaps, sharply presented in Hartley's study of the attitudes of 500 students, using a slightly modified form of the Bogardus Social Distance Scale with the names of some 35 ethnic groups. In the list were included the names of three entirely imaginary nationalities: Danirean, Pirenean, Wallonian. It was found that on the average there was as much prejudice directed against the "none-such" groups as against any other. One concludes that the thinking was in terms of the words, since there were no facts on which the thinking could be based. Or as the investigator puts it: "From the point of view of the experience of students, they must represent groups completely unknown in reality. Even if some students may have chosen to consider the Pireneans to be people who live in the Pyrenees; the Wallonians, Walloons; and the Danireans something else; the fact that they tended to do this is in itself significant. In reality there are no such groups, and for the attributes an individual may assign to them, we must look to the individual for the explanation, not to the group." [9]

[9] Eugene Hartley, *Problems in Prejudice* (Morningside Heights, N. Y., 1946), p. 26.

The identification of these two broadly characterized modes of thinking in the discussions was rarely as neatly etched or as readily explainable as in these examples, in which the point of conflict is readily evident and from which the heat of controversy is absent. For the most part the misevaluation was concealed by the complexity of the subjects under discussion. When the topics had to do with government and religious activities, labor unions, propaganda, prejudice, taxation, health and social insurance, etc., the argument on even the local and specific issues was often observed to develop around a backlog of readily defined associations which the participants had on the terms "communism," "bureaucracy," "labor racketeers," "big business," "government spending," "Wall Street," etc., quite apart from the fitness of their formulations with the immediate and particular aspect of the topic being talked about.

In one group during the course of the study an attempt was made to correct the misunderstanding$_7$ of the participants. That group, which was observed in five different discussions, was made up of people who manifested to an unusual degree this orientation by definition. The leader, a man of some experience, had on occasion sought to move the talk from the definition to the factual level and for his effort was accused of taking sides. In an attempt to explain the type of reaction which was producing unnecessary strains he set up a simple demonstration by means of a conventional formula. They had been discussing the advisability of continuing the Fair Employment Practices Commission. Three recorded speeches, each favoring the continuation of the FEPC, were played. The group was then asked to rank the speakers A, B, and C according to the effectiveness, logical soundness, etc., of the argument. B was judged the best with A and C following. A month later the three speeches were replayed for the group with but one change in the instructions. It was explained that speaker B was a Negro. A was then judged the most effective with C second and B third. Such a result can, perhaps, be accounted for in many ways. But the notion that the members of the group in the second playing of the records were diverted from the speeches to a concern with the definition-associations of the word Negro is nevertheless suggestive.[10]

[10] In this group there was an occasion when there were signs of what could be called "pathological misunderstanding$_7$." This occurred when the leader tried to account for their different responses to the same recorded speeches. A highly verbalized, aggressive member pro-

CONCLUSIONS

These three types of reaction which lead to misunderstanding$_7$ by no means exhaust those which have been catalogued. They are presented as indications of a source of conflict and breakdown in a rather limited series of discussion situations.

Suppose participants could be so trained that they did not project their own values into variables, did not respond inferentially as if they were responding factually, and did not identify definition with fact-thinking, etc., would it follow that problems and disagreements in discussions would be thereby solved or resolved? Little in our findings so far could either support or raise doubts about such a conclusion. What is conceivable is this: the study of the sources of misunderstanding$_7$ might, if the lessons were well learned, keep people from the moments when their talk leads to unnecessarily created controversy. Such antisepsis might, perhaps, create the atmosphere in which solutions become possible. Only then would it be desirable to explore the means leading to understanding$_{4,5}$.

It is not yet clear to what extent on-the-ground training in the patterns of proper evaluation will lead to a reduction in the points of disintegration in group discussions. The possibility of locating and charting such points, however, suggests that discussion leaders might well be made more sensitive to the signs of their development. Study might then move to the investigation of means by which such oncoming conflicts can be arrested or deflected.

One further conclusion seems inescapable. Where the basic orientation of a culture makes few semantically critical demands, it will not be surprising if men are isolated from each other by their very modes of communication. This is but a way of implying that progress in "understanding" does not require either the correction or simplification of the language in use, or the creation of special abridgments, but rather that

---

ceeded to lose his temper, even threatening the leader with physical harm for his statement that "to change one's attitude because of the word Negro was not quite sensible." Such an occurrence leads one to wonder whether a person, when unaware of the distinction, can become so immersed in definition-thinking, so habituated to identifying it with fact-thinking, that he may be rendered incapable of facing facts even when they are shown–much less talked about. In this state, identifications become evidence of a kind of unsanity.

progress depends instead on a reorientation of attitudes toward the verbalizing process itself.

The late Irving J. Lee (1909–1955) was professor of public speaking, School of Speech, Northwestern University, and author of Language Habits in Human Affairs *(1941),* The Language of Wisdom and Folly *(1949),* How to Talk with People *(1952), and* Customs and Crises in Communication *(1954). His posthumously published* Handling Barriers in Communication *(1957), a workbook in the application of general semantics to practical business situations, written in collaboration with Laura L. Lee, is widely used in management training programs.*

Barriers to Communication Between Men

F. J. ROETHLISBERGER

IN THINKING about the many barriers to personal communication, particularly those that are due to differences of background, experience, and motivation, it seems to me extraordinary that any two persons can ever understand each other. Such reflections provoke the question of how communication is possible when people do not see and assume the same things and share the same values.

On this question there are two schools of thought. One school assumes that communication between A and B, for example, has failed when B does not accept what A has to say as being fact, true, or valid. The goal of communication is to get B to agree with A's opinions, ideas, facts, or information.

The position of the other school of thought is quite different. It assumes that communication has failed when B does not feel free to express his feelings to A because B fears they will not be accepted by A. Communication is facilitated when on the part of A or B or both there is *a willingness to express and accept differences.*

As these are quite divergent conceptions, let us explore them further with an example. Bill, an employee, is talking with his boss in the boss's office. The boss says, "I think, Bill, that this is the best way to do your job." Bill says, "Oh yeah!" According to the first school of thought, this reply would be a sign of poor communication. Bill does not understand the best way of doing his work. To improve communication, therefore, it is up to the boss to explain to Bill why his way is the best.

From the point of view of the second school of thought, Bill's reply is neither a sign of good nor bad communication.

Bill's response is indeterminate. What Bill means, the boss has an opportunity to find out if he so desires. Let us assume that this is what he chooses to do, i.e., find out what Bill means. So this boss tries to get Bill to talk more about his job while he (the boss) listens.

For purposes of simplification, I shall call the boss representing the first school of thought "Smith" and the boss representing the second school of thought "Jones." In the presence of the so-called same stimulus, each behaves differently. Smith chooses to *explain,* Jones chooses to *listen.* In my experience Jones's response works better than Smith's. It works better because Jones is making a more proper evaluation of what is taking place between him and Bill than Smith is. Let us test this hypothesis by continuing with our example.

THE ASSUMPTIONS, PERCEPTIONS, AND FEELINGS OF SMITH[1]

Smith assumes that he understands what Bill means when Bill says, "Oh yeah!" so there is no need to find out. Smith is sure that Bill does not understand why this is the best way to do his job, so Smith has to tell him. In the process let us assume Smith is logical, lucid, and clear. He presents his facts and evidence well. But, alas, Bill remains unconvinced. What does Smith do? Operating under the assumption that what is taking place between him and Bill is something essentially logical, Smith can draw only one of two conclusions: (1) either he has not been clear enough, or (2) Bill is too damned stupid to understand. So either he has to "spell out" his case in words of fewer and fewer syllables, or give up. Smith is reluctant to do the latter, so he continues to explain. What happens?

If Bill still does not accept Smith's explanation of why this is the best way for him to do his job, a pattern of interacting feelings is produced of which Smith is often unaware. The more Smith cannot get Bill to understand him, the more frustrated Smith becomes and the more Bill becomes a threat to his logical capacity. Since Smith sees himself as a fairly reasonable and logical chap, this is a difficult feeling to accept. It is much easier for him to perceive Bill as uncooperative or stupid. This perception, however, will affect what Smith says and does. Under these pressures Bill comes to be evaluated more and more in terms of Smith's values. By this

[1] For the concepts I use to present my material I am greatly indebted to some very interesting conversations I had with my friend, Irving Lee.

process Smith tends to treat Bill's values as unimportant. He tends to deny Bill's uniqueness and difference. He treats Bill as if he had little capacity for self-direction.

Let us be clear. Smith does not see that he is doing these things. When he is feverishly scratching hieroglyphics on the back of an envelope, trying to explain to Bill why this is the best way to do his job, Smith is trying to be helpful. He is a man of good will and he wants to set Bill straight. This is the way Smith sees himself and his behavior. But it is for this very reason that Bill's "Oh yeahs" are getting under Smith's skin. "How dumb can a guy be?"

Unfortunately, Bill will hear this more than Smith's "good intentions." Bill will feel misunderstood. He will not see Smith as a man of good will trying to be helpful. Rather he will perceive him as a threat to his self-esteem and personal integrity. Against this threat Bill will feel the need to defend himself at all cost. Not being as logically articulate as Smith, Bill expresses this need by saying, "Oh yeah!"

ASSUMPTIONS, PERCEPTIONS, AND FEELINGS OF JONES

Let us leave this sad scene between Smith and Bill, which I fear is going to terminate by Bill either leaving in a huff or being kicked out of Smith's office. Let us turn for a moment to Jones and see what he is assuming, seeing, hearing, feeling, doing, and saying when he interacts with Bill.

Jones, it will be remembered, does not assume that he knows what Bill means when he says "Oh yeah," so he has to find out. Moreover, he assumes that when Bill said this, he had not exhausted his vocabulary or his feelings. Bill may not necessarily mean one thing; he may mean several different things. So Jones decides to listen.

In this process Jones is not under any illusion that what will take place will be essentially logical. Rather, he is assuming that what will take place will be primarily an interaction of feelings. Therefore, he cannot ignore the feelings of Bill, the effect of Bill's feelings upon him, or the effect of his feelings upon Bill. He cannot ignore his relationship to Bill. He does not assume that Bill's attitude toward him makes no difference to what Bill will hear or accept. Therefore, Jones will be paying strict attention to all of the things Smith has ignored. Jones will be addressing himself to Bill's feelings, his own, and the interactions between them.

Jones will, therefore, realize that he had ruffled Bill's feelings with his comment, "I think, Bill, this is the best way to do your job." So instead of trying to get Bill to understand him, he decides to try to understand Bill. He does this by encouraging Bill to speak. Instead of telling Bill how he should feel or think, he asks Bill such questions as, is this what you feel, is this what you see, is this what you assume? Instead of ignoring Bill's evaluations as irrelevant, not valid, inconsequential, or false, he tries to understand Bill's reality as Bill feels it, perceives it, and assumes it to be. As Bill begins to open up, Jones's curiosity is piqued by this process. Instead of seeing Bill as stupid, he perceives Bill as quite an interesting guy.

This is what Bill hears. Therefore, Bill feels understood and accepted as a person. He becomes less defensive. He is in a better frame of mind to explore and re-examine his own perceptions, feelings, and assumptions. In this process he perceives Jones as a source of help. Bill feels free to express his differences. He feels that Jones has some respect for his capacity for self-direction. These positive feelings toward Jones make Bill more inclined to say, "Well, Jones, I don't quite agree with you that this is the best way to do my job, but I'll tell you what I'll do. I'll try to do it that way for a few days, and then I'll tell you what I think."

Conclusions

I grant that my two orientations do not work themselves out in practice in quite as simple or neat a fashion as I have been able to work them out on paper. Bill could have responded to Smith in many other ways. He might even have said, "O.K., boss, I agree that your way of doing my job is better." But Smith still would not have known how Bill felt when he made this statement or whether Bill was actually going to do his job differently. Likewise, Bill could have responded to Jones in a way different from my example. In spite of Jones's attitude, Bill might still be reluctant to express himself freely to his boss.

The purpose of my examples has not been to demonstrate the right or wrong way of doing something. My purpose has been to provide something concrete to point to when I make the following generalizations:

1. Smith represents to me a very common pattern of misunderstanding. It does not arise because Smith is not clear enough in expressing himself. It arises because of Smith's

misevaluation of what is taking place when two people are talking together.

2. Smith's misevaluation of the process of personal communication consists of certain very common assumptions. Three of these very common assumptions are (a) that what is taking place is something essentially logical; (b) that words in themselves apart from the people involved mean something; (c) that the purpose of the interaction is to get Bill to see things from Smith's point of view.

3. Because of these assumptions, a chain reaction of perception and negative feelings is engendered which blocks communication. By ignoring Bill's feelings and by rationalizing his own, Smith ignores his relationship to Bill as one of the most important determinants of the communication. As a result, Bill hears Smith's *attitude* more clearly than the logical content of Smith's words. Bill feels that his individual uniqueness is being denied. His personal integrity being at stake, he becomes defensive and belligerent. As a result, Smith feels frustrated. He perceives Bill as stupid. As a result he says and does things which only provoke more defensiveness on the part of Bill.

4. In the case of Jones, I have tried to show what might possibly happen if we made a different evaluation of what is taking place when two people are talking together. Jones makes a different set of assumptions. He assumes (a) that what is taking place between him and Bill is an interaction of sentiments; (b) that Bill—not his words in themselves—means something; (c) that the object of the interaction is to give Bill an opportunity to express freely his differences.

5. Because of these assumptions, a psychological chain reaction of reinforcing feelings and perceptions is set up which facilitates communication between him and Bill. When Jones addresses himself to Bill's feelings and perceptions from Bill's point of view, Bill feels understood and accepted as a person; Bill feels free to express his differences. Bill sees Jones as a source of help; Jones sees Bill as an interesting person. Bill in turn becomes more co-operative.

6. If I have identified correctly these very common patterns of personal communication, then some interesting hypotheses can be stated:

(a) Jones's method works better than Smith's not because of any magic, but because Jones has a better map than Smith of the process of personal communication.

(b) The practice of Jones's method, however, is not merely

an intellectual exercise. It depends upon Jones's capacity and willingness to see and accept points of view different from his own, and to practice this orientation in a face-to-face relationship. This practice involves an emotional as well as an intellectual achievement. It depends in part upon Jones's awareness of himself; it depends in part upon the practice of a skill.

(c) Although our colleges and universities try to get students to appreciate intellectually points of view different from their own, very little is done to help them to implement this general intellectual appreciation in a simple face-to-face relationship—at the level of a skill. Most universities train their students to be logical, lucid, and clear. Very little is done to help them to listen more skillfully. As a result, our educated world contains too many Smiths and too few Joneses.

(d) The biggest block to personal communication is man's inability to listen intelligently, understandingly, and skillfully to another person. This deficiency in the modern world is widespread and appalling. In our universities, as well as elsewhere, too little is being done about it.

In conclusion, let me apologize for acting toward you like Smith. But who am I to violate a long-standing academic tradition!

Presented on October 11, 1951, at Northwestern University's Centennial Conference on Communications, and published in ETC. *in 1952. F. J. Roethlisberger is co-author of* Management and the Worker *(1939), author of* Management and Morale *(1941) and* Training for Human Relations *(1954), and co-author of* The Motivation, Productivity and Satisfaction of Workers *(1958). He is the Wallace Brett Donham Professor of Human Relations, Harvard Graduate School of Business Administration.*

Semantic Difficulties in International Communication

EDMUND S. GLENN

IT IS too often assumed that the problem of transmitting the ideas of one national or cultural group to members of another national or cultural group is principally a problem of language. It is likewise assumed that that problem can always be solved by the use of appropriate linguistic techniques—translation and interpretation. A constant and professional preoccupation with the problem of international communication has convinced me of the fallacy of this point of view.

Patterns of Thought

Both an eminent professional philosopher, Professor Max Otto, and a very prominent layman, President Eisenhower, have stated that each man has a philosophy, whether or not he is aware of that fact. This means of course that people think in accordance with definite methods or patterns of thought. The methods may vary from individual to individual and even more from nation to nation.

Philosophical controversy is a historical fact. It is a mistake to believe that philosophical differences of opinion exist only at the level of conscious and deliberate controversies waged by professional philosophers. Ideas originated by philosophers permeate entire cultural groups; they are in fact what distinguishes one cultural group from another. The individuality of, for instance, Western culture, or Chinese culture, cannot be denied. The fact that when speaking of the English, the Americans, the French, or the Spanish, we tend to use expressions such as "national character" should not blind us to the fact that what is meant by "character" is in reality the embodiment of a philosophy or the habitual use of a method of judging and thinking. Thus the French describe themselves as Cartesian; the English and the Americans seldom describe themselves, but still they act consistently in such a manner as to be described by others as pragmatic or empirical. Professor Karl Pribram writes,

> Mutual understanding and peaceful relations among the peoples of the earth have been impeded not only by the multiplicity of languages but to an even greater degree by differences in patterns of thought—that is, by differences in the methods adopted for defining the sources of knowledge and for organizing coherent thinking.
>
> No mind can function to its own satisfaction without certain assumptions regarding the origin of its basic concepts and its ability to relate these concepts to each other. These assumptions have undergone significant changes in the course of time and have varied more or less among nations and among social groups at any given time. These differences in methods of reasoning have generated tension, ill-feeling, and even hatred.

The determination of the relationship between the patterns of thought of the cultural or national group whose ideas are to be communicated, to the patterns of thought of the cultural or national group which is to receive the communication, is an integral part of international communication. Failure to determine such relationships, and to act in accordance with such determinations, will amost unavoidably lead to misunderstandings.

Soviet diplomats often qualify the position taken by their Western counterparts as "incorrect" *nepravilnoe.* In doing so, they do not accuse their opponents of falsifying facts, but merely of not interpreting them "correctly." This attitude is explicable only if viewed in the context of the Marxist-Hegelian pattern of thought, according to which historical situations evolve in a unique and predetermined manner. Thus an attitude not in accordance with theory is not in accordance with truth either; it is as incorrect as the false solution of a mathematical problem. Conversely, representatives of our side tend to propose compromise or transactional solutions. Margaret Mead writes that this attitude merely bewilders many representatives of the other side, and leads them to accuse us of hypocrisy, because it does not embody any ideological position recognizable to them. The idea that there are "two sides to every question" is an embodiment of nominalistic philosophy, and is hard to understand for those unfamiliar with this philosophy or with its influence.

Or again, on a slightly different plane: a simple English "No" tends to be interpreted by members of the Arabic culture as meaning "Yes." A real "No" would need to be emphasized; the simple "No" indicates merely a desire for further negotiation. Likewise a nonemphasized "Yes" will often be interpreted as a polite refusal.

Not all patterns of thought, or rather not everything in patterns of thought, is due to the influence of well-defined methodologies. Association of ideas plays a great part in thought; thus, clearly, each man's thought is to a large extent a function of this man's past.

Thus for instance, the word "colonialism" carries particularly irritating connotations to most Americans whereas it carries no such connotations to most Englishmen, Frenchmen, or Dutchmen. The reason for this is obviously anchored in history. It may not necessarily be, on the part of the Americans, the effect of a fully thought out political theory, but may be a simple association of ideas based on verbal habits which describe the American Revolution as the rising of "colonies" against an "empire."

DENOTATION AND CONNOTATION

Problems of this type appear in a much more complicated form whenever two words in two different languages have the same denotation but different connotations.

Thus for instance, the French word *"contribuable"* and the English word "taxpayer" denote the same thing, but their connotations are not identical. "Taxpayer" is a word descriptive of physical action, of something which might have been seen with the eyes. It evokes the image of a man paying money at, for instance, a teller's window. *"Contribuable,"* on the contrary, embodies an abstract principle. It evokes not an image but a thought, the thought that all citizens must contribute to the welfare of the nation of which they are a part.

Let us consider for a moment the connotations of these two words in the context of the North Atlantic Treaty Organization. A normal reaction on the American side will be: Does the man who pays get a fair return on his money? Or, in other words, is the Mutual Assistance Program really the best way of getting the most security for the least cost? A typical reaction on the French side will be quite different: Does everyone contribute equally to the common cause? Are the Americans as deeply and personally involved as the

French? I would be surprised if some of the differences of opinion which arose at various moments within NATO between the United States and France were not due to a large extent to this particular semantic difficulty.

The Role of Language

The preceding paragraph showed how patterns of thought may influence language and in turn be influenced by it. Both "taxpayer" and "*contribuable*" are comparative neologisms. If a certain method of word formation—by intension—was chosen by the French, it is because it corresponded to the pattern of thought prevalent in France. If another method of word formation—by extension—was chosen by the English, it is because it corresponded to their most general pattern of thought. Thus, peculiarities of language may constitute good indications of the prevalent manner of thinking.

However, once created, words and expressions assume an active role and contribute to the fashioning of thought. Thus two types of situations arise:

1. Cases where a given language is capable of expressing various shades of meaning and where the pattern of expression selected by given individuals provides a clue for the determination of their pattern of thought.

2. Cases where a certain combination of denotation and connotation cannot be obtained in a simple manner in a given language.

An example of the first case may be found in the following expressions: "What should we do under the circumstances?" and "What does the situation require?" Although the denotations of these two questions are just about identical, the answers, influenced in part by connotations, may tend to be different. The point is that although one of these two forms will appear more natural than the other, the English language is capable of using both.

The following occurrence may be presented as an example of the second case: At an international conference which took place a few years ago and in which both the United States and the Soviet Union participated, it became rapidly apparent that the Soviet Union would not sign the agreement in preparation. The reason for it was a disagreement in substance, which would not be overcome. The Russians, however, continued to participate in the work of the various committees, and in particular of the drafting committee, mainly it seemed in order to preserve diplomatic niceties. Their representatives were seldom heard from.

Thus, considerable surprise was created when a seemingly unimportant proposal by the U.S. delegate resulted in an outburst of violent Soviet opposition. Even more surprising was the attitude of most Europeans and in particular of the French who publicly supported the United States but privately stated that it was a mistake to have backed the Soviets against the wall by an attitude which they described as rigid and overbearing. The proposal of the U.S. delegate consisted in inserting in the preamble to the proposed agreement a clause taken from another instrument and containing the expression "expanding economy."

I would suggest the following explanation for this incident: the expression "expanding economy" is neutral with respect to the aristotelian categories of accident and essence. An

Disputants Unscathed after a Volley of Semantic Blanks at Close Range

"expanding economy" may be an economy which happens to be expanding because of various outside influences, or else an economy which is expanding because of characteristics inherent to its nature.

In Russian "expanding economy" becomes *rasshiryayushchiyasya ekonomiya*" in which the reflexive form is used. Although it would be incorrect to say that "*rasshiryayushchiyasya*" has the denotation of the English expression "self-expanding" it unquestionably carries a connotation which will lead a Russian-speaking listener to conclude that "expanding economy" means an economy expanding for reasons inherent to its nature.

Thus in this case language itself directed the attention of the listener away from one possible explanation and in the direction of another. To compound the confusion the difference between accident and essence is much more important to a person whose mind follows the Marxist-Hegelian patterns than to a person whose mind follows an empirical or pragmatic bent. The fact that an economy is expanding may warrant a certain type of action in the eyes of the empiricist, whichever be the cause of the expansion of the economy. To a Hegelian an economy expanding for accidental causes is bound to reverse itself unavoidably and rapidly.

Now it so happens that Marxist theory rules that the economy of the Western world must contract and cannot expand. Thus the recognition of an inherently expanding character in this economy, and this is an official document, could not fail to appear completely unacceptable to a Soviet delegate.

CLASSIFICATION OF PATTERNS OF THOUGHT

The problem of defining, describing and analyzing patterns of thought is not the only one which needs to be faced in the field of international communications. Questions such as translation *proprio motu*, choice of media and levels of approach, etc., also deserve attention. However, as they have been less neglected than were the problems of basic philosophical, ethnical, anthropological and linguistic determinations, they will be considered outside the scope of this paper.

I will deal here only with the analysis of pronouncements made by persons belonging to the Western cultural world and using one of the European languages. I do not feel competent at the present moment to do any work which would extend beyond the boundary defined above. In consequence, the classifications suggested below will be such as to help in analyzing a field limited to one culture, albeit an important one. Three basic groups of criteria will be used in the sample analysis at the end of this paper.

1. PATTERNS OF REASONING. Professor Karl Pribram, who has pointed out the importance of linguistically determined assumptions in the formation of concepts, distinguishes, in his book *Conflicting Patterns of Thought*, the following four patterns of reasoning.

A. *Universalistic reasoning.* Universalistic reasoning is based on the premise that the human mind is able to grasp directly the order of the universe. Reason is credited with the power to know the truth with the aid of given general concepts and to establish absolutely valid rules for the organization of human relationships in accordance with these concepts. Universalistic reasoning proceeds from the general to the particular; it believes that general concepts, or universals, possess a reality independent from those of their components or constituents. The best way to determine what will happen in a given case is to know what happens in a more general category and then to determine what particular modifiers make the case in question a slight exception to the general rule.

B. *Nominalistic, or hypothetical, reasoning.* Nominalistic philosophy rejects the belief that general concepts have a reality of their own; instead it considers them merely as names, as convenient categories, more or less arbitrarily established by human minds. Reasoning proceeds from the particular to the general. Any exercise in pure reason establishes merely a hypothesis which must be verified by concrete experience.

Although these descriptions of patterns of thought may give the impression of dealing with abstract and complex reasonings, the influence of the patterns of thought described above may be found also at very concrete levels. Thus, for example, French visitors to New York are in general highly critical of the New York subway. What repels them is not the dirt or the crowding, but the evident lack of comprehensive planning in the geographical distribution of lines. For instance, there is no subway line which would take one from the business district around Wall Street to the new business district around Rockefeller Center, or from the Cloisters to the Metropolitan Museum of Art. The argument that the New York subway is the one which carries the greatest number of persons the most rapidly over the greatest distances from home to work and from work home does not impress the French visitors overly much.

On the contrary, the Paris Métro covers all of Paris like a spider web. Convenient changeover stations make it possible to go from any monument to any other. At the same time the Métro strikes the American visitor as almost unbelievably slow. It does not reach very far into the suburbs, where many people live, and its routes do not necessarily follow the pattern of home-to-work and work-to-home connections.

I will put it that the Paris Métro is based on the universalistic concept of a means of transit designed to provide for the needs of a city, considered as such, or as a universal, a collective noun. Lines run from one point of interest to another, no part of the city being deprived of a means of communication with all of the other parts; at the same time considerations such as the density of traffic are almost completely disregarded. On the contrary the New York subway is nominalistic; there is no network planned to cover a collective entity, the city; on the contrary, lines are built in such a way as to do the most possible good to the greatest possible number of individuals considered as such. It is not much help to those who want to go from one residential area to another—but then people go fairly seldom from one residential area to another. On the contrary, it is every day that people go from home to work and from work home, and the New York subway is planned according to this consideration.

The names selected in each case by popular usage express the same preoccupation as the planning. "Metro" is an abbreviation of "*métropolitain*" or "metropolitan." The French language has resources which would have enabled Parisians to have selected a name such as "subway," but they did not choose to do so. Likewise English has the word "metropolitan," and the official titles of the various subway organizations in New York include words such as "transfer," "transit," and "system," yet the names chosen by the public are "subway," "el," or in Britain, "underground" or "tube."

It might be noted that "*chemin de fer*" is etymologically as well as factually similar to "railroad." But then, French railroads have the same characteristics from the point of view of planning as does the New York subway. Rail lines follow lines of probable maximum density which in France means that they radiate from Paris to the provinces. At the same time the network is not completed by transversal roads; the shortest way of getting from one provincial town to another may very often be the long way through Paris. This state of affairs was always considered illogical by the French and was violently criticized by them. As a result of this criticism it has been corrected to a large extent. The same criticism might have been leveled against American railroads. I remember being told that the best way to get from Sheridan, Wyoming, to San Francisco was through Seattle. Yet the criticism which might have been leveled at the American roads are in fact never heard. The American public understands that it is not economical to provide trains for occasional travel along low-demand routes.

Now it so happens that the French railroads were started by English capital and planned under English inspiration:

they even run on the left whereas everything else in France runs on the right. Thus even this exception seems to confirm the rule: the fact that France is by and large a universalistic country does not mean that nominalism is entirely without influence there.

C. *Intuitional or organismic reasoning.* This type of reasoning stresses intuition rather than systematic cogitation. It is thus in a position to ignore some of the basic opposition between nominalism and universalism. It considers that the relationship between a collectivity and its members may be compared to the relationship between a biological organism and its component cells. Organismic reasoning opposes intuitive to discursive consciousness and claims that reliance on one's intuition enables man to be "independent yet subject to one's duties" (Joel). It is often associated with extreme nationalism and is prevalent in Germanic and Slavic Central Europe.

D. *Dialectic reasoning.* Hegelian dialectics are derived from universalism and, like universalism, believe in the possibility of a full understanding of the universe through reason. "But, according to the principles of dialectics, comprehension of the ever-changing nature of the phenomena and the flux of events can not be achieved with the aid of rigid concepts, alleged to be implanted in the human mind. The course of events is believed to be determined by the operation of antagonistic forces and must be understood with the aid of concepts adjusted to the contradictions logically represented by these forces" (Pribram).

Marxist dialectic materialism follows the Hegelian pattern which it modifies by the dogma of the predominance of materialistic factors.

2. THE VERB "TO BE" AND THE VERB "TO DO." The classification described above has been used very successfully by Professor Pribram in the analysis of a broad historical evolution of the patterns of thought. Other types of classification may be useful in supplementing it in cases of a more concrete nature.

One such method of classification may be found in the difference which separates the logic of the verb "to do" from the logic of the verb "to be."

The logic of the verb "to be" is basically two-valued: things are either thus or not thus. Propositions are either true or false. Meaningless propositions may generally be eliminated and reasoning presented in such a way that a two-valued logic applies.

On the contrary the logic of the verb "to do" is essentially multivalued: one does not do things truly or untruly, one does them more or less well.

All men are confronted with situations in which they tend to reason in terms of the verb "to be" and with other situations in which they tend to reason in terms of the verb "to do." There are, however, still other situations which may be studied by either of the methods correlated with these two verbs. Choices made by various individuals are indicative of the patterns of thought followed by them.

Quite obviously a prevalence of reasoning in terms of

Discussion: Peaceful Resolution of International Conflicts

the logic of the verb "to do" ties in with nominalism, while a prevalence of reasoning in terms of the logic of the verb "to be" ties in with universalism. Thus an analysis undertaken in terms of these two verbs will be helpful in detecting patterns of thought. More than that, such an analysis will also show why it is that in some cases nominalists and universalists reach different conclusions even when starting from identical premises.

Let us take as examples the two concepts of compromise and intervention. If A wishes to paint the wall black and B wishes to paint it white, they may reach an honorable compromise by painting it gray. If A now states that the wall is black, and B states that the wall is white, they may not compromise by calling it gray, as this would make liars of both of them. They may try to convince one another, they may try to fight it out, or they may drop the subject.

I believe that the instability of the French cabinets is due to the fact that, when faced with an issue, the French tend to ask themselves, "What is right?" That is why there are so many issues which often come up for debate and seldom reach the stage of solution. That is also why action can be undertaken only at the expense of excluding from the cabinet for the time being those who do not agree with the majority and who can compromise only by being absent, even temporarily.

It may be noted that the verb "to compromise" has a dual meaning both in French and in English, as for instance in "compromise the difference" and "compromise one's integrity." The first of these two meanings is by far the more frequent in English, the second one by far the more frequent in French.

Let us turn now to the concept of intervention. A and B intend to have lunch together but have not agreed on the choice of a restaurant. They discuss the question in terms of their likes and dislikes, one saying that he would like to go one place and the other that he would like to go to another. C, who has not been invited, overhears the conversation, steps in and tells them what to do. C's attitude would be unanimously considered extremely rude: the action taken by a group to which he doesn't belong, in a case when this action does not affect him, is none of his business.

Once more A and B intend to have lunch but are not in agreement on the choice of a restaurant. This time, however, they conduct their discussion in terms of the verb "to be," A saying that food is better at one place and B that it is better at another. C, who still has not been invited, again overhears their conversation, again steps in offering some factual information about either or both of the two places. This time C's attitude will probably be quite acceptable.

Yet in fact there is no difference between the two situations. If a person wants to have lunch at a certain restaurant, it is probably because the person in question believes that the food is good there. Conversely, to say that food is good at a place means simply that one likes what is served there. As for factual information, one might do well to remember Goethe's saying: that which we call facts are nothing but our own pet theories. Thus again the difference is not in the situation, but in the patterns of thought.

It may be noted that French has several words which

more or less mean intervention, for instance "*intervention,*" "*immixion,*" "*ingérence.*" The two latter have a pejorative meaning. If now we pass from the nouns to the verbs, we see that the verbs corresponding to the pejorative nouns take the reflexive form, thus: *"s'immiscer," "s'ingérer,"* but *"intervenir."* Thus clearly what brings in the pejorative meaning is an insistence on the intervener, the doer, as opposed to an insistence on the situation.

Let us now consider the hypothetical case of the country A which wishes another country B to take a certain step of a very controversial nature. Country A is basically nominalistic, country B is basically universalistic. Country A will not try to influence public opinion in country B; its government thinks of intervention in terms of the verb "to do" and considers it *a priori* as an unfriendly gesture. Country A will try to negotiate directly this issue at government level, offering perhaps some inducements in another field as basis for a compromise, which being nominalistic, it considers honorable. Unfortunately country B, being universalistic, cannot accept a barefaced compromise. At the same time it would not necessarily have resented an intervention, even addressed directly to its own public opinion, if such intervention were made in sufficiently theoretical and impersonal terms.

3. DENOTATION AND CONNOTATION. Of the two methods of classification suggested above, only one may be qualified as linguistic. Yet language may influence thought or else be used as an indication of an existing pattern of thought correlated with a pattern of expression in many more ways than one. Unfortunately the field of the mutual influence of language and thought is as yet largely unexplored. In consequence purely linguistic manners of classification will need to be developed slowly, through experience.

It appears clear, nevertheless, that a search for connotation as distinct from denotation may clarify many concrete situations. Some examples of situations of this kind have been given previously, some others will be found below.

In seeking to systematize the influence of connotations particular attention will have to be paid to the formation of names of sets or classes, or of representatives of sets, either through extension or through intension. Extensives or descriptive formation will generally indicate the prevalence of nominalist patterns and of multivalued logic. On the contrary, intensive formation will indicate the prevalence of universalistic patterns. Both types of word formation will be found in most languages. Areas in which words are formed by one or the other system will in general correspond to areas in which a corresponding type of reasoning is prevalent.

Analysis of connotations should go beyond simple words. It should also embrace sentence structure, set expressions made up of several words, current metaphors, proverbs, and manners in which groups of words may be formed around the same root.

For instance an expression such as "*faire faire*," which can never be properly translated into English—"to have something done" lacks both spontaneity and generality—is in itself an indication of a certain contempt toward action and at the same time is an expression of respect toward the thought which precedes action; in other words it is an expression of universalistic thinking.

The use of the verb "to do" as the principle auxiliary verb in English is also a program in itself.

The systems of classification suggested above are not intended to cover the entire field. They are, rather, examples of lines which can be followed. No analysis should neglect the possibility of finding other explanations such as the ones which may be derived from the implications of history, even where those implications cannot be expressed in terms of semantic or philosophical categorization.

Thus, for instance, of all the great democracies the United States is the one which shows the greatest intolerance of domestic Communism. I believe that an explanation of this fact may be found in the very tradition of the beginnings of an American nationality. Most European countries are founded on a tradition of indigenous ancestry. There are naturalized Frenchmen and Britons, and other Frenchmen and Britons who are descendants of immigrants, but people of these descriptions constitute very small minorities of the citizens of their respective countries. In consequence it is difficult for European countries to consider unwelcome the exponent of any political ideology as long as he can point out a long line of indigenous ancestry. On the contrary, the United States as a nation was created by men and women who had come to a new continent in order to establish a society based on certain definite ideals. It may be interesting to note in that connection how much more important is for American tradition the settlement of the Pilgrims in 1620 than is the settlement of the gentlemen adventurers of Virginia in 1607. The United States thus bases its tradition on the establishment of an ideology on virgin soil. It is thus quite normal for

Americans to think that those who wish to establish some other ideology should go and do it somewhere else.

A DAY IN THE SECURITY COUNCIL

In the paragraphs below I will try to analyze the complete stenographic record of the first part of the one-hundredth meeting of the Security Council. The record used is in three languages—English, French, and Russian. Analysis will start in all cases with the consideration of statements in the original language, then pass on to the translations.

In that connection it should be noted that (1) the differences of opinion of the various representatives are due primarily to questions of a political nature the discussion of which falls outside the scope of the present paper. At the same time the type of arguments chosen by the participants and the manner in which those participants present their arguments are considered indicative of patterns of thought and will be the subject of the present analysis.

(2) The translations by linguists of the United Nations Secretariat are invariably excellent. Although I have spent many years in work of this type, there is not one single aspect of these translations on which I feel I could improve.

Translation

In order to facilitate reading the various points being analyzed will be numbered consecutively.

1. The President, a Belgian, says, "*Aucune proposition n'étant faite dans ce sens, j'en déduis. . . .*"

The last word becomes "I assume" in the English translation. "I deduce" would have been stiff, "I conclude" almost impolite, implying that no change of opinion or of interpretation on the part of the Assembly would be welcome. "I assume" is correct because that is the word which an English-speaking chairman would have chosen in all probability, and also because, in a nominalistic or hypothetical reasoning, one acts upon assumptions. Assumptions become certainties only after action has resulted in their verification.

The President could not have used the French equivalent of "I assume." If one considers that reason is capable of reaching entirely valid conclusions one does not act upon assumptions. "*Je suppose*" would have implied that the members of the Council have not made their positions sufficiently clear to allow the President to reach a clear conclusion.

The Russian translation uses "*zaklyuchaiyu*"—"I conclude." The strength of this word may be best evaluated if one realizes that the participle form "*zaklyuchonnyi*" means a prisoner and is often used in the subsequent remarks of the Russian delegate.

In that respect it may be interesting to note that Slavic languages tend to create groups of words using the same root with different prefixes and suffixes. Thus for instance "*zaklyuchit'*" to conclude, "*izklyuchit'*" to exclude, "*vyklyuchit'*" to switch off, "*vklyuchit'*" to switch on or to include. A still better example is found in the Polish verbs "to read." There is one such verb in English, and twelve in Polish, to wit:

czytać	to read
czytywać	to read habitually
przeczytać	to read completely
przeczytywać	to read completely and habitually
odczytać	to read aloud to a group, to communicate a written text
odczytwać	the same thing habitually
wyczytać	to read excerpts, to interpret (a meaning)
wyczytywać	the same thing habitually
wczytać	to read a meaning into a text
wczytywać	the same thing habitually
zaczytać sie	to bury oneself in one's reading
zacytywać sie	the same thing habitually

It is not difficult to imagine how such a manner of expression would encourage a manner of thinking prone to a certain subtlety in distinctions and to a certain rigidity of categorization. Situations should fall into one of several clearly defined patterns; whenever they fail to do so, they would be considered with disbelief or at least skepticism.

2. An intervention of the Australian delegate, who alludes to the need of investigating "the situation which is before us."

"Which is before us" becomes *"qui nous est soumise"* in French and *"rassmatrivayemym nami"* in Russian. "Which is before us" is neutral. *"Qui nous est soumise"* means literally "which is submitted to us" and implies the assumption of authority of a body of men—the Security Council—over a situation. The Russian expression means "which is under consideration" but with the connotation of "which is being taken apart" or "in regard to which the precise category into which it falls has to be determined." Both the establishing of a hierarchy and that of fixed categories are characteristic of universalism.

3. Where the Australian delegate says that the situation needs to be investigated, the Soviet delegate says that the question is already decided. It is the "same" situation as the one which was discussed before. The difference of opinion between the two delegates is due to the fact that the Australian looks at it from the point of view of procedure while the Soviet delegate looks at it from the point of view of substance. (Once again it is realized that they may have political reasons for adopting the attitude which they have taken. Nevertheless the manner of argumentation remains indicative of the pattern of thought.) An insistence on the procedural aspect is well in keeping with the nominalist attitude, as after all it is procedure which will determine the manner of action—if not necessarily the direction of such action—of a body such as the Security Council. On the contrary an insistence on the broad substantive aspects of the situation is well in keeping with a manner of thinking according to which historical development falls in a predetermined course, and the main task of the statesman is to recognize and diagnose correctly a substantive situation. The "correct" action to be undertaken will follow more or less automatically from a correct diagnosis.

4. The Soviet delegate claims that the present situation is part and parcel of a more general situation and should not be discussed separately. In doing so, he uses the expression *"opryedyelyennaya stadiya"* which becomes *"phase nouvelle"* and "another aspect" in English. Literally it means "a well-

defined phase." Even such an expression as "another phase" might have conveyed to an English-speaking listener the idea that special measures should be taken, as it is perfectly normal to treat each phase of a situation separately. An expression such as "a well-defined or well-determined phase" would have even accentuated this idea of separateness from the more general question, and thus expressed an intention exactly contrary to that of the speaker. *"Phase nouvelle"* is faithful to the meaning but *"phase bien determinée"* would have again given the impression that this phase should be separated from the broader aspects of the problem. As a matter of fact the expression *"opryedyelyennaya stadiya"* would have conveyed an intention somewhat contrary to that of the speaker even to a non-Communist Russian listener. If used by the Soviet delegates it is because it fits in with the Marxist interpretation of history according to which evolution proceeds necessarily from one "well-determined phase" to another; the fact that the phase is well determined, and not merely vaguely outlined, proves that it is indeed an integral part of a correctly diagnosed and described over-all situation.

5. In the same intervention the Soviet delegate said that the decision of the Council *"dolzhen reshat'sya avtomaticheski."* As "should be reached automatically" is ambiguous in English, it becomes "the question settles itself automatically" in the English translation, and *"pouvons trancher d'office"* in the French translation. The English translation is a wee bit stronger than the original Russian, the French quite a bit weaker. But both convey clearly the dialectical meaning: once the correct diagnosis is reached, the manner of action is determined automatically.

6. The Australian delegation again takes the floor and spells out his meaning: the substantive situation is irrelevant for a moment as the Council must first of all settle a question "concerning the operations" of one of its subsidiary organizations.

7. The President, speaking in French, states that a commission has requested a certain government *"de faire ajourner"* certain measures. This becomes "requested to postpone" in the English translation. In French, a government acts directly only at a very high level. In regard to questions of a less exalted nature, it merely causes an action to be taken. Thus a clear hierarchy between principle and mere action is established. (In Russian this becomes "a request in regard to postponement.")

8. The United States delegate finds that the situation is clearly one of procedure. The question is "simple" because the "only concrete" action which may be taken is a procedural one. The procedural situation should not be "seized upon" in order to introduce long arguments about substance.

9. It might be noted that the expression "draft resolution" becomes *"projet de résolution"* in French and *"proyekt rezolyutsiyi"* in Russian. A draft is something you work upon and try to perfect. The implication is that it is only the final product which will be judged. A project is something which may be rejected *in toto;* the implication is that the desirability of such a project should be decided upon theoretically before any work is spent in trying to reach perfection.

10. The Soviet delegate reiterates that *"otvyet mozhet byt' tol'ko"*—there is but one answer to the question. Once again the Soviet delegate asks how is it possible to consider a question of procedure—about which nothing is said in the theory of historical evolution—independently from the question of substance, which is the one to which an answer can be found through dialectics.

11. The Russian *"utvyerzhdyeniye"* appears as "assertion" in English and as *"avis"* in French. *"Avis"* means in this context merely "opinion." "Assertion" is stronger, but not as strong as "affirmation" which would be the closest to the original Russian. However the very strength of "affirmation" would tend to give it an ironical or even pejorative connotation. *"Utvyerzhdyeniye"* is very strong; it derives etymologically from *"tvyerdyi"*—"hard" and the obsolete *"tyerdynya"*—"fortress." The contrast between the weakness of the French expression and the strength of the Russian one is particularly striking, the more so that we tend to consider both nations as following a more or less universalistic bent. Incidentally, it is quite as easy to express the meaning of "opinion" in Russian as that of "affirmation" in French. The present choice of words, on the part of the Russian delegate and on the part of the very competent French translators, is probably due to the absence in pure universalism and to the presence in Hegelianism of an element of systematic strife: thesis versus antithesis.

12. The Soviet delegate further states that he "cannot understand" how his opponents can consider a procedural aspect as being distinct from the more general question of substance.

13. The Russian *"sootvyetstvovat'"* becomes "to signify"

in English and *"appeler"* in French. It literally and also etymologically means "to correspond" (*so-otvyet, cum—respondere*). This again shows a predilection for rigid categories.

14. The representative of France takes the floor. For obvious reasons he sides with the Australian and the American and gives his own very brief restatement of their position. The only thing which he introduces and which was not contained in the earlier speeches of the Western delegates is one little word: *"donc"*—"therefore." The effects of this little word will be seen in some of the subsequent remarks.

15. For the French delegate the question is *"la question dont il s'agit."* This is translated into Russian by the equally impersonal *"ryech idyet,"* but becomes in English "the question with which *we* are concerned" with a shift of emphasis from the situation *per se* to the people dealing with it.

16. *"Il est naturel"* remains "it is natural" in English but

Language of East–West Diplomacy

becomes *"yestyestvenno"* in Russian. This word derives from the root *"yestyestvo"* meaning "substance" and itself deriving from the word "to be." It is much closer in its connotations to the aristotelian original than is "natural."

17. There are two French words which correspond to the English word "probable." These are *"probable"* and *"vraisemblable,"* the latter containing the connotation of a judgment as to truth value which is absent from the first. It might be interpreted as meaning "something similar to the established scheme of truth." The one Russian word translating "probable," *"vyeroyatno,"* corresponds to the French word *"vraisemblable."*

18. The delegate of the United States takes the floor to "concur with the opinion expressed by the delegate of France." Now, as we have mentioned before, the delegate of France merely restated the position taken by the delegates of Australia and of the United States. He did, however, add the little word "therefore," which made the position so much

clearer and more forceful that it becomes from now on known as the French position.

19. The delegate of the United States presents a draft resolution for the purpose of "giving concrete form" to opinion and to enable "the Council to dispose of this matter." It would be "the acme of futility" to discuss questions of substance when there is need for an immediate procedural decision.

20. The President says, *"Je ne voudrais préjuger en rien la décision que le Conseil de securité va prendre."* *"Préjuger"* remains *"pryedugadyvat'"* in Russian (etymologically, "to guess before my turn") but becomes "to prejudice" in English, thus implying that prejudging by a President could not fail to influence the action of the Council. Once again emphasis is shifted from situation to action.

21. The delegate of Australia also expresses his agreement with the delegate of France.

22. "To have no claim" becomes *"ne pas pouvoir prétendre"* in French and *"nye imyeyet' prava,"* "to have no right," in Russian. The English word "claim" is extremely difficult to translate, as it expresses an entirely nominalistic idea: that of a juridical situation which is neither clearly white nor clearly black, but which on the contrary takes into account the legitimacy of practical adjustments.

In trying to present an over-all evaluation of the meeting described above, one should remember that the various delegates were faced indeed with difficult political problems. On the other hand, however, the men who engaged in the debate described were unquestionably far above the average in preparation for and experience in handling international communication.

The impression obtained is that whereas the French and the Belgian members of the Assembly on the one hand and the American and the Australian on the other have retained their individuality, communication between them has been established; in particular the Frenchman and the Belgian have conclusively shown that they understood not only the position, which would be a political matter, but also the reasoning, which is a semantic matter, of the Australian and the American. On the contrary, the degree of communication between the Soviet delegate and the delegates of Australia and of the United States appears to be nil. Once again political situations may not be disregarded. When the Soviet delegate states that he does not understand the attitude of his opponents, he may be simply seeking to gain some rhetorical advantage. At the same time, however, the very fact that this form of argumentation should have occurred to him shows that he genuinely believes that it is at least conceivable that people of good will might find the attitude of the Australian and the American delegates difficult to understand.

At the same time no attempt is made by anyone to explain the basis of his manner of thinking; all that the various speakers do is to present arguments which appear pertinent once a certain manner of thinking is accepted.

Thus for instance nobody has made a speech along these lines: "It is true that the basic problems which we are supposed to discuss here are the political problems of the world. Those problems, however, are complex, and their solution

Words—Returning from an International Conference

cannot be expected to be reached rapidly. In consequence we must separate from those problems questions pertaining to our day-to-day operations within the Council. If we did not do so, we would be unable to accomplish any useful work whatsoever."

The converse was not heard either: "Operations can be fruitful only if they are in agreement with the substance of the situation to which they pertain. Thus it is better to postpone any action than to undertake an action which might make it more difficult for us to analyze the situation correctly and to take in the end such measures as the situation dictates." The precise point under dispute in this meeting was whether the delegates of certain nonmember countries should be invited to participate in the debate. This participation was at first opposed by the Australian delegate in extremely conciliatory terms. It does not appear to be necessary "for the present." The Council should however be ready to reconsider in accordance with possible developments. After the Soviet delegate has taken the floor to suggest that an invitation be extended, this invitation is again opposed by the delegates of the United States and Australia in terms much stronger than those used previously. The Soviet delegate had based his arguments on the subordination of the procedural aspects to substantive ones; as the nonmember nations are interested in the substantive aspects, they should participate in all the discussions, and in fact the debate should bear on substance principally. The Western delegates reply that the question is one of procedure over which only members of the Council have jurisdiction. The increasing acrimony of the debate leads to the impression that the Australian and the American delegates oppose more the pattern of thought of the Soviet delegate, with his insistence on discussion and inaction, than they do the actual invitation which he champions.

To sum up, it appears that all difficulties of international communication have not been solved in the case above. The purely linguistic problem was solved superbly, insofar as translation and interpretation may solve it, by the staff of the United Nations Secretariat. The question of patterns of thought, however, does not appear to have been given any attention whatsoever.

CONCLUSION

In presenting this paper I do not wish to say that it is possible to arrive at a rigid classification of patterns of thought which would apply in all cases. Neither do I wish to imply that national or cultural groups are characterized by a rigid and constant adherence to definite patterns of thought. Nor again do I wish to imply that there is a rigid correspondence between languages and patterns of thought.

What I hope to have shown is:

1. That there exist correlations between patterns of thought and patterns of expressions and that those correlations may be used in the analysis of patterns of thought.

2. That patterns of thought will be more easily recognized through the connotations appearing in the patterns of expression than in the denotations of statements.

3. That forms taken by language tend in many cases to encourage certain patterns of thought and to discourage others.

4. That connotations appearing in language have at least as much a part in influencing thought as do denotations.

5. That even an imperfect method of classification may greatly help in analyzing patterns of thought as they appear in concrete cases, and thus to make it easier to overcome some of the obstacles inherent in international communications.

Presented at the Conference on General Semantics, Washington University, St. Louis, June 10-12, 1954, and published in ETC. *immediately thereafter. Edmund S. Glenn is Chief of the Interpreting Branch of the Division of Language Services, U.S. Department of State. His paper also formed the basis of the Scientific Conference on Interpreting and Intercultural Barriers to Communication, held in Washington, D.C., January 4, 1956, under the auspices of the State Department and the Josiah Macy, Jr., Foundation. The Winter 1957-58 issue of* ETC. *("Special Issue on Interpretation and Intercultural Communication") reports the proceedings of the latter conference.*

How to Attend a Conference

S. I. HAYAKAWA

THE purpose of a conference is, of course, the exchange of ideas, the enrichment of our own views through the support or the challenge provided by the views of others. It is a situation created specially for the purposes of communication.

Since I am a student of semantics, I am going to venture some observations on the process of communication in the hope that, whether my observations are correct or not, the very fact that I make them may at least help to make the reader aware of the problems of communication that confront participants at any conference in addition to the problems inherent in the subject matter.

There are two aspects to communication. One is the matter of output—the speaking and writing, involving problems of rhetoric, composition, logical presentation, coherence, definition of terms, knowledge of the subject and the audience, and so on. Most of the preoccupation with communication is directed toward the improvement of the output, so that we find on every hand courses in composition, in effective speaking, in the arts of plain or fancy talk, and how to write more dynamic sales letters.

But the other aspect of communication, namely, the problem of intake—especially the problem of how to listen well—is relatively a neglected subject. It does not avail the speakers to have spoken well if we as listeners have failed to understand, or if we come away believing them to have said things they didn't say at all. If a conference is to result in the exchange of ideas, we need to pay particular heed to our listening habits.

A common difficulty at conferences and meetings is what might be called the *terminological tangle,* in which discussion is stalemated by conflicting definitions of key terms.

Let me discuss this problem using as examples the vocabulary of art criticism and the discussion of design. What do such terms as "romanticism," "classicism," "baroque," "organic," "functionalism," etc., *really* mean? Let us put this problem into the kind of context in which it is likely to occur. For example, a speaker may talk about "the romanticism so admirably exemplified by the Robey House by Frank Lloyd Wright." Let us imagine in the audience an individual to whom the Robey House exemplifies many things, but *not* "romanticism." His reaction may well be, "Good God, has he ever *seen* the Robey House?" And he may challenge the speaker to *define* "romanticism"—which is a way of asking, "What do *you* think 'romanticism' really is?" When the speaker has given his definition, it may well prove to the questioner that the speaker indeed doesn't know what he's talking about. But if the questioner counters with an alternative definition, it will prove to the speaker that the questioner doesn't know what *he* is talking about. At this point it will be just as well if the rest of the audience adjourns to the bar, because no further communication is going to take place.

How can this kind of terminological tangle be avoided? I believe it can be avoided if we understand at the outset that there is no ultimately correct and single meaning to words like "romanticism" and "functionalism" and "plastic form" and other items in the vocabulary of art and design criticism. The same is true, of course, of the vocabularies of literary criticism, of politics and social issues, and many other matters of everyday discussion. Within the strictly disciplined contexts of the languages of the sciences, exact or almost exact agreements about terminology can be established. When two physicists talk about "positrons" or when two chemists talk about "diethylene glycol," they can be presumed to have enough of a common background of controlled experience in their fields to have few difficulties about understanding one another. But most of the words of artistic and other general discussion are not restricted to such specialized frames of reference. They are part of the language of everyday life—by which I mean that they are part of the language in which we do not hesitate to speak across occupational lines. The artist, dramatist, and poet do not hesitate to use the vocabularies of their callings in speaking to their audiences; nor would the physician, the lawyer, the accountant, and the clothing merchant hesitate to use these words to one another if they got into a discussion of any of the arts.

In short, the words most commonly used in conference, like the vocabulary of other educated, general discussion, are public property—which is to say that they mean many things to many people. This is a fact neither to be applauded nor regretted; it is simply a fact to be taken into account. They are words, therefore, which either have to be defined anew each time they are seriously used—or, better still, *they must be used in such a way, and with sufficient illustrative examples, that their specific meaning in any given discourse emerges from their context.*

Hence it is of great importance in a conference to listen to one another's statements and speeches and terminology without unreasonable demands. And the specific unreasonable

A Spade Calling a Spade a Spade

demand I am thinking of now is the demand that everybody else *should* mean by such words as "romanticism" what I would mean if I were using them. If, therefore, the expression, "the romanticism of the Frank Lloyd Wright Robey House" is one which, at first encounter, makes little sense to us, we should at once be alerted to special attentiveness. The speaker, by classifying the Robey House as "romantic," is making an unfamiliar classification—a sure sign not that he is ill-informed but that he has a way of classifying his data that is different from our own. And his organization of his data may be one from which we can learn a new and instructive way of looking at the Robey House, or at "romanticism," or at whatever else the speaker may be talking about.

Since a major purpose of conferences is to provide ample opportunity for conversational give-and-take, perhaps it would be wise to consider the adoption, formally or informally, of one basic conversational traffic rule which I have found to be invaluable in ensuring the maximum flow of information and ideas from one person to another, and in avoiding the waste of time resulting from verbal traffic snarls. The rule is easy to lay down, but not always easy to follow: it is that *we refrain from agreement or disagreement with a speaker, to refrain from praise or censure of his views, until we are sure what those views are.*

Of course, the first way to discover a speaker's views is to listen to him. But few people, other than psychiatrists and women, have had much training in listening. The training of most oververbalized professional intellectuals (which would include most people who attend conferences) is in the opposite direction. Living in a competitive culture, most of us are most of the time chiefly concerned with getting our own views across, and we tend to find other people's speeches a tedious interruption of the flow of our own ideas. Hence, it is necessary to emphasize that listening does not mean simply maintaining a polite silence while you are rehearsing in your mind the speech you are going to make the next time you can grab a conversational opening. Nor does listening mean waiting alertly for the flaws in the other fellow's arguments so that later you can mow him down. Listening means trying to see the problem the way the speaker sees it—which means not sympathy, which is *feeling for* him, but empathy, which is *experiencing with* him. Listening requires entering actively and imaginatively into the other fellow's situation and trying to understand a frame of reference different from your own. This is not always an easy task.

But a good listener does not merely remain silent. He asks questions. However, these questions must avoid all implications (whether in tone of voice or in wording) of skepticism or challenge or hostility. They must clearly be motivated by curiosity about the speaker's views. Such questions, which may be called "questions for clarification," usually take the form, "Would you expand on that point about . . . ?" "Would you mind restating that argument about . . . ?" "What exactly is your recommendation again?" Perhaps the most useful kind of question at this stage is something like, "I am going to restate in my words what I think you mean. Then would you mind telling me if I've understood you correctly?"

The late Dr. Irving J. Lee of Northwestern University has suggested another form of questioning which he describes as "the request for information concerning the uniqueness of

The Speakers Are Prisoners of Their Vocabularies

the particular characteristics of the condition or proposal under consideration." I shall simply call these questions "questions of uniqueness." All too often, we tend to listen to a speaker or his speech in terms of a generalization, "Oh, he's just another of those progressive educators," "Isn't that just like a commercial designer?" "That's the familiar Robjohn-Giddings approach," "That's the old Bauhaus pitch," etc. It is a curious and dangerous fact—dangerous to communication, that is—that once we classify a speech in this way, we stop listening, because, as we say, "We've heard that stuff before." But *this* speech by *this* individual at *this* time and place is a *particular* event, while the "that stuff" with which we are classifying this speech is a *generalization* from the past. Questions of uniqueness are designed to prevent what might be called the functional deafness which we induce in ourselves by reacting to speakers and their speeches in terms of the generalizations we apply to them. Questions of uniqueness take such forms as these: "How large is the firm you work for, and do they make more than one product?" "Exactly what kind of synthetic plastic did you use on that project?" "Are your remarks on abstract expressionism and Jackson Pollock intended to apply equally to the work of De Kooning?"

Something else that needs to be watched is the habit of overgeneralizing from the speaker's remarks. If a speaker is critical of, let us say, the way in which design is taught at a particular school, some persons in the audience seem automatically to assume that the speaker is saying that design shouldn't be taught at all. When I speak on the neglected art of listening, as I have done on many occasions, I am often confronted with the question, "If everybody listened, who would do the talking?" This type of misunderstanding may be called the "pickling in brine fallacy," after the senior Oliver Wendell Holmes's famous remark, "Just because I say I like sea bathing, that doesn't mean I want to be pickled in brine." When Alfred Korzybski found himself being misunderstood in this way, he used to assert with special forcefulness, "I say what I say; I do not say what I do not say." Questions of uniqueness, properly chosen, prevent not only the questioner but everyone else present from projecting into a speaker's remarks meanings that were not intended.

All too often, the fact that misunderstanding exists is not apparent until deeper misunderstandings have already occurred because of the original one. We have all had the experience of being at meetings or at social gatherings at which Mr. X says something, Mr. Y believes Mr. X to have said something quite different and argues against what he believes Mr. X to have said. Then Mr. X, not understanding Mr. Y's objections (which may be legitimate objections to what Mr. X didn't say), defends his original statement with further statements. These further statements, interpreted by Mr. Y in the light of mistaken assumptions, lead to further mistaken assumptions, which in turn induce in Mr. X mistaken assumptions about Mr. Y. In a matter of minutes, the discussion is a dozen miles away from the original topic. Thereafter it can take from twenty minutes to two hours to untangle the mess and restore the discussion to a consideration of Mr. X's original point. This is the kind of time-wasting which I should like to help avoid.

All this is not to say that I expect or wish conferences to avoid argument. But let us argue about what has been said, and not about what has not been said. And let us discuss not for victory but for clarification. If we do so, we shall find, I believe, that ultimately agreement and disagreement, approval and disapproval, are not very important after all. The important thing is to come away from a conference with a fund of information—information about what other people are doing and thinking and why. It is only as we fully under-

Prejudice Listening to Reason

stand opinions and attitudes different from our own and the reasons for them that we better understand our own place in the scheme of things. Which is but another way of saying that while the result of communications successfully imparted is self-satisfaction, the result of communications successfully received is self-insight. Let us attend conferences and take part in them not only for the sake of increased self-satisfaction, but also for the sake of increased self-insight.

Presented at the opening session of the International Design Conference, Aspen, Colorado, June 13, 1955. S. I. Hayakawa is professor of English, San Francisco State College, and author of Oliver Wendell Holmes *(1939),* Language in Action *(1941),* Language in Thought and Action *(1949),* Language, Meaning and Maturity *(1954),* Our Language and Our World *(1959). He has been editor of* ETC.: A Review of General Semantics *since its foundation in 1943 to the present. In 1960 he served for ten weeks as a lecturer under the U. S. State Department's specialist program in Scandinavia and Germany. In 1961 he served for three months as Alfred P. Sloan Visiting Professor at the Menninger School of Psychiatry in Topeka, Kansas.*

SEMANTICS AROUND US

General Semantics and the Reporter's Job

DONALD M. SCHWARTZ

FOR some time the daily slogan of the *New York Times*—"All the news that's fit to print"—has stirred up among publishers and journalism professors much moralistic debate over "fit." What concerns me more in the slogan is the "all." The *Times,* as everyone knows, weighs a great deal, particularly on Sundays. But even if the *Times* weighed three or four pounds instead of two, it couldn't justify its "allness" slogan. (Unless, of course, its editors think there is an *awful* lot of nasty news around.) If there is doubt about this statement, consider, for instance, James Joyce's job as a reporter in *Ulysses,* a *partial* account of just a few persons' actions (mostly one man's) in one town in a day; it weighs almost as much as a Sunday *Times.*

The *Times,* though, isn't the only news-giver that stresses completeness to the extent of imitating "allness" for its coverage. The Atlanta *Journal,* for instance, has the slogan, "Covers Dixie Like The Dew," and I know a Chicago *Tribune* reporter who says—I don't know with how much of a smile—"It hasn't *happened* until it's been in the *Tribune.*"

Many programs in the radio news business have painted themselves into a verbal corner by striving after the "allness" effect with the phrase, "And now here is a *complete summary* of the day's news . . ."

Because of the physical structure of the news-getting-and-giving business I suspect that most journalists in the field are aware of the abstracting process; but somewhere in the high towers where most journalistic policy is made the idea seems to be to try to kid the public into thinking each news medium is telling all.

Abstracting is constantly going on in the news. I would

like to see the press—which, I believe, is aware of the fact—admit it. What I have called the "physical structure of news" is apparent in most high school trips through the local newspaper plant—complete with explanations of how the reporter gets a digest of the facts, phones part of them to the rewrite man, who selects some of the facts for the story, which he slides over to the copy desk, where it is checked for accuracy, spelling, etc., and in the process usually is chopped down a bit.

If the story isn't of a "policy" nature so that the managing editor, editor, executive editor, and publisher, etc., have to get in a few licks, it may go to type. Now the make-up editor exercises his own particular brand of abstracting with his recognized ability to make a big story into a little one (or vice versa) by the kind of headline he assigns it and where he "buries" it in the paper. Finally, even the pressroom worker, who locks the type into place, may at the last moment throw out a few lines of type (carrying facts of the story) if they won't fit into the allotted space. Journalistic writing, with its prescription of who-what-where-when-why coming first, makes unconscious abstracting easy. The story trails off into tail-end facts which the make-up man or compositor lops to any convenient length.

This process of abstracting through selection usually is explained in academic or public relations journalism lectures. However, another and equally important abstracting factor is seldom noted. That is the selecting done by the reporter, or "legman" as he is known in the trade, and the selecting that's already done before the reporter gets started.

Laymen generally seem to think reporters go out and cover events—events happening and observable. All too often, though, especially for the regular beat reporter, that isn't true; he merely reports words about other words, spoken or written. The handing of news up the abstraction ladder in, say, the routine automobile accident is likely to go like this. The policeman goes to the accident *after* it happens, listens to the stories of the two drivers, who are too scared and involved at best to tell much of what went on, and usually are interested in presenting only the facts that prove "it was all the other guy's fault." The cop also may talk to witnesses if any are available. He takes notes on what he thinks he hears, returns to the station, and turns the material over to a records-writing sergeant, who writes up what he wants of it.

Then our ground-floor man of the radio station or newspaper, the reporter, arrives on the scene—not the scene of the accident, but the police station. Unless he decides to do some digging, the sergeant's report will be the basis of his story.

The "Washington story" apparently follows much the same route to front pages and broadcasts, if James Reston of the *New York Times* is any judge. *Time* recently reported a speech Reston gave at the University of Kansas School of Journalism, in which he criticized Washington reporters for a growing tendency to do their reporting by rewriting the handouts or abstractions prepared by government officials.

And so the police reporter, city hall man, and other legmen often work from reports, or reports of reports—e.g., city council minutes, housing survey studies, etc. What has to be "covered" is sometimes the product of years of work, an account of which might run thousands of pages without telling every detail of what was done.

But not only is the reporter usually reporting on a fraction of the events, but often, by accepting the statements of "responsible officials," he passes along words that have little or no relation to the extensional facts.

During 1950 I was reporting the running story of the Gary Municipal Board of Censors, who were concerned at the time with allegedly obscene literature available in local newsstands. I reported on one broadcast:

> Now one of the questions raised at this week's Censor Board meeting was: who is to be protected from this so-called lewd and lascivious reading? Is it the youth the mayor is trying to protect? It would appear so from the discussion at the Censors' meeting . . . [The] Board chairman . . . asked Gary's acting librarian . . . about teen-age reading habits. Both agreed that library reading falls off at about 16. That, thought [the chairman], was the point where the "bad" reading takes up . . . The mayor agreed with that general position of needing to protect the late teen-age group. The mayor said he felt the "bad" reading "incited" them.

As I said on the air, I became curious, and asked: "Who actually read this 'bad' literature—the much-damned younger generation?" A partial answer came, as I reported, from:

> . . . a talk at one of the biggest and busiest corner newsstands in Gary . . . [with] the newspaper boy . . . Only he didn't know our conversation . . . was being recorded. We got his unrehearsed views on censorship: how it may affect his business,

his comments on legality, and one of the things we've been talking about here: who reads the forbidden or about-to-be-forbidden literature?

After the newsboy (who was no boy) told me he thought the censoring idea was illegal, I suggested:

"Well, the mayor . . . they say they want to protect these teen-agers from those magazines." (And I indicated a rack of magazines of the type under question.)

"Naw, they don't buy 'em," said the newsboy.

"Really? You mean the young kids don't buy 'em?"

"Naw, they don't buy 'em," said the newsboy. "Too expensive. Cost twenty or twenty-five cents."

"That right? Then who does buy 'em?"

"Forty-, fifty-year-old men, that's who."

"Yeah?"

"Yeah!"

This passage isn't quoted primarily to show that the Censor Board and mayor were on a wild-goose chase in their desire to protect the teen-agers. Because of my curiosity, and because I was fortunate enough in this instance to have had both the time and the opportunity, I was able to correct, or at least to bring sharply into question, the prevailing notion, held by the Board of Censors and therefore reported as news, that *here was a problem affecting Gary teen-agers.* This incident suggests how reporters (including myself), often cut off from firsthand observation and therefore relying upon the inferences and evaluations of others, may, without knowing it, pass along false information.

In countless stories the kind of statements made by the board and mayor are reported with no attempt to check facts. Both journalists and readers ought to be aware of this possibility if they want to have a more accurate idea of what they are giving to and getting from the news media. Among the more gullible, statements that would be regarded as asinine if heard personally are accepted as facts when dignified by type or by a convincing voice.

The battle cry of the news-givers is "authoritativeness." A look at almost any issue of *Broadcasting,* one of the trade journals of radio and television, is instructive. In the want-ad columns, newscasting job seekers are constantly telling possible employers they have "authoritative" voices—while in adjoining columns employers seeking newscasters are demanding "authoritative" voices. And the promotion for printed news-dispensers—the Kiplingers, Pearsons, et al.—is similar. "Get the last word, the King James version of the news. You don't have to shop around after you've got the straight dope from us—we're *authoritative!*"

But who is authoritative? Who ever has the final word on anything that moves as fast as the news? What reporter ever asks the last question and gets the last answer and the last development? Compare the handling of any story by several news media.

For example, Lake County, Indiana, elected a Republican prosecutor, David Stanton, who was committed to an investigation of politics and gambling in his campaign; as a special deputy in charge of the investigation he appointed a Democrat, Metro Holovachka. One night, about a month after his appointment, when Holovachka was sitting in a private Gary club (of which he had been a member for some time), several Gary policemen entered the club and carried off four illegal slot machines. The same night Gary police raided a policy-wheel press at a different place.

Next day the Gary *Post-Tribune* carried a story of the two raids under a one-column headline, "SEIZE POLICY WHEEL, SLOTS IN TWO RAIDS; FOUR MACHINES TAKEN IN SLOVAK FORAY," and in the sixth paragraph, mentioned Holovachka's presence. Further down the *Post-Tribune's* story said, "Police officials who would not permit the use of their names disclosed that Holovachka was in the club." The story was on the sixth page of the second section. (The *Post-Tribune* had strongly supported Holovachka's boss, Stanton, in the election.)

The story made the front page of the Chicago *Tribune* under a one-column headline, "CRIME FIGHTER IN RAIDED CLUB CRIES: POLITICS." And "Metro Holovachka" were the first two words in the story. The *Tribune* story had the policy-wheel information in the last two paragraphs. And the *Tribune* account quoted Holovachka directly, "This was obviously a political move on the part of the Gary city administration to place me in an embarrassing position."

The *Tribune* reporter got his quote from Holovachka after I had got mine. For my WWCA story Holovachka said only, "I'm an innocent victim of a set of circumstances," and he said a couple of times that the timing of the raid looked strange to him. The *Tribune* reporter talked with Holovachka immediately after I did; perhaps the deputy, after having talked to me, remembered to tell the next caller some of the things he had forgotten to tell me, or perhaps the *Tribune* man was a better prodder that morning than I was. In the WWCA story Holovachka was in the lead, and the policy-wheel raid was made a separate story.

Next, chronologically, came the *Times* from nearby Hammond, Indiana, which put the story in its late Saturday edition under an eight-column front-page headline: "HOLOVACHKA 'FRAMED' IN SLOT RAID!" Here the lead was what Holovachka's boss prosecutor Stanton told the *Times* about the slot raid. The *Times* reported Stanton as saying that he "suspected a frame-up." The paper also quoted Stanton's allegation that the "city administration of Gary would give anything to embarrass me." (In the Chicago *Tribune* story the raid was an attempt to embarrass Holovachka, according to Holovachka.)

Obviously these are four different stories, not only in the sense that they appeared physically in four different places, but especially in the sense that they were developed by different reporters, with different questions, from different sources (even Holovachka was different when he talked to the *Tribune's* man from what he was like when he talked to me), at different times, were written differently, and played differently—by make-up and placement in the papers, and on the air, by tone of voice, etc.

If one allows these variables inherent in abstracting to show up in reporting the news, the reports will have naturally a tone of tentativeness quite different from the "authoritativeness" sought by most reporters.

There are some reporters who show some humility in giving the news. Whether it comes from a consciousness of abstracting or from a realization that yours is only one man's version, or one newspaper's I don't know. Nevertheless, NBC radio-TV commentator Clifton Utley, for one, often says things like "Now, I don't pretend to be an expert on this, but from the wire reports I get, and based on, etc., etc., it seems to me . . ." Mr. Utley is unusually aware of the methods by which he arrives at his comments; this is clear not only from his broadcasts, but also from his published reflections on his profession, "Can a Radio Commentator Talk Sense?" in the Spring, 1946, issue of *ETC.* (III, 217–223).

Nineteenth-century journalism, practiced when communication of the news was slower, seemed more inclined toward tentativeness and the guarded statement than is journalism today. Headlines like "RUMOR PRESIDENT LINCOLN CAPTURED—SIGNIFICANT IF TRUE" were more in use. Even the use of the word "account" in place of today's more common "story" seems to carry with it the recognition of the subjectiveness of all reports—including those by "our reporter." But today, when the teletypes move hot copy fast, journalists act as if they no longer need to talk cautiously—that is to say, accurately.

During the fall 1950 political campaign, I happened to be in the Gary Philip Murray Steelworkers Union building the night of a labor rally with all Democratic speakers on the announced program, when in walked the Republican candidate for first-district congressman for Indiana, Paul Cyr. He sat down in the front row while his opponent, incumbent Democrat Ray Madden, finished his talk. Then, as I reported:

> When Madden finished, GOP candidate Cyr started toward the speakers' stand, saying he wanted an opportunity to answer Madden. Madden sat there smiling, and *if this reporter isn't mistaken,* the Congressman even said hello to his opponent. However, *it's hard to say just what happened,* because about here the audience caught on that a Republican candidate was trying to get the floor at this solid Democratic rally, and began yelling words to the general effect of "Throw the bum out!" Some took the advice. About three or four grabbed Cyr, one applying an arm lock, and escorted him up the aisle and toward the exit.[1]

The fact that I was the only reporter in the hall did not prevent other newsmen from reporting the incident with much more "authoritative" sounds than I made. One writer, who reconstructed the event from Cyr's next-day account of it, did have the good grace to enclose most of his story in quotes.

One out-of-town paper (Indianapolis *Star*) wrote: "Paul Cyr, Republican nominee for Congress in Lake County, was manhandled by 'labor goons' in the presence of top officials of the Democratic party when he sought to address a political rally here Wednesday night." The *Star,* which datelined its story "Gary, Spl," then went on to tell what had happened, with no attribution to anyone, although it had no reporter in the hall, and its "Spl" probably reconstructed his version from someone who was there—probably Cyr. The *Star* later took

[1] Perhaps this is as good a place as any for me to say, in taking credit for the words in italics, that I was introduced to general semantics by Professor Earl English (now dean) of the School of Journalism of the University of Missouri. His instruction and inspiration and his views on the social responsibility of journalism have been deeply influential in shaping my views.

off on the incident in an editorial, saying, among other things, that ". . . Ray Madden [First district Indiana, Representative], John Watkins [Lieutenant-Governor of Indiana], and Frank McHale [Democratic National Committeeman from Indiana] sat idly by and watched the brutality and unfairness of these labor goons without protest . . ."

The fact was that while Madden was in the hall Cyr was told he could speak at the end of the program and had sat down to wait; then Madden left, and it was after that that most of the fireworks with Cyr took place. McHale from the first had suggested that Cyr be allowed to speak.

Cyr's wife was surprised to read in the same paper that *she* was under a doctor's care, which bit of erroneous information that paper reported immediately after saying that her husband had visited a doctor next day for treatment of a wrenched arm. The Associated Press story on the Indiana wire, provided by one of its Lake County correspondents, went through another step of abstracting and became even more "authoritative" because the wire service was carrying it. One of the most striking experiences I have watching abstracting and intensionalism at work in the news is watching stories that originate in Gary come over the state AP wire. Sometimes they are so different from what I think I have seen and heard that I cannot in conscience use them.

It is my personal feeling that mere accurate reporting is almost nowhere admired in journalism as it used to be. Once it was a feat for the reporter who was able by shorthand to report the Lincoln-Douglas debates accurately word-for-word. Today Lincoln and Douglas would have publicity men, and if they wanted to make the big dailies and wire services they would have to provide "advances" on the debates. They'd probably do it, too, since people don't go to political meetings as they used to. And that raises for me a rather crucial point: while "straight reporting" isn't admired as it used to be, it is more essential than ever that it be done well, since people are much more stay-at-homes than they formerly were, depending more and more on radio, television, and the press to give them their picture of the world.

There has been much comment on *Time* magazine's "*Time*-style" from a stylistic point of view, but unraveling *Time's* report-inference-judgment-affective-connotation maze appears to me much more important for the reader. *Time's* admitted job of interpretative writing leads it to the necessity of "goosing itself" (as one writer put it) to intensional conclusions that are hard to square with even what little can be checked. In "reporting" the Dewey dinner incident, in which the New York governor told off the Russian guests, who promptly left, *Time* said Dewey may have been rude but nobody except the Communists and their friends were very excited about the rudeness. In the meantime, Eleanor Roosevelt spent a column following the episode telling how upset she for one felt about it.

Time's opposition, *Newsweek,* at least makes an attempt to separate its reports from its opinions by telling its stories first and saving its interpretative writing for the end, announcing it with italic type and calling it "significance." This is not to say there is no subjective element in so-called "straight reporting"; I already have demonstrated that there is. I say only for practical purposes that this matter of varnishing the truth must be examined in terms of how many layers are being used.

One of the most outstanding examples of spreading it on thick I've ever seen occurred in 1951 when an American Broadcasting Company commentator, Paul Harvey, was caught by a plant guard trying to sneak into the Argonne National Laboratory in Chicago, which is very much off limits for Mr. Harvey. People in and around Chicago seemed to be primarily interested in figuring out what Harvey was up to—boosting his Hooper rating, testing security safeguards, both, or what?

What many missed, I think, was the chance to watch an advanced word-to-word manipulator caught with his intensionalism down. (Incidentally, Harvey sounds very, very authoritative to lots of people.) In one of the many stories carried by Chicago papers after Harvey was caught, Jack Starr wrote for the *Sun-Times:*

> News commentator Paul Harvey, in advance of his "Operation Backfire" had prepared the script of an exposé intended to show up security safeguards at the Argonne National Laboratory. . . . But the whole thing was hung up on a fence around the Laboratory where the hefty Harvey lost his overcoat. . . . His project . . . ended . . . with his hands in the air and a guard's gun in his face. But the script of what might have been told was found in the car he drove to the atomic research installation. . . . The script was planned for Harvey's radio or television programs Sunday. It described how he and a friend, both big men and easily identified, mind you, were driving a little past midnight Monday—just driving. And what do you think? They ran

out of gas. They left the car and walked toward a place from which a light was shining. There was a fence around the place. They climbed the fence, presumably without wear and tear on a single overcoat. . . .

On and on went the advance verbalization of the never-to-be-accomplished escapade. The payoff, according to Starr's report of the Harvey script, was to be when Harvey would reveal that he and his friend left a note inside the plant to be discovered by the "chagrined guards."

Harvey's kind of work of necessity makes his symbol of reality the teletype machine that delivers him his words, just as the rewrite man's symbol of reality is the telephone receiver. The radio commentator's job is mostly putting the words together and delivering them so that they "sound good."

It is not stretching things too far, I believe, to say that what appears to have happened in Harvey's case is that having *verbally* climbed the Argonne Laboratory fence and sneaked past the guards *in his prepared script,* he deluded himself into a conviction that what is easily *said* is as easily *done*. Whether or not this is what actually occurred in this instance, there is no doubt of the high degree of intensionality in Harvey's regular broadcasts. This intensionality is demonstrated in another *Sun-Times* story a few days after the attempted gate-crashing. At a press conference to "explain" the incident, said the *Sun-Times,* Harvey "waved a figurative American flag and talked of patriotism. . . . Actually . . . the commentator explained nothing to the press, his employers, and his sponsors." He said something about not wanting to jeopardize security in government agencies. "What government agencies are you talking about?" he was asked. "I cannot comment on that," Harvey answered. "After much sparring," said the *Sun-Times,* "Harvey ended the conference by handing out a seven-page statement. It quoted Representative Fred Busbey (R., Ill.) as saying, 'Paul Harvey is one of America's most brilliant and patriotic radio commentators.' " This was the extent of the "explanation."

A certain amount of intensionalism is inevitable, of course, in news reporting. Certain events have a routine quality about them, in that the routine expectations on the basis of which a reporter makes his inquiries are fulfilled by unstartling and routine facts. Nevertheless, to be constantly on guard against intensionalism, to be aware of the nature of the abstracting process, to be aware of the endless variety and complexity of human events, are necessary to the reporter. In the first place, these semantic cautions make a reporter or commentator less "authoritative." Furthermore, they give him the means whereby his news reports become far more interesting. The interest is in the *differences* between one railroad wreck and another railroad wreck, between one murder and another murder. The extensional attitude alerts one to these crucial differences.

Once I covered a murder story in Gary, Indiana. I look back on this incident with some gratification, because I feel that it was a good story, and because I feel too that this was an occasion on which my training in general semantics was noticeably helpful to me in observing the uniqueness of the situation.

This particular murder was notably different from other murders from the start in that the murderer was found before the body was. The police spent a day trying to break down their suspect, and finally in the late afternoon he took them to a clay pit where he had thrown the body. Around this water-filled pit some people were fishing under the late afternoon sun. Suddenly the police, leading the murder suspect, walked on the scene. The suspect was told to throw a stone in the water where he had thrown the body. At the spot where the stone landed, a fishing line was dangling, held by a priest sitting in shirt sleeves on a log jutting out over the water. The police went to work pulling out the body. The fishermen around the bank withdrew their lines and watched. While the work went on and the crowd stood around waiting, a train ran by on the far side of the pit. The engineer leaned out and waved to the crowd, as engineers do.

In my report of this part of the murder story, I included along with the routine details of names, addresses, time, and so on, the unique situation of the group of people around that pit in those circumstances—the sudden appearance of police among a group of peaceful fishermen, the finding of the body directly under the line of the shirt-sleeved priest, and the engineer, certainly unaware of what was going on, waving in his friendly way. I still feel it was a good story—at least there is no other murder story exactly like it, because there is no other murder exactly like it.

It is said that a reporter gets the story he is sent after, and a good reporter gets the story he is not sent after. Hence the principle of extensionalism is recognized—at least to the extent of a well-known adage—in my profession. It only remains that more of us act on the principle more of the time.

Donald M. Schwartz is a graduate of the University of Missouri School of Journalism, where general semantics is a required course of study. At the time this paper was written, he was on the staff of the South Bend (Indiana) Tribune. *He is now with the Chicago* Sun-Times.

Can a Radio Commentator Talk Sense?

CLIFTON M. UTLEY

I SHOULD like, right at the outset, to say a few words about the genesis of tonight's discussion. Several months ago, Dr. Hayakawa phoned to ask if I would address your society on the subject "How Can One Be a Radio Commentator and Still Talk Sense?" I replied that my ignorance of semantics was abysmal and that I had no place on your platform. He insisted that that made no difference and urged me to undertake the engagement. Though he did not so state, I had the impression that he regarded me as an interesting case study from whose presence the society might derive some profit in a clinical sense from such semantic fallacies as I might exemplify, much in the manner that a patient with a difficult disease has interest for a group of doctors even though the patient has no knowledge either of medicine or of the significance of his disease. It is in that role alone—and not as one who claims any knowledge of your special field of competence—that I am glad to be here tonight.

Now that I have made clear the reasons for my presence, and warned you not to expect much, let me hasten to add that I am very glad to be here and to discuss a question which is to me both fascinating and vitally significant.

As phrased by Dr. Hayakawa, the somewhat slanted title of this address reveals a good deal regarding both his beliefs and his approach to problems. It reveals first that he thinks much nonsense is broadcast by those styling themselves radio commentators. In this, he is, of course, entirely right.

The title further discloses that he is no pessimist. He does not believe radio commentators have to utter nonsense merely because they are commentators. It is possible, he appears to think, for them to talk sense. Sense in radio comment is therefore not unattainable. It is merely harder.

At this point he crosses the threshold of true optimism. For having ruled that the objective is attainable, he seeks to find out how it is achieved. On its face, this quest is an analytical process, and thus falls into the province of pure research—of the quest for truth.

I suspect, however, that Dr. Hayakawa's objectives reach beyond research and that as a social therapist he expects that if one can discover how one can be a radio commentator and still talk sense, one will then know *why* so much nonsense is being talked, and that knowing this, it will then be possible to do something about the nonsense. I wish him luck in his endeavors. Tonight, I cannot hope to make more than the most microscopic contribution to them, but I shall at least attack the problem in the spirit he has posed it. To talk sense, a radio commentator must first have the qualifications that enable him to do so, and second he must have the inclination—no, it is more than that; he must have the determination to talk sense no matter how great the temptations and pressures that might incline him to do the contrary.

Let us attack the question of qualifications first. The necessary qualifications are quickly apparent if one considers the material the commentator must handle and the function he is expected to perform. He must deal with the most complex political, social, and economic issues on all levels from local to international; he must inform the public of the basic facts the public needs to know, and he must interpret these facts so that relationships between them and relative significances become apparent to the busy listener. I believe—though here I am on very controversial territory and flying directly in the face of the announced policy of one great network—that the commentator at times also has the additional function of passing that degree of judgment on social issues that is implicit when one indicates where the weight of evidence lies.

But even if one drops this last point for the moment, it is clear the profession of the commentator is still sufficiently difficult, and that its responsible practice requires educational qualifications fully as rigorous as those required of persons practicing medicine, law, or any of the other learned professions.

I am not so concerned over formal education—university degrees and the like, but it seems to me that it is not enough for a commentator simply to read the teletype, the *New York Times,* and the Kiplinger letter. Behind that, if he is to speak of economic issues—and today no commentator can avoid it—there should at least be some knowledge of Adam Smith, David Ricardo, and John Stuart Mill—yes, and of the rest of the great classical economic tradition, as well as of Marx, Veblen, Keynes, and the contemporary neoclassicists. There must be historical knowledge, lack of which will lead into many pitfalls in the evaluation of current developments. There should obviously be training in political theory, and by this I do not mean simply a hasty reading of Dunning and Vernon Parrington, commendable as both those works may be. One could continue this list of specifications at much greater length, but I think you will see what I mean.

Since he will be dealing frequently with international affairs, it is desirable that the commentator should have experience in handling them, and that means, preferably, that he should have had the benefit of study or residence abroad, and, of course, a knowledge of languages other than his own; otherwise he may find he is not fully able to manipulate his own. The more training in the precise use of any language the commentator can have, the better, for remember, *it is much easier to give a false impression unintentionally over the air than elsewhere.* The radio speaker cannot watch his audience. He lacks the public speaker's opportunity to sense from audience reaction when he has not communicated his ideas effectively. He cannot therefore go back and clarify when communication is incomplete.

But now let us assume that our commentator has these or similar background qualifications. They alone will not enable him to talk sense over the radio, though they will certainly help.

Let us follow our commentator as he enters the newsroom of a major network at six o'clock some evening to begin preparation of a broadcast for later in the evening. He arrives at his desk where he finds between 100,000 and 150,000 words of United Press International and Associated Press and radio service copy awaiting him, with more constantly coming in. Earlier in the day he has read the local papers, *The New York Times,* and perhaps even the *Christian Science Monitor,* and, if he is curious as to what possible listeners are thinking in the more rural areas, he may also have glanced through the Des Moines *Register* as well. I should also mention that the British, French, Greek, Polish, Soviet,

Lithuanian, Chinese, Indian, Swedish, Norwegian, Hungarian, Arab, and other news services will have flooded his desk during the day with a wealth of mail, the best of which will contain significant texts and background material, and the poorest of which will be special pleading of the worst sort. The commentator skims through this. Something catches his eye. He reads. The rest goes into a mounting pile on the shelf behind him.

Subject to what may later come in on the wires, he now has the material for the night's broadcast, and he has anywhere from three to five hours to assimilate the current material and write a fifteen minute program.

From what has been said, you will see that the pressure under which the commentator works is considerable. It is now too late for leisurely reflective thought. That is where training and background come in. From two hundred or more stories, the relevant must be quickly separated from the irrelevant. In doing this, the commentator, whether he consciously realizes it or not, is constantly asking himself a series of questions; questions something like the following, which, when collectively answered make up news judgment. In which of these items is the public interested? In which ones should it be interested, to be able to perform its function as citizens in a democratic society? What items will the listener probably have heard on previous broadcasts? To what extent can I, through interpretative material, interest the listener in an item about which he is going to need to have knowledge, but the need for which knowledge is not yet apparent to him?

Once these questions are answered—and the answers come almost unconsciously—then a host of others arise. I have decided to include a certain subject in the broadcast. Let's say that the subject is Spain. The teletypes are carrying ten reports about Spain, some of them confusing, some actually contradictory. What is my duty? I cannot include them all. Do I seek to balance the reports on both sides, giving some from each side and letting it go at that? That sounds reasonable, but suppose I know from experience that one source has been habitually unreliable or slanted? In that event the apparent balancing, when served up cold to the listener who lacks sophistication in appraising sources, may be the worst form of distortion, in the sense that it may completely mislead him.

So my own judgment must go into the process of selection and weighing. To the extent that judgment is based on adequate background, experience, and training, it is more likely to be correct than the judgment which the listener might apply to contradictory reports. Yet in the last analysis, the judgment has its subjective elements that cannot be avoided. It may prove wrong.

And that brings me to one very vital rule which it seems to me that a commentator should follow if he is to talk sense over the radio. It concerns the controversial subject of expression of opinions by radio commentators. Judgments, at least those of the type I have mentioned, are clearly opinions. They are also necessary if the public is to be adequately and correctly informed. Yet, since they are opinions, and as such are fallible, the commentator with a true sense of responsibility to his audience will not give them as facts. In a case where this sort of judgment is rendered the commentator will not say, "This is so," or "This is a fact." Rather he will say, "This appears to me to be so," for this and this reason. The listener then has the advantage of the commentator's judgment, but he knows it is a judgment. Being aware of that, he is encouraged to apply his own critical faculties to it. Doing this, he may accept or reject the judgment, but in any case he has used his own thought processes, and that in itself is a gain. When that relationship is achieved between the commentator and the listener, the commentator is no longer talking *at* the listener. He is communicating *with* him. We commentators do not achieve that often enough, but it is an end to which we should constantly aspire.

On the side of the commentator, what this largely comes down to is the possession of a sense of modesty about one's opinions. If one possesses that, the tendency to put forth one's opinions as fact will be minimized. For a commentator, however, modesty of this sort is not easy to achieve or to retain. Even assuming the commentator possesses it to start with, the daily sitting before a microphone with the opportunity it presents for uttering statements without fear of immediate contradiction, makes it very difficult for the commentator to avoid developing the oracular when-I-open-my-mouth-let-no-dog-bark manner of speech.

I have suggested that the commentator who would talk sense should present his judgments, not as facts, but as judgments that might be fallible, documenting the judgments by whatever evidence the limits of available air time and the requirements of the issue under consideration make possible and necessary.

There is a related rule, equally important, which can perhaps be phrased as follows: The commentator should, at all times, keep his political or economic *science* rigidly separated from his political or economic *philosophy* or *morality*. A friend of mine, discussing a certain commentator, once said, "Poor So-and-so has an awfully hard time finding out which way is up, and the reason is he is so sure which way *ought* to be up." He meant, of course, that the commentator was letting his beliefs as to what ought to be interfere with his analysis of what actually was. Any commentator who does this will confuse both himself and his audience. He will not talk sense.

For example, suppose the run of the news causes the commentator to discuss problems of monopoly. He would logically have occasion to explain to his audience how the monopolist operates, how monopoly makes possible the setting and obtaining of different prices in different markets, or even in the same part of the same market. Economists will recognize this as the old split-demand problem in a different form. If, at the time he is seeking to explain the operation of this particular example of economic pathology, the commentator also renders judgment, if his vocabulary is charged with words of moral disapprobation, he is not going to make his listener understand the process involved. He may produce heat in the listener. He will not engender light. The commentator has a legitimate function both as a social scientist and as a social philosopher, but he must not confuse the two. He must not begin the second role until he has completed his function in the first capacity, and the audience must be able to see that the reality of his thinking is not injured by his social desires. To illustrate the point further, imagine the confusion that would be caused by a physicist who, addressing a classroom of students, began a lecture on hydrogen with the observation that really the atomic weight of hydrogen *ought to be* 14.

If these rules that have been suggested are followed, there is still no guarantee that the commentator will talk sense, but he is much more likely to be able to do so than if he violates them, and, in addition, he is much more likely to be able to do so than if he is forced into some sort of intellectual strait jacket by the laying down of a rule that he shall have no opinions.

If I seem to recur too frequently to the opinion-no-opinion

question, it is because it is a controversial and important one within the profession. To me a commentator with no opinions is of no value. Granted that the privilege of expressing opinions, drawing conclusions, and making judgments on the air can be and often is abused, the solution to the problem is not to prohibit them. Rather it is to obtain commentators with background, training, and intelligence, who will use the right to express opinions with discretion and balance. A quack doctor with a scalpel in his hand can do a lot of damage too, but we don't meet this danger by prohibiting surgery. We do it by seeing to it that unqualified persons do not practice medicine.

I think it is clear that, in the last analysis, the no-opinion rule is unenforceable anyway. But it may be worth indicating some of the absurdities that an attempt to enforce it can lead to.

At the time of the bombing of the Vatican, I suggested that when the final truth was discovered, it might well be found that the bomb in the Vatican gardens might prove to have been dropped by neither the Germans nor the Allies, but rather by some of the Catholic-hating Italians of the Roberto Farinacci stripe. In my script, I referred to Farinacci as a confirmed Catholic-baiter. The news editor said I could not say this on the air because after all it was only my opinion that Farinacci was a Catholic-baiter. I replied that that was my opinion, but that it was also a fact, and that I would submit the issue to any scholar in the field on Italian affairs. This shook the news editor a bit, but knowing the no-opinion rule, and being a good soldier, he still demurred. Then he brightened, for he saw the light of compromise. "You can," he volunteered, "say that Farinacci *is reported to be* a Catholic-baiter." He was quite pleased by this, because that put the responsibility on somebody else; it implied somebody else was being quoted. I pointed out that if it implied *that,* or if it implied that our teletypes had carried some such statement from Italy, then the use of the proposed compromise statement would perpetrate a falsehood on the audience, because no such report had been carried from Rome. I do not recall with any certainty how we finally did settle the issue. My recollection is that we decided to drop the item from the commentary. No great damage was done thereby, but to the extent that the judgment which I had attempted to offer was correct—and subsequent history proved it was—the audience was deprived of some degree of understanding of the issue in question.

I have tried to indicate thus far some of the qualifications and practices that will enable the commentator to talk sense. Lacking these, the commentator will hardly be able to talk sense, but possessing them there is still no assurance that he will do so. For in addition he must possess the will to talk sense, and the determination to do so in the face of all the pitfalls and temptations that will beset him. We will see what some of these temptations are when we turn—as we shall now do—to a consideration of why there is an appreciable amount of nonsense poured into microphones under the label of commentary.

The first reason for nonsense commentary is, of course, that certain commentators lack qualifications. They may have been selected because they have golden voices. This would be analogous to a situation in medicine where doctors would be selected on the basis of whether they looked well in that type of white medical coat that doctors always seem to wear, when, peering out at you from the advertisements, they point an admonitory finger into space while the accompanying legend proclaims "science says" to use this or that product.

Or again, the commentator may have been selected because the sponsor is willing to pay for a rather expensive and not otherwise easily salable block of time only if the particular commentator he wants is put on the air.

In either event, the remedy is clear. Note the word *clear,* but not always *easy*. It is for the facility involved—meaning the station or network—to step in, exercise its editorial prerogative, and refuse access to the air to the unqualified practitioner. In the financially stronger part of the industry much progress has been made along these lines, but where the financial structure is weaker, considerable abuses still prevail. One cannot escape the fact that financial strength is directly related to policy on such matters. Although I did not hear it said directly, a salesman for one facility was quoted to me recently as saying, "When we get rich we'll be moral too. In the meanwhile, whatever sells, goes on."

But now let us assume that we have rid the profession of the unqualified and that those practicing are fully competent by the most rigid standards. There are still pitfalls.

All of us, whether we admit it or not, are seeking to maximize our audiences, and it is a rare commentator who does not sneak an occasional look at the Hooper ratings, both at his own, and at those of his competitors.

It sometimes happens that a commentator may feel the

maximum audience can be obtained more readily if he deviates from some of the highest standards of the profession. This can be true for a variety of reasons. Many of the situations with which the commentator deals are complex in the extreme, and the commentator may feel that just a dash of oversimplification may pull his audience through better. Understand, I am not objecting to simplification. Simplification and lucidity, so as to make complex issues understandable to the listener, should always be attempted by any commentator. But oversimplification, by which is meant the elimination of facts that are essential to give the listener evidence he needs to make his own judgments, or the short circuiting of essential analysis through the substitution of heat for reason—these things are not compatible with talking sense. But, as stated, the commentator may be tempted to yield to them because he thinks they will raise his audience.

On the point of emotional heat, one commentator once said, "The Hooper is slipping. I'll have to begin raising hell with somebody again." Maybe hell should have been raised. But the raising of it for the reason assigned represents prostitution of the profession of the worst sort.

But let us assume the commentator escapes these pitfalls. There are still others which may come from the sponsor. I know of one commentator who was forbidden by his sponsor to say anything about labor on his program, which, by the way, was a network commentary. In another case, which also involved a network, the sponsor's representative phoned his commentator immediately after the broadcast on the night of D-Day and criticized him strongly for devoting all the broadcast to the war. "There is other news of importance," the representative told the commentator. On that night, of course, there was no other news of importance. But the sponsor "didn't like war" and it pained him to hear about it on his program.

Here again, the remedy is clear, though here again, it may not always be easy. Abuse of position by sponsors is not as frequent as some think, and it is decreasing as sponsors obtain a clearer view of what is their legitimate role, and as the various facilities become stronger financially and are able and willing to risk loss of revenue rather than to permit pollution of their news report.

I have by no means exhausted the pitfalls that confront even the most qualified commentator. One should also mention perhaps the possibility that the commentator, though qualified, will become lazy and simply not do his work adequately even though no adverse pressures are brought to bear on him. He may fail to keep up with the developing background material, and thus find himself unable to interpret new situations as they arise. In that event, he may take shortcuts—make wild guesses, and mislead his audiences. In that case, of course, the commentator in reality removes himself from the ranks of the qualified. He no longer talks sense, and the remedy is clear. Get rid of him.

We are near the end of our journey. I have tried to suggest that while it is not easy to talk sense over the radio, it is certainly not impossible. In my opinion, the industry, particularly in its more responsible units, has made great progress in recent years toward the goal of talking sense, and while there is still much nonsense on the air under the name of radio comment, we are making progress. Where, to cite only two conspicuous examples, will you find a higher level of interpretation of the current scene than that provided by Edward Murrow or Elmer Davis?

Admitting all our faults, and they are many, I feel that at its highest level, radio comment has made a substantial contribution to understanding and has produced much good sense. I think you can see it in the development of the level of national political intelligence. As a nation we have given up some of the most conspicuous attributes of our former ostrich-like isolation. Radio, I believe, has made at least some contribution to the achievement of this end by increasing the national fund of understanding of world affairs.

As to the abuses, there is no simple remedy that will eliminate them all; or perhaps I should say, I can see no such remedy. But there is progress being made, and in time I am confident the abuses will be minimized. It took medicine a long time to get rid of quack doctors, and I have heard it suggested there are still a few lurking on the periphery of the profession. Radio commentary is a profession much newer than medicine.

Presented before the Society for General Semantics at Thorne Hall, Northwestern University Chicago Campus, March 1, 1946, and published in ETC. *immediately thereafter. Until overtaken by illness, Clifton M. Utley was news commentator for the National Broadcasting Company in Chicago, widely known for his perceptiveness in international affairs and the thoroughness of his background knowledge. At present he continues his convalescence in Chicago.*

You Can't Write Writing

WENDELL JOHNSON

THE late Clarence Darrow, while speaking one day to a group of professors of English and others of kindred inclination, either raised or dismissed the basic problem with which his listeners were concerned by asking, "Even if you do learn to speak correct English, who are you going to talk it to?"

What Mr. Darrow was contending can be summarized in the statement that the effective use of the English language is more important than the "correct" use of it, and that if you can speak English "correctly," but not effectively, it does not matter very much "who you talk it to." I agreed that day, ten years ago, with Mr. Darrow's contention, and I still do, but whereas ten years ago his remarks served to dismiss for me the problem of the teaching of English, they serve now, in a new context of experience, to raise that problem to a position of peculiar educational and social significance. For, like many others, I have come to take a serious view of the apparently astonishing discrepancy between the opportunity and responsibility of the teachers of English and the actual contributions which they appear to make to the efficiency and well-being of individuals and of society.

The point of view which I have to present with regard to this problem has gradually developed during the decade that I have spent, sitting near the end of the educational conveyer belt, helping to put certain finishing touches on the human products of the scholastic mill. This is a way of saying that my experience has been chiefly with graduate students. When they arrive in the graduate college they have had, as a minimum, sixteen years of formal education. During practically every one of those sixteen (or more) years they have undergone some kind of training specifically designed to enhance their skill in the use of the English language. In spite of this, there falls upon me, as upon other directors of masters' and doctors' dissertations, the task of teaching graduate students how to write clear and meaningful and adequately organized English.

What are the linguistic shortcomings that the teachers of English seem unable to correct? Or do they in some measure nurture them? First of all, it is to be made clear that grammatical errors are not particularly serious. Whether or not they find anyone to "talk it to," the majority of graduate students have been taught most of the rudiments of "correct" English. In fact, it appears that the teachers of English teach English so poorly largely because they teach grammar so well. They seem to confuse or identify the teaching of grammar with the teaching of writing. In any event what they have failed to teach my graduate students about writing is not grammar. It is skill in achieving factually meaningful statements, and skill in organizing statements into an order consistent with the purposes for which the statements are made. The students have not been taught how adequately to achieve either precision or systematic arrangement in the written representation of facts. This can be stated in another and more significant way of saying that they have not been taught how to use language for the purpose of making highly reliable maps of the terrain of experience.

These students exemplify the simple fact that although one may have learned how to write with mechanical correctness, one may still have to learn how to write with significance and validity. One of my friends, who is a particularly astute investigator of the psychology of reading, has stated essentially the same problem by saying that the one place in which a child is not likely to learn to read is the reading class, for the simple reason that one cannot read reading. One can only read history or geometry or biology, etc. If the child reads such material in the reading class, then it is difficult to see how the reading class differs appreciably from the classes in history, geometry, and other subjects. If the child does not read such material in the reading class, then the reading class must differ from these others, but in a puzzling way, for it may be that the reading teacher is actually making the amazing effort to get the child to read reading.

In the teaching of writing, or any other of the language skills, the same problem appears. One cannot write writing, any more than one can read reading. One can only write, just as one can only read, history, or geography, or physiology, or some other such subject about which writing can be done. One can, of course, write about writing, but what one writes about writing will have little, if any, significance, except insofar as one writes about writing about something else. We have to deal here with a very general, and a very crucial, problem. What is true of reading and writing is true, also, of speaking. It holds for any kind of symbolizing. Just as one cannot, with significance, read reading, or write writing, or speak speaking, except insofar as one reads about something, or writes about something, or speaks about something, so one cannot, with significance, symbolize symbolizing in general except insofar as one symbolizes the symbolizing of something.

It seems clear to me, as I attempt to analyze the writing difficulties of graduate students, and as I ponder over my own experiences as a student of English, that these considerations, sketched immediately above, are crucial. The teacher of English appears to attempt to place the emphasis upon writing, rather than upon writing-about-something-for-someone. From this it follows quite inevitably that the student of English fails in large measure to learn the nature or the significance of clarity or precision and of organization in the written representation of facts.

He learns grammatical correctness reasonably well, because that is emphasized. But so long as the student's primary anxieties are made to revolve around the task of learning to spell, punctuate, and observe the rules of syntax, he is not likely to become keenly conscious of the fact that when he writes he is, above all, communicating. If he is to learn to communicate effectively, he must realize that his first obligation to his reader is not to be grammatically fashionable, but to be clear and coherent. One does not just communicate; one communicates something to someone. And the something communicated is not the words used in the communication, but whatever those words represent. Moreover, the degree to which there is communication depends precisely upon the degree to which the words represent the same thing for the receiver or reader that they do for the sender or writer. And the degree to which they do is an index of the clarity of the communication or written statement. Thus, clarity can be *measured,* not just "felt" or "appreciated," but measured, in terms of the ascertainable agreement between writer and reader, and among various readers, as to precisely what the words of the writer represent.

My graduate students have not been taught this. They write as if they had been trained to observe a principle of *caveat lector.* Such a principle, strange as it may seem, is championed, in one form or another, by certain teachers of English. Mr. Cleanth Brooks, Jr., writing on the subject of communication in poetry in the journal, *American Prefaces,* in 1940, expresses this curious point of view in these words:

> The theory of communication throws the burden of proof on the poet, overwhelmingly and at once—the reader tells the poet: here I am; it's your job to get it across to me—when he ought to be assuming the burden of proof himself. Now the modern poet has thrown the weight of responsibility on the reader.

I have quoted Mr. Brooks because he has succeeded in stating with unusual conciseness this strange notion that the writer is properly under no obligation to be communicative. I do not wish, on the other hand, to be understood as saying that a reader has no obligation to try to meet a genuinely original (and therefore difficult) writer halfway, for obviously many writers and poets, dissatisfied with the clichés of their time and trying to create new ways of feeling (i.e., to recanalize the reader's semantic reactions), must necessarily rely upon the reader's willingness to accept a revised vocabulary of an unfamiliar set of symbols. But this is a problem only in extremely advanced levels of artistic composition. In undergraduate instruction, even to imply that a writer has no obligations to his readers is to become, whether one wishes to or not, an advocate of obfuscation.

Such advocates of obfuscation apparently teach fairly well, if it is they who have instructed my graduate students. They have never learned, so far as I can see, to take the reader seriously into consideration. They do not, to be sure, artfully avoid clarity; they artlessly fail to achieve it. The contention that in writing they are communicating, that they are addressing a reader, simply strikes them as a novel point of view. They do not rebel against it; many of them just don't understand it.

This basic notion of communication, however, is not extraordinarily difficult to explain, and as it begins to sink in, and when the students have seen a few demonstrations, not of the reading or criticizing of communications, but of the *process* of communicating by means of writing, they are at least prepared to understand that there are techniques of clarity. Moreover, they are able to understand that these techniques have something to do with effectiveness in writing—unless one means by writing a gyring and gimbling in the wabe of literary slithy toves, or unless one believes the excuse offered by frustrated literary midwives: namely, the "only-God-can-make-a-tree" theory that effectiveness cannot be taught at all. But this definition of "writing" and this theory of "effectiveness" have practically nothing to do with the kind of writing that involves communication. For communication is achieved by virtue of clarity, as this is defined in terms of agreement between writer and reader, or among various readers, as to what the writer is referring to. The ability to achieve clarity in this sense, and thus communicative effectiveness, is a tree that others besides God can make, at least in a rough fashion.

This discussion is not designed to take the place of a textbook for the teaching of effective communicative writings, but it is offered in the hope that a brief statement of a few simple principles upon which such writing is based might serve at least to raise the question as to why these principles are not more adequately taught by English instructors.

The first of these principles has already been given in the statement that clearness depends upon, and can be measured in terms of, the degree of agreement between the writer and his readers as to what the words of the writer represent. Simply by striving for a high degree of such agreement, the writer discovers, in some measure, his ingenuity in achieving it. He discovers the usefulness of conditional and quantifying terms, the confusion created by leaving out significantly differentiating details, the degree to which the meaning of a term varies from context to context, and the kinds of differences he must allow for among his readers' habits of interpreting words. He learns to rely less on the dictionary and more on the linguistic habits of the people for whom he writes. He discovers that literary posing, pleasurable as it may be, usually can be enjoyed only at the expense of effective communication—that Chesterton's paradoxes or Paul de Kruif's chronic astonishment are more titillating than informative. He discovers that there are various levels of abstraction, and that if he goes systematically from lower to higher levels he can use so-called abstract words and still be reasonably clear.

Above all, perhaps, he discovers the basic significance of order, or relations, or structure, or organization. This matter of structural relationships has wide ramifications, and no writer ever exhausts it, but the student quickly grasps some of its more obvious aspects, if he is striving for agreement between himself and his reader. It does not take him long to understand that the organization of what he writes should correspond to the organization of what he is writing about if the reader is to follow him readily. The graduate students with whom I work frequently have difficulty organizing their descriptions of experimental techniques or procedures, and I have found that it is more helpful to refer them to a cookbook than to a textbook on composition. By examining a cookbook they see at once that the organization of a description of procedure is determined simply by the order of the events that make up the procedure. First you do *a*, and then *b*, and then *c*, and you write it in that order because you do it in that order. This simple principle of order is fundamental in practically all descriptive, narrative, and expository writing, and it is obvious to anyone who is attempting to be considerate of the reader.

One might suppose that graduate students would know this, but in spite of the years they have spent in English courses most of them seem not to have learned much about it. The more significant fact is that, as a rule, they learn quite readily to apply this simple principle, once it is clearly explained and demonstrated to them. In this case, certainly, one can make a tree that either God or the English teachers forgot to make.

One aspect of organization that seems to have eluded practically all graduate students is that involved in the making of transitions. Even those who have been taught how to lay beads in a row have not been taught how to string them. Just as the order of what one writes is determined by the order of the parts or events involved in what one is writing about, so the ways in which transitions are made in the writing are determined by the ways in which the parts or events are related in the realities one is describing, narrating, or explaining. The ability to move from one sentence or paragraph or chapter to the next, in such a way as to blend them into a unified whole, is largely dependent upon an understanding of the reasons for going from one to the next, of why one statement should follow another instead of the reverse, of why one should say, "It follows, then," rather than "But." And these reasons are found in the character of the relations existing among the details of that about which the writing is being done. This becomes obvious to one who is not trying to write writing, but who is attempting, rather, to write-about-something-for-someone.

Another principle underlying communicative writing is that clarity is a prerequisite to validity. It is to be considered that statements that flow beautifully and are grammatically superb may be, also, utterly devoid of factual meaning, or meaningful but vague, or precise but invalid. For writing to be effective, in the sense in which I am using this term, it may or may not be grammatically correct, but it must be both clear and valid. It can be clear without having validity, but if it is unclear its validity cannot well be determined. It must, then, first of all, be clear; it must be that before the question of its validity can even be raised. We ask the writer, "What do you mean?" before we ask, "How do you know?" Until we reach agreement as to precisely what he is writing about, we cannot possibly reach agreement as to whether, or in what degree, his statements are true.

Only to the extent that the various readers of a statement agree as to the specific conditions or observations required for ascertaining its validity can the question of its validity have meaning. And the extent to which the readers of the statement agree on these conditions is, of course, indicative of the extent to which the statement is clear. If a statement is such that its readers do not agree at all as to how it might be verified or refuted, the statement may be "beautiful" or "rich in meaning" or grammatically irreproachable, but it is also, from the point of view of scientific courses such as I am teaching, nonsense. It cannot be demonstrated to be valid or invalid, and is meaningful, therefore, to its author, possibly to his English teacher, and perhaps to his psychiatrist.

My graduate students have not learned this, either. They show this in a particularly disturbing manner when they first attempt to state the topics or problems they propose to investigate in undertaking their theses. The quite characteristically propose problems which preclude the possibility of clear discussion. They propose questions for investigation, for which they desire to obtain precise answers, but which are so stated as to be unanswerable. Apparently they have never been taught that one cannot get a precise answer to a vague question—that the terminology of the question limits the clarity and thus the validity of the answer. Many students are so befuddled on this point that they do not recognize any relation at all between clarity and validity. They actually assume, for example, that they can ask, "What causes personality maladjustments?" without specifying what they mean by "causes," or by "personality," or by "maladjustments," or what observations one is to make in order to comply with their definition of "what." Many of them appear to have been taught that to eliminate the vagueness of a question or statement is to destroy its "richness of meaning"—that for a statement to be "full of meaning" it must not mean anything in particular!

Even though they have been so taught, and come, therefore, to the graduate college quite untrained in the writing of valid statements, they can be taught, to a considerable degree, to gauge the validity of what they write. They can be trained to do this by being trained, first, to write clearly. For when a statement is made clearly—when there is reasonable agreement among its readers as to what it represents in the realm of fact—its validity can be judged, or a procedure for determining its degree of validity can be devised.

In summary, then, what graduate students, as I know them, have been well taught—and what, in my judgment, their English instructors should have been able to teach them, because the students do learn readily—is the ability to write a clear, organized, unified, and valid document. They have been made familiar with grammar, for the most part, and they have picked up a few tricks of literary flavoring. The grammar can be used to advantage; most of the literary condiments have to be chucked.

There appear to be three main reasons for the English instructors' failure. The first is that they do not appear to utilize to any considerable extent the principle of teaching by example. They tell the student how to write and how not to have written, but they don't, as a rule, do any actual writing for him or with him. They show him examples of what has been written, but no examples of something being written.

To try to learn to write by reading literature that has already been written and thoroughly jelled, instead of by observing the actual writing of literature, is much like trying to learn to bake a cake by eating one, instead of by watching the baker. One should teach by example, and what the teachers of English forget is that there are no examples of writing in the grammar book or the anthology; there are only generalized blueprints of statements yet unwritten and examples of something already written—cakes that were baked yesterday. The teacher herself has to provide the examples of writing to demonstrate the process. She must bake the cake of written English, not merely eat the cake that Hawthorne baked, as she stands before the class.

The second, and a more grave, reason for their failure is that they appear to place the emphasis on "writing," rather than on writing-about-something-for-someone. You cannot write writing. Or, at least if you do, you are not likely to learn how to write with clarity and validity, because they are not important to one who merely writes writing. Unless the emphasis is placed upon writing as a form of communication and directed very definitely, therefore, to an actual, live reader, the importance of clarity, organization, and validity is not likely to become very apparent. Their importance becomes obvious, and the means of achieving them suggests themselves more or less readily, the moment one begins seriously to write about-something-for-someone.

The third and final point in this "diagnosis" of English instruction is that teachers of English, with apparently only a few exceptions, cling tenaciously to two strange theories. The first is that writing is an art, and the second is that it cannot be taught. What they seem to mean when they say that writing is an art is that writing does not have to say anything—except to the reader who has "appreciation"—that writing is at its best when it is a form of expression *qua* expression.

In teaching the student to write, if one takes this view of "writing as an art," there is no point—in fact, there is a strong argument to the contrary—in training the student to express himself clearly or with validity. For truth that is "not art" would be of no value, and if art that is clear is regarded as a contradiction in terms (and it seems to be so regarded by some), there would remain only truth that is vague as the ideal of the teachers of English whom we are here discussing. But in communicative writing, truth is never vague, for unless a statement is clear, the degree to which it is true cannot be determined. All of which goes far to explain how students can reach the graduate college without learning how to produce effective communicative writing.

The explanation is extended when we recall the other theory, so popular among some teachers of English, that real effectiveness in writing, since it is an "art," cannot be taught at all. Only God can make a tree; the teacher of English can only water the tree with verbal dew in the hope of keeping it green, and even the value of doing that is debatable. Teachers frequently boast of having "discovered" a writer; it seems that this in itself is regarded as no mean accomplishment. It is also to be noted that writers are sometimes said to have been "influenced" by a teacher. But when a teacher has "discovered" a writer and "influenced" him, he cannot further add to what the genes have done, nor detract from what the fates will do. Presumably, then, he doesn't try. And this pedagogical swooning by the teachers of English, on the theory that you can't make a silk purse out of a sow's ear, results in their making a great many sows' ears out of silk purses. It is not a question of the truth or falsity of their theory that effective writing cannot be taught, although this theory is probably not as largely true as many teachers of English suppose. The significant point is that the theory makes for unimaginative and lackadaisical teaching. Even God's trees might benefit from some systematic pruning and spraying.

My own narrow concern with all this lies in the fact that the ineffectiveness of the English instruction in our schools makes for a serious difficulty in the graduate college in all its branches. But the problem has an importance far more vast than this fact could ever give to it. For the ability of the individual, and of groups of individuals, to use language clearly and with validity is basic to personal efficiency and general development—it is basic to sanity itself—and it is fundamental to intelligent social organization and to the adequate management of national and international problems. The teachers of English in our schools and universities have been and are being entrusted with the heavy responsibility of training the members of our society in the effective communicative use of our language. It is not a responsibility that they can meet appropriately merely by teaching the formalism of grammar, or superciliously disclaim by asserting that effective writing is an art and cannot be taught.

Effective writing is a human necessity in anything resembling a democratic culture, and this becomes increasingly true as the culture becomes increasingly complex. If the effective use of language cannot be taught, or if it is not to be taught to a far greater extent than it has been, we may well have occasion to despair of the grand experiment dreamed by Voltaire, championed by Washington and Franklin, and cherished by the American people through many generations. And if we must despair of that, then truly, even if you do learn to speak correct English, it may well not seem to matter very much "who you talk it to." For when the people cannot adequately speak or write their language, there arise strong men to speak and write it for them—and "at" them.

The issues of which I write are by no means to be regarded as academic issues. We are a symbolic class of life. To say that we are human is to say, above all and with incalculable significance, that our problems, as individuals, as groups, and as a world culture, are symbolic problems. They are problems that center around the symbols of government, the symbols of finance and general economy, of social status, of power and prestige, of class and race. They are the problems involved in the great institutionalized symbol systems of the Church, the Law, the State. They are problems of meaning, of evaluation, or orientation, processes which, on human levels, are predominantly symbolic in character. It is not the vestige of some forebear's whim that the whole structure of our educational system is founded squarely on the three R's, for reading, writing, and the use of numbers are forms of behavior in the absence of which *human* society would disintegrate and vanish. The degree to which these forms of behavior are cultivated and made adequate determines, more than does anything else, the degree to which a symbolic class of life may escape the threat of self-destruction and achieve cultural maturity. Our maladjustment, no less than our genius, as individuals and as groups, lies in our way of responding to and with symbols.

The place of the teacher of English in the structure of a symbolic society is, thus and indeed, not one to be occupied by petulant little men engrossed in verbal "fancy work." It is not too much to say that our possibilities for progress are determined, and limited, by those who instruct us in the use of our language. This view is as disheartening, perhaps, as it is challenging, but the more challenging it is to some, the less disheartening it need be to others.

Wendell Johnson is professor of psychology and speech pathology at the University of Iowa. He is the author of Language and Speech Hygiene *(1939),* People in Quandaries *(1946),* The Onset of Stuttering *(1959), and* Stuttering and What You Can Do About It *(1961). He served as President of the International Society for General Semantics from 1945 to 1947.*

The Process of News Reporting

KEN MACRORIE

IN FEBRUARY, 1949, Joseph T. Klapper and Charles Y. Glock published in *The Scientific American* an incisive content analysis of the newspaper reporting in the case of Edward U. Condon, head of the Bureau of Standards, who was called a weak security risk by the House Committee on Un-American Activities. In their study, entitled "Trial by Newspaper," Mr. Klapper and Mr. Glock said:

> Bias may be shown . . . in the manner in which a paper reports an event and in its selection of which events to report and which to omit. An outside observer, lacking the newspapers' access to the events on which they based their reporting, can only judge their treatment of the Condon case by comparing the way in which the various newspapers dealt with the same events.

But must an outside observer lack the newspapers' access to events on which they base their reporting? Can he judge reports fairly when he has no notion of how they emerged through the complex process of modern reporting?

A communicative act may be thought of as a *transaction*, involving manifold relationships between persons, their pasts, and their present situations—as suggested by the explorations of John Dewey and Arthur F. Bentley in *Knowing and the Known* and Adelbert Ames, Jr. and his followers in perception experiments.[1] Looked at in this way, one of the most crucial elements in a communication becomes the very selection of subjects, which Mr. Klapper and Mr. Glock suggest is outside the content analyst's purview.

Surely a description of the whole process of a news report

[1] See *ETC.*, Vol. XII, No. 4 (Summer, 1955), "Special Issue on Transactional Psychology."

in the making will tell more than a mere examination of printed reports in the paper. Here is an example of how an actual news report may be studied *in process*.

At 11:15 A.M., Friday, May 21, 1954, in the newsroom of *The New York Times*, Robert E. Garst, assistant managing editor, told me that I could probably accompany Peter Kihss, a city reporter, on a news assignment. Marshall E. Newton, assistant city editor, got in touch with Mr. Kihss, who agreed to meet me that afternoon at the Customs House annex at 54 Stone Street in lower Manhattan.

The hearing of the Senate Subcommittee of the Judiciary Committee took place in a locked room containing hundreds of canvas mailbags piled in rows, stacks of packages wrapped in brown paper, and dozens of magazines spread on a large table. About fifteen people were present, some looking over the literature on the table, which proved to be foreign Communist publications, many printed in English. A few rows of folding chairs were lined up, facing the table. The place looked more like the back room of a post office than a setting for a Senate investigative hearing.

Soon a man wearing a gray-blue suit and black-and-white shoes entered and loudly greeted several men, his entourage following him. He was addressed as "Senator." Someone said his name was Welker [Idaho]. He told one of his assistants, who had been awaiting him, that he wanted someone to make a call for him to a hotel. He gave instructions for getting in touch with one or another of two men connected with the Pittsburgh baseball club who he said would get him some tickets to a game the Pirates were playing. "If you can't get him," he said, "ask for Vernon Law." The Senator moved to the back of the room where a man began to brief him, saying, "Now, Senator, what we have here on the table is . . ."

A few minutes later, at 1:25, Mr. Peter Kihss, the *Times* reporter, arrived. We introduced ourselves and I explained my purpose. He said he was going to introduce himself to the Senator, adding that he used to know the members of this committee. He talked to a number of the principals, including the Senator and Deputy Collector Irving Fishman, who knew most about the details of handling the Communist propaganda coming through Customs to the Port of New York. One of the officials said that approximately three-quarters of a million pieces of Communist propaganda were in the room and that they represented just two days' accumulation. Mr. Kihss greeted other newspapermen who arrived, and they exchanged what information they had on the purpose and personnel of the hearing. It was scheduled to begin at 2 P.M. At approximately 1:45, photographers began to take pictures. First they shot stills of the Senator and his associates looking at magazines on the table. They asked him to take one that was boldly titled *Soviet Union* and hold it as if he were reading, yet so they could see his eyes and the title. Then a Telenews crew, after rigging lights, blowing a fuse or two, and rearranging the principals at the table as well as the news reporters sitting nearby, photographed the Senator while he made a statement about the purpose of the hearings. Without explaining the issues, he emphasized the increasing flood of propaganda that was "pouring" into the United States.

Since, as the cameraman put it, the Senator "fluffed" some of his lines while partially improvising his speech and looking up into the camera, a retake was necessary on one lengthy part of his statement. He uncomplainingly posed for all the cameramen, while they maneuvered and rearranged him and his associates like mannequins. Finally, on one cameraman's insistence that he again hold up a piece of literature, he showed some irritation and said that that was enough. About forty-four minutes after picture-taking had started, the camera crew packed up and left. At 2:32, the hearings began.

In his opening statement, Senator Welker said there were 34 million pieces of propaganda in the room (perhaps he had read "¾ million" as "34 million"). No one corrected him although his words were being recorded both by a stenotype operator and a tape recorder. The Senator swore in as the first witness the Collector of Customs, Robert W. Dill, who said that the room held a two-day supply of mail. From this point on, I had difficulty following the details of the hearing.

Witnesses from the Customs House testified and discussions of the laws under which they were operating were carried on, seldom to any clear resolution. At one point, Senator Welker dramatically asked the members of the press to pick out any sack of mail in the room for inspection. The reporters said they were content to have any one of them opened which was handy. One of the Customs workers cut the seal on one bag and spilled the contents on the table before everyone. The principals and the reporters began looking over the addresses on the packages. Under Senator Welker's questioning, Deputy Collector Fishman read off the names on several of the packages, saying that he recognized one as that of a man at the Soviet United Nations delegation, who frequently received such mail. All of these comments were being made a part of the record.

At 2:59, when the reel of tape in the recorder needed to be changed, Senator Welker arose, announced that the hearings would be suspended for a few minutes, and went out to complete his call about baseball tickets.

When the hearings resumed, Deputy Collector Fishman asked permission to correct his sworn testimony about the name on the package. He said that on further check he had found that the man named was not the person he had identified as belonging to the Russian UN delegation. Other names from packages were read off. One of these, that of a library, and another, of a committee, later appeared, accompanied by addresses, in the tenth paragraph of an Associated Press account of seventeen paragraphs sent over the AP wire. Mr. Kihss later implied to me that he did not approve of reading names in this way. The public might infer that those named were Communist sympathizers when perhaps they were simply students of Communism. Mr. Kihss examined more packages than anyone else at the table. At times throughout the hearing, he asked questions, confirmed or corrected factual statements made by officials, and showed such an active knowledge of the proceedings, past and present, that one reporter chided him for having so much interest in them.

When one of the principals spoke of labeling material "Communist propaganda," Mr. Kihss attempted to straighten him out on the wording of the 1938 Alien Registration Act, which he said did not require the labeling of mailed material as "Communist propaganda," but simply as "political propaganda." Mr. Arens, the committee counsel, and Mr. Fishman, Deputy Collector of Customs, discussed this point further and read portions of the McCarran Act ordering labeling of material. From time to time, Mr. Kihss consulted papers he carried in a brown envelope, including a printed copy of the proceedings of the executive session hearings of the subcommittee headed "Communist Underground Printing Facilities and Illegal Property, March 6—July 11, 1953." Mr. Kihss had said earlier that because that day was his father's birthday, he would have preferred not to work, but he was the logical choice for the story since he had covered this subject on November 12 and 13, 1952, and October 11, 1953. At that time, he said, he had been concerned about the problem of the Federal law preventing the mailing of Communist propaganda to recognized anti-Communist scholars at such centers as Columbia and Harvard universities. As the law stood, the Customs officials were only supposed to let mail go through to people registered as foreign agents or to embassies, consulates, etc. Yet those same agents might, if they wished, distribute the material to book shops which could sell it to any individual in the country who cared to buy it. Customs officials had let some of the mail go through to university scholars—as anyone can see by visiting libraries and centers for Russian study—but they knew they were disobeying the letter of the law in doing it, even though they were acting in the best interests of the United States. Both officials of the Customs and the Post Office in the past, Mr. Kihss said, had made recommendations for legislation legalizing such distribution, but no legislation had resulted.

This point was never raised at the hearing. Instead, Senator Welker and his counsel made much of the bill the Senator said he had proposed for the stamping of "Communist propaganda" on the material so that readers would know what they were getting. Under Mr. Kihss's questioning, the Senator admitted that actually his bill did not provide for this. Rather it applied to propaganda coming from any country, including England or France, for example, and provided for that material to be labeled "political propaganda" only. Mr. Kihss complained to a reporter friend that the point about the scholars receiving the material was one of the central issues in the whole affair, and yet it had never been taken up during the hearing.

Under persistent questioning by the counsel, one of the Customs officials testified that the bags in the room at the time were in part mail that had been there for a month. Under further questioning, he said that about 30 per cent of it had been there a month and the rest was current—had come in the last few days and would be moved out as soon as possible. The reporters, especially Mr. Kihss, were irritated by the shifting statistics that were being given on the amount of mail coming in, especially since the increase was being made one of the important points in the hearing. One of the women who testified for the Customs said that for the two-week period, May 5 to 18, about 600 bags of mail, or 100,000 pieces of published material, reached the port. The Associated Press and United Press dispatches later said that such mail was arriving in New York at the rate of 300 bags a week. Apparently the reporters or editors had

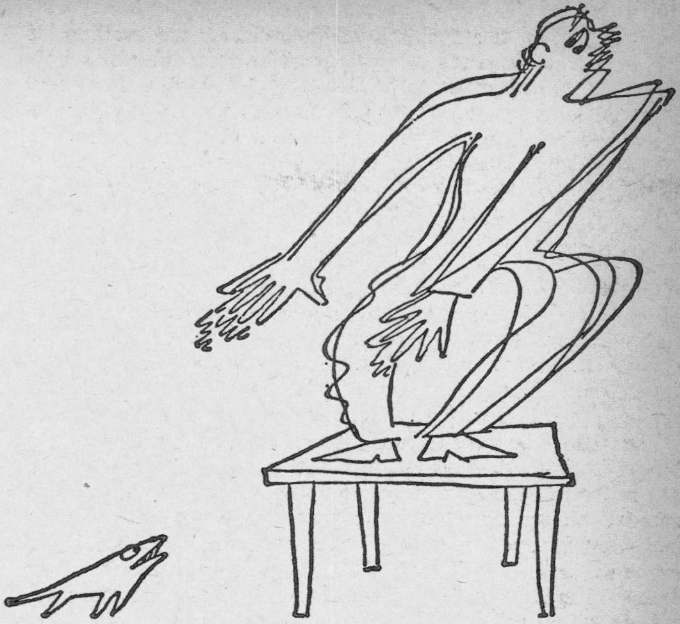

The World's Most Powerful Nation Reacts to a Certain Word

averaged the 600 bags for two weeks, which was probably not a long enough period to yield a representative average. Mr. Kihss, when he later wrote his story, stuck to the more precise statement: "From May 5 to 18, 100,000 pieces of published material . . ."

Senator Welker asked the Customs officials what they thought of his proposed legislation requiring all political propaganda to be so stamped. Mr. Fishman, the Deputy Collector, agreed that it would be helpful in reducing the volume of mail they received from foreign countries. Earlier, witnesses had testified at length on the inadequacy of the Customs House staff to process the mail. Some of it was in Russian and Chinese and had to be interpreted before it could be judged for propaganda content. Mr. Fishman told of an inspection trip he had made of American ports handling such material. He said that in St. Paul one official who did not know Russian was attempting to process the flood of propaganda with the aid of a Russian dictionary and his own efforts to learn the language.

The hearing, I gathered, was designed to put down for public record the salient facts of the matter of propaganda mailings into the Port of New York. It often confused rather than enlightened me. For example, when Collector of Customs Robert W. Dill testified as the first witness, he said that about sixty ships were coming or going every day at the port, but he did not say that all of them carried Communist propaganda. The wire story sent out by the United Press included these words, "Communist propaganda is arriving here from behind the Iron Curtain on 60 ships daily." It further stated:

> Any material addressed to individuals, institutions or any other addressee not on the list of registered agents supplied the customs service by the Department of Justice, it was testified, are returned to the Postmaster designated as material which cannot be forwarded and which is to be returned to the sender.

The New York *Herald Tribune* story, "300 Bags Weekly of Red Mail Here," on page 4, and the *Daily News* story, "Reveal Red Literature Flooding U.S.," page 5, and the New York *Journal-American* story, "Bare Flood of Red Propaganda Here," page 4, repeated this assertion in different words. Mr. Kihss said that the mail which was not forwarded was actually confiscated rather than returned to the sender, a fact which he had reported in an earlier article.

At one point, a Customs House film reviewer was interrogated about Communist propaganda films. He read some of the reviews he had prepared, and under questioning admitted that he knew some of these films were being shown at the Stanley Theater in Times Square, New York City. Mr. Kihss told me that this fact had been brought out at preceding hearings and was "old stuff." I knew that any reader of the *Times* could examine daily advertisements for the Stanley Theater, read reviews of its films, and like me, trot over to the Stanley and see a film on ballet—or even a faked-up propaganda film—without being converted to the Communist party.

At 3:47 Senator Welker officially concluded the hearing, but not before he and Customs officials had exchanged elaborate compliments, the Senator praising the officials' cooperation and the officials assuring him that he was always welcome. Earlier in the afternoon the Senator had complimented Mr. Dill and his "gallant men" of the Customs.

When the principals arose from the table, the reporters

sought them for further questioning. Mr. Kihss asked the Senator and his counsel for specific information about his bill which they had mentioned. When asked for a copy of it, the Senator and his counsel said they had none with them, but the counsel said it was "S-37," and the Senator nodded in agreement. After talking with others, Mr. Kihss again returned to the Senator, who was about to leave, and asked him whether he had been considering including in his bill anything to clear up the trouble the Customs encountered in being legally denied the right to send these important Communist documents to recognized American scholars. The Senator said that it did not. Mr. Kihss asked whether he could say in his story that the Senator was aware of this problem—that he was working on it. The Senator reflected and answered yes.

Mr. Kihss, another reporter, and I left the building. On the way to a drugstore telephone, Mr. Kihss emphasized what a poor story this was. When the other reporter left, Mr. Kihss called the *Times*. Then we headed for the nearest subway, and boarded a train. After one stop, I noticed that the subway car was identified as the Lexington Avenue line. We realized that in our absorption with the story—Mr. Kihss had been poring over his finely written personal shorthand in his notebook—we had boarded the wrong train. He suggested that we could get off at Grand Central and shuttle across to Times Square. On the way, he told me that this was the kind of story he liked to think about a long time before he wrote, to let it jell. It had him stumped, he said, because the most important issue was not even taken up in the hearings. He had two alternatives, he thought: to write a short, straight story giving the facts, which were really old stuff except for the increased flow of material, or to write a long article in which he editorialized constantly in order to explain to the lay reader the significance of the whole controversy, and he would not be allowed to do that. He really did not know what he would do, he said. He looked over his notes, which he held in a secretary's stiff notebook. He underlined in pencil the portions he thought important.

When he arrived at the newsroom, he found in his mailbox an office memorandum stating that, "Space requirements make it necessary that stories should run 15 to 20 per cent shorter than they have been recently. Our goals should be simplicity and clarity, through the use of short sentences, careful organization and the elimination of unnecessary details." He went to the newspaper's library and with the help of a librarian found that "S-37," the bill the counsel had said was Senator Welker's, was in reality one introduced by Senator McCarran. Further checking in congressional records shed no light. Next he went to the morgue and checked quickly through recent clippings on Senator Welker. Again no light. He got out his own notes and files on past Customs stories he had done, and again said he did not know what to do with the story, adding that perhaps no story at all would be best. Then he went to the desk of the national editor. Later, he wrote me what happened there:

> When I reported to Ray O'Neill, who handled the written story as the national news editor, the substance of the conversation as I recollect it now [one week later] went like this. I said:
>
> "Ray, I was assigned to the Welker Senate Internal Security subcommittee hearing on Communist propaganda. The story today was that we're getting an increasing flow of Communist propaganda. We had some new statistics, about 100,000 pieces coming in by mail alone between May 5 to 18, and there was a show of about hundreds of mail bags piled up in the Customs House annex where the hearing was held. But otherwise, the hearing didn't get very far. I asked Welker after the hearing about the problem of the scholars who need this stuff—you know we studied this in 1952 and 1953. He said he was studying it. The customs fellows tell me their legislative recommendations seem to be stalled in Washington. The scholar issue didn't come up in the hearing itself."
>
> "How much space do you need—we don't have much tonight," he rejoined.
>
> "Anything from one paragraph up—it wasn't too important," I said.
>
> "All right, 400 words, but we may have to cut it back to an M head," he said. (An M head runs 200-250 words.)

At 5:15, he began typing a summary of the story, which the *Times* requires to help editors see what they have to work with. When he finished, he began typing a scratch version of the story itself. He looked this over, made some changes, and then began writing the story on special copy paper with attached carbons. He bent over the typewriter, typing quickly. At 5:32, when he was on page 3, a man dropped on his desk the first "take" of the Associated Press wire report on the story. He stopped typing, read the dispatch, and told me that it was pretty close to what he was writing. When he finished, he had more than three pages,

Postage
Will Be Paid
by
Addressee

No
Postage Stamp
Necessary
If Mailed in the
United States

BUSINESS REPLY MAIL

FIRST CLASS PERMIT No. 13923 SAN FRANCISCO, CALIF.

ETC.
San Francisco State College
540 Powell Street
San Francisco 2, California

with his copy triple-spaced. He penciled out several sentences. "Still too much," he said, and slipped a new set of copy sheets into the typewriter. On the edge of the unoccupied next desk, a telephone—almost touching the one on his desk—began to ring insistently. He never looked up, but clattered on with his story, his head bent over the keyboard.

By 6 P.M., he had finished the final version, six paragraphs, which ran to exactly 321 words, 79 under his prescribed limit. I told him that the fifth paragraph, which included Senator Welker's comments on scholars, made the story valuable because it showed what his knowledge brought to the story. He said that it was an important paragraph, but that he couldn't justify putting it any higher in the story. He checked over his copy and dropped it in a box at the national desk.

A few minutes later, he went over to the copy desk, where several men kidded him about coming over to protect his story from cutting. "If it's 405 words," one copyreader said to me, "we'll cut it." The story had come from the national desk with no changes. Mr. Kihss left after introducing me to men on the copy desk. I sat down next to Jack Randolph, a copyreader, who let me look over his shoulder. He went through the story quickly, and without hesitation drew two diagonal lines through the sixth, and last, paragraph. He broke the first paragraph into two. Then, spending only about five minutes, he made minor changes to conform to *Times* style, such as changing "United States" to "Federal" and the phrase: "In the last two weeks from May 5 to 18, 100,000 pieces of published material . . ." to the simpler and easier to read: "From May 5 to 18, some 100,000 pieces of published material . . ."

Then he crossed out the last clause in the fifth, and now last, paragraph: "but legislative recommendations on this point have been pending in Washington for months." He looked over the whole story again. "Still too much," he said, and marked diagonals through the rest of the fifth paragraph, which contained the scholars' issue. Before cutting, it had read:

After the hearing, Senator Welker said he was studying the need of responsible scholars for such material for research on Communism. At present, the Customs Service and Post Office Department use their own discretion to forward material addressed to these quarters, but legislative recommendations on this point have been pending in Washington for months.

This paragraph differentiated Mr. Kihss's story from accounts by other reporters who had not had his acquaintance with the controversy.

After Mr. Randolph puzzled out a headline for the story, I went back to Mr. Kihss's desk and told him the sad news. He was angry that his story had been cut to 194 words, when he had written 321 for a 400 limit. He told me that he had worked on many papers, some of which had always been tight for space, and that he had learned to write for word limits, which he carefully observed, usually writing fewer words than the limit. In this story, he knew how important the fifth paragraph was. After talking out his feeling for a while, he said he would try to do something about it. At 6:58, he intercepted Mr. Randolph at the drinking fountain. Later he wrote me what happened:

> I told Jack Randolph that for two years in a row, the *Times* had made studies of this problem of Communist propaganda from the viewpoint of the difficulties encountered by scholars and research men, including our own Harry Schwartz. I contended we ought to record what, if anything, was happening on that phase. I said I had been ordered to write up to 400 words, and had stayed in that space—if I'd known the story was to have been less, I could have geared it accordingly. But in any case, I said I could get the scholars' phase into twenty-five words, as a minimum, and that the story had now been cut so hard that it was already well below the 250-word maximum for M heads.

Mr. Randolph agreed to add these two sentences, which Mr. Kihss hurriedly composed:

> Afterward, Senator Welker said he was studying scholars' need for such material. The Customs and Post Office now use their own discretion in research cases.

Mr. Kihss had cut his original paragraph considerably, but he had made the important point. Mr. Randolph said the story had left the copy desk, but that they would send along the "add" and hope that it would get in. The story appeared in the late city edition of the *Times* on Saturday morning, May 22, 1954, on page 6. It was identical with Mr. Kihss's edited copy, except for one misspelling: *progoganda,* a typographical error.

After the story was in, Mr. Kihss and I sat at his desk discussing reporting problems. I said that I thought what a re-

RED MAIL INCREASING FROM FOREIGN PORTS

A Senate Internal Security subcommittee heard yesterday that the volume of Communist propaganda coming here from abroad had increased "very materially" since 1951.

From May 5 to 18, some 100,000 pieces of published material in various languages reached the Port of New York by mail alone.

The Customs House annex at 54 Stone Street was heaped with mail bags containing perhaps 750,000 pieces of material still to be studied to determine its mailability under Federal laws, as a task force composed of Senator Herman Welker, Republican of Idaho, and Richard Arens, counsel, held the hearing.

Senator Welker said he was proposing legislation to require that material be labeled as "Communist propaganda" before being shipped here. Deputy Collector of Customs Irving Fishman, in charge of restricted merchandise, said such a move would probably reduce the admissible flow sharply, on his theory that shippers would refuse to label it.

Collector of Customs Robert W. Dill, Assistant Collector Francis B. Laughlin, Mr. Fishman and three subordinates testified that such material was now admitted when addressed to a registered foreign agent. It may be seized, however, if found to be political progoganda addressed to a non-agent.

Afterward, Senator Welker said he was studying scholars' need for such material. The Customs and Post Office now use their own discretion in research cases.

From New York Times, *Saturday, May 22, 1954, p. 6*

porter decided to emphasize in a story made a great difference—no matter how fair or impartial he was trying to be. Mr. Kihss agreed, and as examples, typed off two possible "leads" for the story he had done. A reporter on one paper, he said, could understandably have written this lead:

> United States' failure to recognize the menace of Communist propaganda was shown today when the Senate Internal Subcommittee brought out that Communist publications were entering the country on a vastly increased scale.

A reporter for another paper could have written this lead, he said:

> The Senate Internal Security Subcommittee got into a competition for anti-Communist headlines with Senator Joe McCarthy's circuses today, when it staged a hearing on Communist propaganda—the first half hour being devoted entirely to posing for television cameras.

Mr. Kihss did not judge the committee one way or the other. He reported what Senator Welker wanted him to report—the increase of mail from Soviet sources, but he went on to suggest the need for Americans to read and study Soviet publications.

In the light of what goes on before a news story reaches print, of which the foregoing is only one illustration, the "objective" content analysis of finished news stories seems to miss the point so completely as to be as unreal as a game—a playing with words as with counters, with no regard for what they stand for or what was omitted before those particular words were chosen. Understanding the perceptual frameworks of those who supply the story and those who write and edit it is infinitely more important than staring at, counting, and otherwise analyzing the little black marks on paper that finally result. "The word is not the thing," we say. How true this is! And the news *report* is not the report*ing*, which is a *process*—complex, perplexing, and human.

Ken Macrorie, who formerly taught at Michigan State University and at San Francisco State College, is the author of The Perceptive Writer, Reader and Speaker *(1959). He now teaches at Western Michigan University in Kalamazoo, and is editor of the* Journal of the Conference on College Composition and Communication.

THE ARTS:
Low, Middle and High

A Grammar of Assassination

MARTIN MALONEY

> *The typical book titles of our age are not* THE AGE OF REASON, *but* THE AGE OF LONGING, THE AGE OF ANXIETY, THE POLITICS OF MURDER, THE STRATEGY OF TERROR, THE AGE OF TERROR.
>
> —PETER VIERECK

> *Let me lend you* THE HISTORY OF CONTEMPORARY SOCIETY. *It's in hundreds of volumes, but most of them are sold in cheap editions:* DEATH IN PICCADILLY, THE AMBASSADOR'S DIAMONDS, THE THEFT OF THE NAVAL PAPERS, DIPLOMACY, SEVEN DAY'S LEAVE, THE FOUR JUST MEN.
>
> —GRAHAM GREENE, *The Ministry of Fear*

IT is an oddity of an odd age that critics of contemporary American society should concern themselves so often with the symbols, rather than the facts, of violence. At a time when his study windows might almost have rattled to the remote explosions on Yucca Flat, or to the coughing of Korean sniper fire, Canon Bernard Iddings Bell was busy citing the current *literature* of violence as another symptom of the Common Man's decline:

> The most popular novelist in America today . . . is . . . almost ludicrously savage in his substance and his style. He writes tales of a violence that is near to madness plus a degenerate sexuality. His best-selling production reaches its climax when a woman, physically beautiful and fascinatingly wicked, undresses herself, with an almost incredible particularity of lascivious description, in the presence of a libidinous and savage hero. When she is quite bare, the hero shoots her twice in the belly. As she dies,

she cries, "How could you?" He replies, "It was easy." End of book. Over one million, two hundred thousand copies of this masterpiece have been purchased. The sale of all his books, essentially the same in plot with minor differences of decoration, has passed the ten million mark in four years. This pander is indeed an exceptionally low creature, but he is at the moment the Common Man's delight.[1]

This is, I suppose, a relatively sophisticated kind of criticism, with which we can agree in principle, at least. Popular literature is certainly, in its own manner, intensional and stereotyped; its enormously wide diffusion suggests that it relates to the structure of social character, or of society. For this reason it is worth study, though perhaps a different sort of study from that which Canon Bell accords it.

A second example: In 1953 Mr. Jack Mabley of the Chicago *Daily News* conducted a spectacular if short lived campaign against the literature of crime available to children on television. Mr. Mabley apparently monitored a good deal of the dramatic programing on Chicago television stations; with loving care he listed and tabulated the symbolic acts of violence, ranging from simple assault through mayhem to homicide, which he found represented on the flickering screens. He was thus able to include in his reports some fairly impressive totals of human destruction, including some detailed and gruesome descriptions of specific examples, which lost very little in the retelling. This information was headlined in the *Daily News* over quite a long period, seemingly, as a demonstration of the depravity of television broadcasters, or of American children, or of parents, or of society in general, with the obvious exceptions of Mr. Mabley and the *Daily News*.

A third and final exhibit is provided by Mr. Edmund Wilson, a literary critic of reasonable distinction and an exceedingly serious-minded man where the literary arts are concerned. A dozen or more years ago, Mr. Wilson read some detective stories—the first literature of this sort, he remarks, that he had sampled since 1907. As a result of this experience, Mr. Wilson wrote:

My final conclusion is that the reading of detective stories is simply a kind of vice that, for silliness and minor harmfulness, ranks somewhere between smoking and cross-word puzzles. De-

[1] Bernard Iddings Bell. *Crowd Culture: an Examination of the American Way of Life* (New York: Harper & Brothers, 1952), pp. 31-32.

tective story readers feel guilty, they are habitually on the defensive, and all their talk about "well-written" mysteries is simply an excuse for their vice, like the reasons that the alcoholic can always produce for a drink. One of the letters I have had shows the addict in his frankest and most shameless phase. This lady begins by pretending, like the others, to guide me in my choice (of detective novels), but she breaks down and tells the whole dreadful truth. Though she has read, she says, hundreds of detective stories, "it is surprising," she finally confesses, "how few I would recommend to another. However, a poor detective story is better than none at all. Try again. With a little better luck, you'll find one you admire and enjoy. Then you, too, may be

A MYSTERY FIEND."

This letter has made my blood run cold; so the opium smoker tells the novice not to mind if the first pipe makes him sick; and I fall back for reassurance on the valiant little band of my readers who sympathize with my views on the subject.[2]

There are two questions which seem to be raised by these quotations. 1. Is crime fiction actually worth all this comment? 2. If so, is the critical apparatus suggested in these quotations adequate to deal with the subject matter? Let us, for a moment, assume that we have made positive answers to the first question, and go on to the second.

I do *not* think that the critical apparatus of Bell, or Mabley, or even Wilson, is adequate to discuss present-day crime fiction, because it seems to me that each of our three critics fails to recognize this form of popular literature as something separate from "serious" writing.

Whoever discusses the present-day, melodramatic tale of crime and violence is talking about a special form of popular art. Popular art, I conceive, may be defined as a kind of communication which uses many of the techniques of the fine arts, and which sometimes has the general appearance of fine art, but which is, in various important aspects, a profoundly different sort of thing. The fine arts normally express the insights of an artist into the nature of his experience, his subject matter, and his medium; for such insights, popular art usually substitutes formula—the formula plot, the formula design, the formula melody. A work of fine art is intended to communicate to others, but it requires that the others contribute importantly in the way of understanding and appreciation. A work of popular art makes no such demand, or at

[2] Edmund Wilson, "Who Cares Who Killed Roger Ackroyd?" in *Classics and Commercials* (New York: Farrar, Straus, 1950), pp. 263-264.

Dawn of Literacy

any rate, as modest a demand of this sort as possible. It is usually directed at the largest possible audience of viewers, listeners, or readers, whether or not they are able to contribute anything to the process of communication. A work of popular art, in practice, is judged by the number of people who consume it.

The popular arts, thus roughly defined, are a new phenomenon in the world. They depend absolutely for their existence upon a highly developed technology; the works of Mickey Spillane, which Canon Bell has read with such horror, would be inconceivable in a society which did not command the technical ability to reproduce them inexpensively some thirteen million times over. Mr. Mabley, for his part, might be struggling with the analysis of sports or politics, were it not for the efforts of Zworykin and Marconi and Fessenden and Conrad. It is thus, I think, a mistake for anyone to talk about the popular arts of the twentieth century as if they were the same as the fine arts of the sixteenth century. And it seems to me that this mistake is precisely the one which our critics usually commit. Mr. Wilson condemns the present-day detective story because it is not as good literature as

Dickens or Poe or Thackeray; Canon Bell finds it vulgar because it seems not to be as sophisticated as the literature which the better people of the eighteenth century enjoyed.

The observations of these critics are accurate enough; they are also unimportant. We shall never understand or control or deal with the popular arts by simple condemnation. A quotation from a recent article by Weller Embler suggests—if we may now proceed to our original question—the vital importance of sound criticism in this area, together with an apparatus for achieving it:

> Though our world of today is one of extreme violence, it is not true that people living the everyday routine lives of our society are either given to or are the subjects of violent acts. Though it would be insane to deny the abundance of rape, murder, mayhem, manslaughter, suicide, torture, assault, arson, enslavement everyday everywhere, still, considering the density of modern society, there is not as much actual overt violence as one would suppose from the evidence of motion pictures, comic books, radio, and cheap fiction. On the other hand there is universal inner violence, fear, and treachery. It is the great inner conflicts and tensions that modern story-telling describes; and it is the translation of fiction's outward beatings, stranglings, stabbings, and shootings into our own inner struggles that we make when we read or listen.
>
> Since the tempest within will not submit to description in words of exact reference, the tempest without must serve as metaphor to tell about the soul's life. Modern fiction has chosen the device of *hyperbole* with which to show forth the inner life—all the shocks the spirit's heir to in our time—the insults, the humiliation, the sacrifice, the moral corrosion. For the most part, the modern story-teller chooses to deal with the extraordinary incident. Being more dramatic, it is more immediately understandable, reflects more directly the conflicts of everyday life. The violence and the fear of violence that is in us and so much a part of our psychological life are amplified many times in the metaphor of melodrama. The terror of the cinema screen and the ferocity of, for example, *Sanctuary* are mirrors held up to the terror and rage of our inner lives. Thus, the age of anxiety gives away its inner tensions in the works of popular writers like Graham Greene, James M. Cain, Dashiell Hammett, Mickey Spillane; in the cartoons of Charles Addams; in the plays of Tennessee Williams and Arthur Miller; in the operas of Carlo Menotti; in the films of Alfred Hitchcock, Billy Wilder, Raoul Walsh, Carol Reed, and Roberto Rossellini. Not that violent death does not occur in daily life, still it occurs but seldom to the 13,000,000 people who read the fiction of Mickey Spillane. Modern novels and motion pictures express our fears, our desires, our anxieties, our hate, all that troubles inwardly—

frustration, fear of poverty, of spinsterhood, of losing status, of loneliness, discrimination, humiliation, shame, heartache, of being sacrificed, of slavery, and of tyranny.[3]

I do not think it matters greatly whether we take the tales of violence as a *History of Contemporary Society* in an unlimited series of volumes, or as a metaphor of the soul's plight in the atomic age. The fact remains, in either case, that here again the symbols of fiction and drama perform their immemorial function: they permit human beings to say the unspeakable, and they make possible the verbal solution of problems which are, in the flesh, insoluble.

The literature of crime and violence, however crude the connoisseur of letters may judge it, however shocking the moralist may think it, is thus no trivial thing. Like most of our entertainments—and especially those which strive to be most entertaining and least meaningful—it conceals some grave and terrible problems. An anatomy of this literature—what I have called here "a grammar of assassination"—remains to be constructed. The chief purpose of these notes is to sketch the bare outlines of such a grammar. To do this, we must examine briefly the history of this special branch of literature.

As everyone knows, the modern crime story begins with a segment of the work of Edgar Allan Poe. Poe wrote only three detective stories—*The Murders in the Rue Morgue, The Mystery of Marie Roget,* and *The Purloined Letter.* As Edmund Wilson correctly points out, Poe was probably interested chiefly in writing a story which should turn about the solution to a puzzle, which should exploit his own keen interest in the processes of reasoning. In so doing, he created the first true hero of detective fiction—a *private* detective, incidentally, and the first watson.[4]

Throughout the last century, the detective story prospered modestly. There was Wilkie Collins, with his rather dull and complex novels, *The Moonstone* and *The Woman in White;* there was Gaboriau with his Inspector LeCoq, whom Sherlock Holmes once called "a miserable bungler." Dickens attempted the detective story, especially in his unfinished novel, *The Mystery of Edwin Drood.* It was not, however, until Dr.

[3] Weller Embler, "The Novel as Metaphor," *ETC.,* X (1952), 3-11.

[4] Dr. John (or James) Watson's last name has become, to detective story writers, a common noun. A watson is the admiring and naïve associate of the detective (usually of the brilliant amateur class).

Arthur Conan Doyle's tale, "A Study in Scarlet," appeared in the *Strand Magazine* in London in the 1880's that the detective story began to show signs of that enormous popularity which it later achieved.

It is possible to name stories of crime and detection which long antedate Poe. Voltaire's *Zadig,* on one occasion, becomes almost indistinguishable from Holmes or Dupin. So does D'Artagnan, in one episode of *Le Vicomte de Bragellonne.* There is even a rather typical tale of deduction in the Old Testament, which tells how Daniel exposed the chicanery of the priests of Baal. But a more important observation is this: all stories of crime appear to embody one of those myths so meaningful and so essential to human understanding of life that they appear in an endless variety of forms back to the remotest antiquity. This is the dual myth of flight and pursuit, the ancient theme of guilt and punishment.

To some extent all stories are embodiments of this theme. No living man fails to pursue, more or less effectively, the goals he is able to construct; nor does any living creature fail to flee destruction, or at least, whatever it can recognize as destruction. And the processes of flight and pursuit seem, in most cases, to be rationalized by the concept of personal guilt and personal responsibility for one's acts. A great number of stories and plays, based largely or wholly on this theme, examine with special care the motives and behavior of pursued and pursuer, and attempt to demonstrate the tragic or comic or melodramatic possibilities of the theme of pursuit. Thus, the story of Telemachus' search for his father in the *Odyssey,* the relentless pursuit of Jean Valjean by the terrible Javert in *Les Miserables,* and the chase sequences in some early American film comedies, all make some use of this theme. So does Francis Thompson in *The Hound of Heaven;* so does Dante in *The Divine Comedy.* So, in a direct and obvious way, does the crime story.

With this general theme of pursuit and flight as a starting point, we may isolate some of the common terms in the detective stories of Conan Doyle. We should first observe that the grammar of the Holmes stories—and of many other, but not all, detective stories—is peculiar. The statement of each story implies a previous statement, which is initially concealed from the reader, but without which the story could not exist. Sometimes these implied statements are exceedingly complex: Enoch J. Drebber must first, in the deserts of Utah, commit a dreadful wrong against Jefferson Hope; Hope in turn must wreak his long-delayed vengeance upon Drebber one foggy London morning at 3, Lauriston Gardens—all this before Mr. Sherlock Holmes can conduct his investigation which Watson so fancifully entitled "A Study in Scarlet." This feature of the grammar of the Holmes stories is crucial; its function is to establish guilt and responsibility for the acts described, and without it the entire character of the pursuit would alter significantly.

As for the stories proper, they involve but a single verb: to pursue. The pursuit is, as a rule, symbolic rather than physical. As Holmes remarks on one occasion, "We have not yet grasped the results which the reason alone can attain to. Problems may be solved in the study which have baffled all those who have sought a solution by the aid of their senses." But on occasion the chase can be active enough; see for instance the pursuit of Jonathan Small down the Thames in "The Sign of Four."

The actions antecedent to pursuit vary a good deal; but they have one characteristic which recurs frequently. A surprising number of the stories hinge on the commission of such minor crimes as theft, embezzlement, arson, fraud, and blackmail. One of the early stories, "A Case of Identity," involves no legal offense at all. In these cases, the stake for the pursued might be exposure, imprisonment, disgrace, or simply the contempt of all right-thinking men. The symbols of death and violence were by no means essential to this world.

As for Holmes himself, the actor in these tales, we may readily see that Doyle invented many adjectives to describe him; he is shown as a musicologist (his monograph on the polyphonic motets of Lassus was the last word on that abstruse subject), as a cocaine user, research chemist, and amateur boxer. Many of these characteristics were dropped or contradicted in later tales; nearly all are individually unimportant. The essential adjectives which describe Holmes are three in number: he is superhuman; he is a private detective, not a public official; and he is a defender of "the right" as "the right" is understood by all right-thinking men. He is not necessarily concerned with the law. James Windibank, in "A Case of Identity," has broken no law; yet Holmes demonstrates the coldest anger and contempt for his somewhat unethical behavior, and even threatens to horsewhip him. On the other hand, Holmes almost jovially permits a certain Captain Jack Crocker, who has—out of the purest motives—crushed the skull of Sir Eustace Brackenstall with a poker, to go free. ("The Adventure of the Abbey Grange," in *The Return of Sherlock Holmes*.) As for the actual officials of the law—

the incredibly bumptious and obtuse Inspector Lestrade, for example—they are obviously beneath anyone's contempt.

We might summarize the world of the Sherlock Holmes stories (which is typical of detective stories of the period, for these tales were widely imitated) in this fashion. It was a world in which law was operative, but in a limited way; it was a world in which a gentleman's code of right and wrong transcended the law when it did not supplement it. It was a world in which the business of upholding the right fell upon the shoulders of private men rather than public officials. And finally, it was a world in which there were few gradations in the moral code; black was black and white was white; a theft discovered might be as fatal to a man's future as a murder discovered.

Let me be quite clear; this world, and the attitudes which informed it, were the peculiarly personal products of Doyle himself, as anyone familiar with his life can attest. But that it was an intelligible and acceptable world to large numbers of person in Britain and America may be inferred from the immediately enthusiastic reception which the stories received, and by their long-continued popularity. Then too we must remember that these stories have added, perhaps permanently, to the language and to our stock of stereotypes, and so to our "knowledge" of human motives and behavior.

Two changes in the grammar of the crime story occurred after the first successes of Sherlock Holmes, but long before Doyle wrote the last of the stories in the *Casebook* (around 1922), both changes being more or less to the same purpose, but quite different in detail.

One of these changes was to slip the story proper from the pursuit back to the action which antedated and motivated the pursuit. This meant, of course, that the chief actor was now the pursued, the offender, the criminal, and that the action concerned chiefly his crime and subsequent flight. Perhaps the best British examples of this changed pattern may be found in the works of E. W. Hornung (*The Amateur Cracksman,* 1899; *The Black Mask*, 1901; *A Thief in the Night,* 1905; *Mr. Justice Raffles,* 1909). Holmes, representing as he does an extra-legal code of ethics, can and does sometimes stand outside the law; his behavior, since it is always directed toward a "good" end, can be rationalized. Raffles' behavior, on the other hand, since it violates not only the law, but to some extent the "gentleman's code," cannot be so lightly treated. Holmes, it is notorious, not only "lived happily ever after" despite his occasional illegal behavior, but seems to be immortal; Raffles, on the other hand, necessarily died young; he atoned for his many misdeeds during the Boer War. As George Orwell points out:

> Raffles is presented to us . . . not as an honest man who has gone astray, but as a public school man who has gone astray. His remorse, when he feels any, is almost purely social; he has disgraced "the old school"; he has lost his right to enter "decent society"; he has forfeited his amateur status and become a cad. Neither Raffles nor Bunny (his friend and accomplice) appears to feel at all strongly that stealing is wrong in itself. . . . They think of themselves not as sinners but as renegades, or simply as outcasts. And the moral code of most of us is still so close to Raffles' own that we do feel his situation to be an especially ironical one. A West End club man who is really a burglar! That is almost a story in itself, is it not? [5]

The British preference in wrongdoing, if we may judge by the Raffles stories and others of similar pattern, is for highly skilled and somewhat genteel thievery. Americans, with a long tradition of horse-trading behind them, seem to have preferred fraud to outright burglary, as examplified in the "Get-Rich-Quick" Wallingford stories of George Chester, or O. Henry's sketches of the chicaneries of Jeff Peters and other con men.

The other grammatical alteration in the crime story pattern is perhaps less interesting. Writers of the conventional (usually British) detective story discovered that no crime save murder was really worth dramatization; here the chase, in itself, had a real point to it. The stake at both ends was death; the killer must be killed lest he kill some more.

But even this use of the most extreme symbols of violence did not save the detective story of the early 1900's, in most cases, from dullness. Most of the stories and plays of this period were highly conventionalized puzzle pieces; see for example the collected works of Agatha Christie, Anna Katherine Green, or Mary Roberts Rinehart. The victim did not bleed genuine blood; and if the hero was sometimes "in danger," it was as if a chess piece had been endangered in a game. I do not bewail simply the absence of blood; the story and the characters were usually missing too. In these stories we usually find a collection of almost excessively respectable authors and genteel readers (the late President Wilson, for one) perpetuating and popularizing a literature of violence, a kind of phenomenon which neither Mary Roberts Rinehart nor most of

[5] George Orwell, "Raffles and Miss Blandish," in *Dickens, Dali and Others* (New York: Reynal and Hitchcock, 1948), pp. 203-204.

her devoted circle of readers ever had the temerity to examine at very close range. The point of the crime story or play was said to be the puzzle it propounded: whodunit? Readers were urged to rationalize their excursions into symbolic murder on the grounds that the experience sharpened their wits.

The next step in the development of the crime story was a natural one. Convinced—and correctly so—that the consumers of crime stories were more interested in vivid, realistically appointed writing than in puzzles, certain American writers began to produce highly realistic and brutal tales of murder; of these, one of the first and the best was Dashiell Hammett. The sawdust-filled baronet with an Oriental dagger planted in the center of his shirt disappeared; in his place appeared the shabby and furtive racketeer shot bloodily to death in a dingy city street. Raymond Chandler says of Dashiell Hammett's early writings that he

> gave murder back to the kind of people that commit it for reasons, not just to provide a corpse; and with the means at hand, not with hand-wrought dueling pistols, curare and tropical fish. He put these people down on paper as they are, and he made them talk and think in the language they customarily used for these purposes.[6]

This new concept of the crime story, which has of course been reflected in film, radio, and television productions of the cops-and-robbers sort, has made some essential changes in our grammar of assassination. The act of pursuit becomes almost exclusively physical, and often extremely violent; it is a long step from Holmes pondering the significance of a flake of cigar ash in his study to Hammett's Continental Op who, on one occasion, stuffs a length of copper wire into his pocket because it's just the right length to go around somebody's neck. The verb "to pursue" now becomes almost synonymous with "to destroy." In addition, the old adjectives of the crime story are lost or discarded, and new ones are found to describe both the antecedent statement (the crime) and the story statement (the pursuit). The black-and-white universe of Holmes vanishes. In the new world, the burden of guilt for crime tends to spread so that no one is free of it; law and conscience alike are shaken—neither the police nor the courts nor his next-door neighbors are necessarily on the side of the good man, who thus becomes a desperately solitary figure. Chandler describes this change admirably:

[6] Raymond Chandler, "The Simple Art of Murder," in *The Pocket Atlantic* (New York: Pocket Books, 1946), p. 210.

> The realist in murder writes of a world in which gangsters can rule nations and almost rule cities, in which hotels and apartment houses and celebrated restaurants are owned by men who made their money out of brothels, in which a screen star can be the fingerman for a mob, and the nice man down the hall is the boss of the numbers racket; a world where a judge with a cellar of bootleg liquor can send a man to jail for having a pint in his pocket, where the mayor of your town may have condoned murder as an instrument of money-making, where no man can walk down a dark street in safety because law and order are things we talk about but refrain from practising; a world where you may witness a holdup in broad daylight and see who did it, but you will fade quickly back into the crowd rather than tell anyone, because the holdup men may have friends with long guns, or the police may not like your testimony, and in any case the shyster for the defense will be allowed to abuse and vilify you in open court, before a jury of selected morons, without any but the most perfunctory interference from a political judge (p. 212).

This is indeed a world of anarchy, in which the act of violence becomes the core. But a completely anarchical universe is difficult to imagine, and still more difficult to write about. What holds the Hammett-Chandler world together? Into this world, Chandler says

> down these mean streets a man must go who is not himself mean, who is neither tarnished nor afraid. The detective in this kind of story must be such a man. He is the hero, he is everything. He must be a complete man and a common man and yet an unusual man. He must be, to use a rather weathered phrase, a man of honor (p. 214).

So we return, by somewhat devious ways, to the essentials of the world of Sherlock Holmes. But where the morality of Holmes was a morality shared with all right-thinking men, the morality of Sam Spade and Philip Marlow is private, unshared, and unspeakable. Nevertheless, the morality of Sam Spade exists—or at least, we are so led to believe.

Since Hammett, no completely defined new patterns have emerged in the crime story. The perpetually interesting question is: what next? What new patterns can the vocables of violence assume?

It appears to me that two patterns have begun, rather tentatively, to emerge. I have been speculating for several years whether the time is not ripe for a new Raffles to appear, his story to be the legend of the "nice chap" who unfortunately goes about killing people. Several attempts have been made in this direction, in published fiction, in broadcasting, and in films. A recent motion picture, *The Sniper,* presented the story of a charming, handsome, all-American boy who went about shooting strange women because they reminded him of his mother. And of course, there was Chaplin's film *Monsieur Verdoux,* the fable of a kindly and dapper little businessman who—unable to find more suitable work—goes into the business of marrying elderly spinsters, and murdering them. Chaplin, a man of rash courage in more ways than one, justifies Verdoux in the film: why should societies either capable or presently guilty of genocide look askance at this little man who, for the best of reasons, has destroyed only twenty or so aged and not very interesting women? In general, of course, this pattern seems rather difficult to popularize; I suspect that our future experience of it will be confined to a few, occasional, and perhaps brilliant examples.

The alternative pattern is, of course, already rather widespread. We remarked a moment ago that the personal and secret integrity of Chandler's and Hammett's heroes is all that holds their universe of violence together. But suppose that that integrity (whatever it may amount to) fails? What then? The answer is that we then get the paranoiac universe of Mickey Spillane, in which the world is a dark, terrifying, and hostile place, where elaborate and deadly plots are commonplace, where no man is free of guilt, and where the only response to any situation is violence, violence first and last. For Philip Marlow's sense of honor, Mickey Spillane's Mike Hammer substitutes a lively gift for hallucination, complete with phantom bells ringing inside his cranium in moments of crisis.

I assume, however, that scholarly readers with a laudable interest in social phenomena will already be familiar with Spillane's works, and with the critical comment about him; so I should like to pass on to another, less familiar work of the same general school. This is a novel by Sterling Noel, entitled *I Killed Stalin* (New York: Farrar, Straus and Young, 1951). The hero of this remarkable book is Alexis Ivanovitch Bodine, born in Brooklyn to White Russian parents, a former OSS man with a record of service in Yugoslavia during World War II. He is abruptly recruited by an American espionage organization referred to as Bureau X, which is so secret that nobody appears to know what its purpose is. As an employee of this organization, Bodine is planted in the American Communist party, where he rapidly qualifies himself as a saboteur. The Communist groups with which he is affiliated are, of course, quite as secret as Bureau X. Eventually he is shipped off to the

Soviet Union, where he becomes almost instantly a colonel in the Red Army and commanding officer of another organization called Arbat 568, which is even more secret than anything he has belonged to so far, but the purpose of which is all too clear. Arbat 568 is the organization which murders and cremates enemies of the regime. Bodine finds this work rather depressing at times, but not beyond his capacities. The sole motivation for this entire rigmarole, from Bureau X through an assortment of assassinations, plots, and counterplots to Arbat 568, is the killing of Joseph Stalin. As presented in Noel's book, this political murder is quite purposeless: the United States and the Soviet Union are not at war when it is projected, and it is not expected that the death of the dictator will accomplish anything very startling. In a rather strained effort to provide some motivation for the killing, Noel shows the Soviet Union attacking the West a day or so before Bodine finally gets Stalin in front of the sights of a rifle.

The interesting thing about *I Killed Stalin* is that in this *reductio ad absurdum* of the crime story, it is no longer possible to tell the pursuer from the pursued, or the good from the evil. Anyone can be anything; characters change their faces with the fluidity of nightmare. Suspicion is the normal evaluation of character, and automatic violence is the signal response to suspicion. The grammar of assassination, at this point, disintegrates almost wholly: what remains is a verb, an endlessly active verb, whose significance is compounded of sterile sexual pursuit, destruction, and torture.

Now why—if at this point I may venture the question—why is the detective story, or any other branch of popular literature, worth all this critical pother? My answer would be along these lines. To a large extent our semantic environment conditions all of us, shapes our goals, our attitudes toward others, toward ourselves, toward society. To a large extent, within the past fifty years or so, our semantic environment has become mechanized: our lives are swamped in the endless flood of symbols poured over us daily by our complex communications network, much of which is beyond our control. No one can wholly avoid contact with the mass media: even those who, by prodigious effort, fail to attend the movies, or to watch television, are brought in contact with the content of these media at second hand, through their children, friends, and neighbors.

The reverse of these observations also appears to be true. If we may correctly remark that our semantic environment (which is now crowded with the symbols of violence) is inescapable, and that it conditions us all to some extent, we may also note that the semantic environment, in a kind of unholy antiphony, supplies the responses to the questions raised by our fears, our anxieties, our unachievable desires. "The tempest without," says Weller Embler, "must serve as metaphor to tell about the soul's life." More than this, we might add: the "tempest without" may be regarded as part of, a complement to, "the soul's life."

Mickey Spillane's work is still being avidly consumed, via film, radio, and books. Sterling Noel has published a second novel, much like his first. A book warning the public of forthcoming invasions of Earth by flying Venusian saucers reached the best-seller lists. Is it too much to suggest that millions of people immerse themselves in this sort of witch's broth because it provides a "normal" intellectual climate for them? that literature which becomes popular does so because it dramatizes and complements most effectively the inner tumult which its readers experience?

We cannot of course transfer literally the symbols of the literature of violence to the life of the soul. And no doubt there are many who would find this literary world incredible and horrifying if they were forced to regard it as in any sense "real." For in this world, the world which we have been examining, a man lives dreadfully alone, clutching the secret of his own goodness to himself. And outside is a world of unfathomable evil, half concealed by grinning masks which only parody goodness. One's next-door neighbors, the cop on the corner, the judge in his chambers, the minister in his pulpit, the huge, mock-heroic, mock-beautiful faces of celebrities, senators, generals, even presidents—one by one they slip their masks to reveal the demon beneath. And yet, one is reassured. In this universe a champion will arise, evil will be bloodily suppressed, and all one's anxieties will be melted in the heat of violence.

Is this world an echo, a reflection, of the inner world in which millions of us live? If it is, then I do not think that censorship or protests directed at broadcasting networks, the Johnston office, book publishers, or the press will avail us much. We are not dealing with the stupidity or malpractice of a small group of communicators, but with a whole society badly in need of therapy. This therapy must be self-administered, and we must rely on the agencies available for the task: schools, churches, such civic, business, and professional organizations as have any direct influence on public attitudes, the media of public communication, and above all, any individuals with a modest preference for sanity and some notion of how to achieve it.

I suppose it to be true that unsanity is catching; it spreads with equal facility from an obscure person with few contacts outside his family, from a great man standing before the television cameras, from the pages of a cheap book or a not-so-cheap magazine, from a classroom lecture or a Sunday morning sermon. But I like to think that—contrary to the normal laws of medicine—sanity can be contagious too. If it is, it will be contracted from individuals, whose range of influence may be great or small. And if that is so, we can scarcely have too many carrying its virus.

Based on a lecture given before the Chicago Chapter of the International Society for General Semantics, March, 1953; originally published in 1954. Martin Maloney is associate professor of radio and television in the School of Speech, Northwestern University. He has written widely on popular culture and mass communications.

Communication in Science Fiction

ROBERT PLANK

GROWING like a mushroom, science fiction has in a few years achieved the status of a major literary genre in its own right. It has hardly yet, however, been subjected to systematic investigation. One of the first problems to be faced would be that its rapid sprouting must, obviously, be a symptom of whatever it is that is peculiar about the present state of our civilization. But what is that? One expects science fiction to be particularly concerned with science, in the usual sense of the word. It is surprising to find that this is not so. These systems of fantasy are, rather, preoccupied with communication.

It may be that this preoccupation is the key to the question of how science fiction reflects broader trends of our times. For it is the same focus of interest which characterizes semantics; and the same preoccupation has played a growing role in our social and political life, coming to the fore in the importance of such concepts as the "iron curtain."

The science fiction literature of the last few years offers an abundance of material to illustrate the various forms that the preoccupation with communication may take. The classical guise is perhaps that displayed in "discontinuity" by Raymond F. Jones (*Astounding Science Fiction*, October, 1950).

The central character of the story is Dr. Mantell, a scientist who has "provided the medical world with its most brilliant technique in thirty centuries of its history. . . . With one sweep he eliminated the centuries old butchery of lobotomy and topectomy which had maimed hundreds of thousands in its long fad" (p. 83). This he achieved by the "Mantell Synthesis": "He could tear apart the brain of a man, cell by cell, and reconstruct it in the image of a living human being" (p. 79). The operation proceeds by building "blank molecules" which are then "punched" with data from "giant pattern molecules." A "semantic selector" is built in.

However, Mantell's experiments had led to "intensifying the very conditions they were designed to heal. In a hundred cases of extensive brain damage, his process had restored life, but only in varying degrees of hopeless aphasia. At first the public hailed the magnitude of his stride, then, revolted by the horror of his failures, they had turned against him with a mighty clamor" (p. 83).

At the beginning of the story, after fifteen years of married life, Alice Mantell, with the help of her lover, has attempted to murder her husband, but has succeeded merely in bashing his head in. Mantell's coworkers, finding him after his wife's assault more dead than alive, decide to put him together again by subjecting him to the "Mantell Synthesis." The result is that he is restored to complete health—in fact, he feels better than ever before—but he finds himself totally unable to communicate with other people, either by speaking or writing.

It is noteworthy that no other symptom is mentioned, yet the reaction to his condition is drastic. Dr. Vixen, Mantell's chief assistant, "was staring, his face reflecting sickness of heart" (p. 85). Dr. Mantell himself "knew what his fate would be. Visual, auditory, ataxic aphasia—schizophrenia—they would put a label on him and lock him in a jail. They'd lock him up for the rest of his life because somehow he had become imprisoned behind an incredible wall of communication failure" (p. 86).

So he escapes from the Synthesis Laboratory to a suburban insane asylum. There he finds several of his former patients who are in custody, and he is overjoyed to discover that he can talk to them. The cause of the *supposed* failures of the Mantell Synthesis is found: having "semantic selector banks" built into them, the brains of the synthesized have been freed of so much ballast that they, far from being schizophrenic, aphasic, etc., are really "the most completely sane people the world has ever known" (p. 97). Their communication system is so nearly perfect that they can have no truck with the poor linguistic systems of communication of us nonsynthesized folk—an astonishing situation which is explained as follows: "All are beyond our comprehension because, as Shannon demonstrated so long ago, a channel cannot pass a message of greater entropy than the channel capacity without equivocation. Since we demand zero entropy and ordinary communication employs so much higher values, we understand nothing" (p. 99).

The rest is easy. Putting the Mantell Synthesis into reverse gear as it were, some "entropy" is reintroduced into the brain of one of the synthesized. Then two people—one of them Alice Mantell—are kidnaped and synthesized. These cases—both striking successes since they are made over into perfect beings—convince Dr. Vixen. "'If those two could be changed,' he whispered half to himself, 'the whole world can be made over. I am next. You'll let me be next?' he demanded urgently. 'And after me, the whole world'" (p. 109).

All this sounds quite puerile. Surely one would not find a story of this sort in a purportedly scientific book. But, as Hayakawa points out,[1] one does. To anyone who has read some of those "case histories" on which L. Ron Hubbard built his doctrine of "Dianetics" (the "Modern Science of Mental Health"), the motifs and the atmosphere of "Discontinuity" have a familiar ring. And one might doubt whether Jones would have displayed so much crusading zeal at the end of his story, were it not for the impression that his fantasy is backed by a new method which can solve the problem of communication once and for all.

What is noteworthy about both Jones's science fiction and Hubbard's fictitious science is that they give expression to the feeling that present methods of communication are unsatisfactory; according to both, not only technical means must be improved but also underlying mental processes. Communication is by definition interpersonal, but both Jones and Hubbard identify it with an inner mental process. The demand for better communication changes in this way into a demand for clearing the mind.

This is to be achieved by a posttraumatic reconstruction comparable to birth—Mantell, awakened from Synthesis, "endured the pains of primal birth" (p. 84). A similar rebirth theme appears in Dianetics. Any person who is not thus reconstructed, or who does not possess that perfect communication system which is actually beyond human reach, is flatly labeled insane. Fear of insanity is an obviously dominant motif, though it is largely disguised as fear of the treatment meted out to the insane—which is distorted beyond recognition. We may note the obsession with the "butchery" of lobotomy, which is referred to as though it were an extremely common psychiatric practice.

[1] "From Science-fiction to Fiction-science," *ETC., VIII* (1951), 280-293.

The world of such stories—many modern science fiction tales as well as Hubbard's "case histories"—is peopled with individuals who are able to exert a powerful influence on human minds, and especially on the mind of the hero. Depending on the place of those persons in the pattern of interpersonal relationships, this influence may be beneficent or sinister. It is, of course, always an essentially magical influence. It is a strongly directive communication, and usually perpetrated by methods which are outside of normal human experience, if not outside of experience altogether.

It would thus seem that there is a compulsive need which forces the author of science fiction to deal with the problem of communication. It must not be overlooked that there is also a technical requirement of his craft which exerts a powerful pressure in the same direction.

Flight from Reality

While the foregoing is true of much of science fiction, it is even more universally true of a literary genre which is not identical with science fiction but has ties with it—utopian fiction. All utopias and a large proportion of science fiction stories are concerned with depicting a society and way of life which is different from that in which the author actually moves. He must therefore transpose his hero into an alien world by letting him sink into a magic sleep to wake up in another century, by letting him travel to a faraway and hidden place, or by some more abstruse method. The preferred vehicle nowadays is, of course, the space ship.

All those travels to distant stars, into the future, or more modestly, just to uncharted islands of the Pacific, raise tremendous problems of interpersonal communications. Older authors generally ignored them. Their globetrotters, space travelers, and shipwrecked sailors land on a foreign shore and begin blithely to talk and to listen to the natives as though the language gulf did not exist—an unrealistic procedure which could only be justified as long as the problem of communications just did not evoke any interest.

This situation changed with Kipling, who included in his collection *A Diversity of Creatures* (1912) a very odd short story, "Easy as A.B.C.," in which he equipped an expeditionary force with all the paraphernalia a signal corps could dream of. This interest in communication has of late become more marked. Communication now plays a paramount role in the works of practically all science fiction writers and utopists.

In one group of them, communication is sinister, technical, and a one-way process. The "telescreen" in the late George Orwell's influential novel *1984* and the "mending apparatus" in "The Machine Stops" (an anti-Wellsian short story by the famous British writer E. M. Forster) are almost diabolical devices by which the powers that rule the world crush the individual. Such contraptions were not known to earlier authors.

In another group, represented by Olaf Stapledon's *Odd John* (a fantasy on the idea of development, by mutation, of a supernormal type of man) and by a host of lesser works, communication means telepathy. This is not a new idea. The motif of telepathy is found in old works like Cyrano de Bergerac's *Voyage dans le Soleil* and in such intermediate works as Wells's *Men Like Gods;* but it is now used much more freely. Telepathic powers, especially as part of the endowment of a new species or of robots, have become quite commonplace in science fiction.

The common denominator of all these devices is that they provide rapid and penetrating communication by short-cutting the more conventional medium of language. It cannot be a matter of mere chance that the shift to this concept coincided with the catastrophe of 1914 which has been conceived of as the great breakdown of understanding, and that it has paralleled the emergence of disciplines specifically dealing with communications, such as significs, semantics, and cybernetics.

Nor is it to be overlooked that these fictitious methods of

communication obviate the necessity of confession. In *1984*, the special twist that confessions are exacted even though the authorities, thanks to their privileged means of communications, have known everything all along, becomes to the author the crowning abomination. In some science fiction stories, telepathy—in the hands of the forces of law—is a powerful weapon against evil schemes. What telepathic forces would mean in a patient-psychotherapist relationship can easily be inferred. It should also be noted that the idea of telepathy is markedly close to the patient's delusion that his mind is being read and influenced, which is so common in paranoid schizophrenia. Herein lies the real connection between the communications problem and psychosis which was dimly seen in Jones's "Discontinuity."

All the elements which have been gradually evolved in science fiction tie in with various phenomena of our culture outside of science fiction. All centering around the problem of communication, they form a complex pattern; we can recognize two strands in it.

One is a well-known phenomenon, though clothed in a new and unusual garb: the desire to be removed from the earth; to be reconstructed; to be able to make confessions without having to put them into words; to escape the consequences of being declared insane—all this is known to the psychotherapist as resistance.

This, however, is but one side of the picture: that same desire to escape from this world; to be reborn; to obtain a clearer mind; to be endowed miraculously with a better system of communication; that paradoxical doubt about the place of sanity (are the psychotic on the outside of reality, looking in, or are we?)—all these are manifestations of the anxiety and discomfort which have characterized the most recent stage of our civilization.

These are the tendencies which flavor the peculiar atmosphere of science fiction. They are, to a surprising degree, identical with undercurrents that characterize much of the actual world in which we all live. The same parallelism which prevails with regard to communications could also be demonstrated as far as some related complexes of ideas are concerned, such as the by now rather trite motif of space travel. Inside science fiction as well as outside it, all these imaginative attempts to escape emotional discomfort may gain even greater importance if present trends continue.

The emergence of a deviant emotional climate in a civilization, as the rise of the Nazis taught us to our sorrow, is not a matter ever to be taken lightly. There is an adage that when a man lies prostrate, if no angel lifts him up, the devil will.

Robert Plank (LL.D., M.S.W.) is social service supervisor, Neuropsychiatric Section, Veterans Administration Hospital, Cleveland, Ohio.

Popular Songs vs. the Facts of Life

S. I. HAYAKAWA

BECAUSE I have long been interested in jazz—its history, its implications, its present developments—I also listen to some extent to popular songs, which are, of course, far from being the same thing. Up to now my interests in general semantics and in jazz have been kept fairly clear of each other. But since both interests are manifestations of the same nervous system, I suppose it was inevitable that someday I should talk about both jazz and semantics at the same time. My present subject is, therefore, an attempt to examine, from a semantic point of view, the *words* of popular songs and jazz songs in order to discover their underlying assumptions, orientations, and implied attitudes.

First, let me clarify the distinction between popular songs and jazz. In "true" jazz, as the jazz connoisseur understands the term, the basic interest on the part of both musician and listener is in the music as music. Originality and inventiveness in improvisation are highly prized, as are the qualities of instrumentation and of rhythm. Popular music, on the other hand, stands in about the same relationship to jazz as the so-called "semiclassics" stand in relation to Bach, Beethoven, and Brahms. Just as the musical ideas of the classics are diluted, often to a point of inanity, in the "semiclassics," so are the ideas of jazz (and of semiclassics) diluted in popular music—diluted, sweetened, sentimentalized, and trivialized.

Now the contrast between the musical sincerity of jazz and the musical slop of much of popular music is interestingly paralleled in the contrast between the literary sincerity of the words of blues songs (and the blues are the basic source of jazz inspiration) and the literary slop in the majority of popular songs. The words of true jazz songs, especially the Negro blues, tend to be unsentimental and realistic in their statements about life. (In saying "Negro blues," I should add that *most* of these are written by Negroes, but some have been written by whites under Negro inspiration.) The words of popular songs, on the other hand, largely (but not altogether) the product of white song writers for predominantly white audiences, tend toward wishful thinking, dreamy and ineffectual nostalgia, unrealistic fantasy, self-pity, and sentimental clichés masquerading as emotion.

We have been taught—and rightly—to be more than cautious about making racial distinctions. Hence let me hasten to explain that the differences between (predominantly Negro) blues and (predominantly white) popular songs can, in my opinion, be satisfactorily accounted for without "racial" explanations. The blues arise from the experiences of a largely agricultural and working class Negro minority with a social and cultural history different from that of the white majority. Furthermore, the blues—a folk music which underwent urbanization (in New Orleans, Chicago, New York, Memphis, Kansas City, and elsewhere)—developed in an economic or market situation different from that in which popular songs, aimed at mass markets through mass entertainment media, developed.[1] With these cultural and economic conditions in mind, let me restate the thesis of this paper, using this time the terminology of general semantics: *The blues tend to be extensionally oriented, while popular songs tend to exhibit grave, even pathological, intensional orientations.*

Perhaps I can make my thesis come to life by discussing a specific area of emotion about which songs are written, namely, love, in the light of what Wendell Johnson calls the IFD disease—the triple-threat semantic disorder of Idealization (the making of impossible and ideal demands upon life), which leads to Frustration (as the result of the demands not being met), which in turn leads to Demoralization (or Disorganization, or Despair). What Johnson says in *People in Quandaries* (Harper) is repeatedly illustrated in the attitudes toward love expressed in popular songs.

First, in looking forward to love, there is an enormous

[1] I might add that I do not know enough about folk music among the whites (hillbilly music, cowboy songs, etc.) to be able to include these in my discussion. Hence in comparing *folk* blues with *commercial* popular songs, I am comparing two genres which are not strictly comparable.

amount of unrealistic idealization—the creation in one's mind, as the object of love's search, of a dream girl (or dream boy) the fleshly counterpart of which never existed on earth:

Will I ever find the girl in my mind,
The girl who is my ideal? [2]

Every night I dream a little dream,
And of course Prince Charming is the theme,
The he for me. . . .[3]

Next of course, one meets a not-altogether-unattractive person of the other sex, and the psychological process called projection begins, in which one attributes to a real individual the sum total of the imaginary perfections one has dreamed about:

I took one look at you,
That's all I meant to do,
And then my heart stood still . . .[4]

You were meant for me, I was meant for you. . . .
I confess, the angels must have sent you,
And they meant you just for me.[5]

Wendell Johnson has commented frequently on what he calls a prevalent belief in magic. Some of his clients in his speech clinic at the University of Iowa, he says, will do no drills, perform no exercises, read no books, carry out no recommendations; they simply seem to expect that now that they have come to THE right speech clinic their stuttering will somehow magically go away. The essence of magic is the belief that you don't have to do anything—the right magic makes all effort unnecessary.

Love is depicted in most popular songs as just this kind of magic. There is rarely an indication in the accounts of love euphoria commonly to be found in these songs that, having found the dream girl or dream man, one's problems are

[2] "My Ideal," by Leo Robin, Richard Whiting, and Newell Chase. Copyright, 1930, by Famous Music Co.

[3] "The Man I Love," by George and Ira Gershwin. Copyright, 1924, by Harms, Inc.

[4] "My Heart Stood Still," by Lorenz Hart and Richard Rodgers. Copyright, 1927, by Harms, Inc.

[5] "You Were Meant for Me," with lyrics by Arthur Freed, melody by Nacio Herb Brown. Copyright, 1929, by Robbins Music Corp.

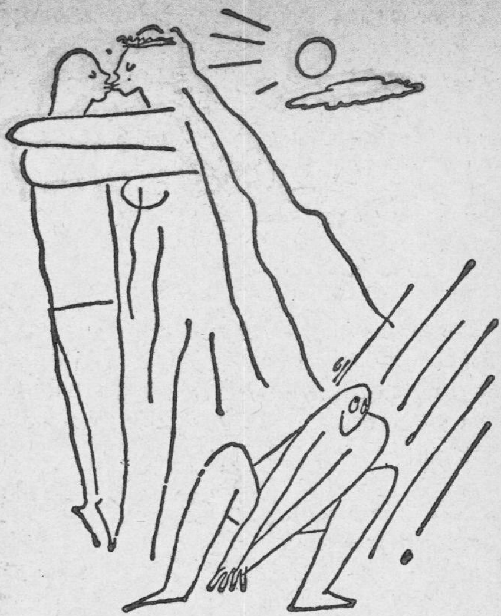

just beginning. Rather it is explicitly stated that, having found one's ideal, *all* problems are solved:

We'll have a blue room, a new room, for two room,
Where every day's a holiday, because you're married to me. . .[6]

The "Blue Room" song hints at what other songs often state, namely, that not only are emotional problems (and apparently economic problems) automatically solved by finding "the sweetheart of all my dreams"; the housing problem is also solved:

> *You'll find a smiling face, a fireplace, a cozy room,*
> *A little nest that's nestled where the roses bloom. . .*[7]
>
> *In a bungalow all covered with roses,*
> *I will settle down I vow,*
> *I'm looking at the world thru rose-colored glasses,*
> *And everything is rosy now.*[8]

6 "Blue Room," by Lorenz Hart and Richard Rodgers. Copyright, 1926, by Harms, Inc.

7 "My Blue Heaven," by George Whiting and Walter Donaldson. Copyright, 1927, by Leo Feist, Inc.

8 "Looking at the World Thru Rose Colored Glasses," by Tommy Malie and Jimmy Steiger. Copyright, 1926, by Pickwick Music Corp.

That, then, is the idealization. And students of general semantics know from reading Wendell Johnson what *that* leads to. The unrealistic expectations—for love is never expected to last for any shorter a period than "forever"—result inevitably in disappointment, disenchantment, frustration, and, most importantly, self-pity. Hence:

I'm all alone every evening,
All alone, feeling blue,
Wondering where you are, and how you are,
And if you are all alone too.[9]

What if it turns out that he wasn't all alone at all, but two-timing her? She complains bitterly:

You were only fooling,
While I was falling in love.[10]

Little you care for the vows that you made,
Little you care how much I have paid. . . .[11]

But in spite of the disappointments he has caused, she still loves him:

Yesterday's kisses are bringing me pain,
Yesterday's sunshine has turned into rain,
I'm alone because I love you,
Love you with all my heart.[12]

Am I blue, am I blue,
Ain't these tears in these eyes telling you? [13]

How can I go on living, now that we're apart? [14]

[9] "All Alone," by Irving Berlin. Copyright, 1924, by Irving Berlin.

[10] "You Were Only Fooling," with words by Billy Faber and Fred Meadows, music by Larry Fotine. Copyright, 1948, by Shapiro, Bernstein & Co.

[11] "Somebody Else Is Taking My Place," by Dick Howard, Bob Ellsworth, and Russ Morgan. Copyright, 1937, by the Back Bay Music Co.–assigned to Shapiro, Bernstein & Co. Copyright, 1941, by Shapiro, Bernstein & Co.

[12] "I'm Alone Because I Love You," words and music by Joe Young. Copyright, 1950, by M. Witmark & Sons.

[13] "Am I Blue," by Grant Clarke and Harry Akst. Copyright, 1929, by M. Witmark & Sons.

[14] "Have You Ever Been Lonely?" with words by George Brown (Billy Hill) and music by Peter de Rose. Copyright, 1933, by Shapiro, Bernstein & Co., Inc.

She admits vociferously, "I'm a fool to care," but she wallows nevertheless in self-commiseration:

No day or night goes by,
That I don't have my cry. . . .[15]

The next stage in the progress from disenchantment to demoralization and despair is, of course, another popular song theme, "I'm through with love, I'll never love again" —a theme which has such variants as these:

I'll never love again,
I'm so in love with you.
I'll never thrill again
To somebody new. . . .[16]

And if I never fall in love again, that's soon enough for me,
I'm gonna lock my heart and throw away the key.[17]

And what is the final stage? Students of general semantics are familiar enough with psychiatric concepts to know that when the world of reality proves unmanageable, a common practice is to retreat into a symbolic world, since symbols are more manageable and predictable than the extensional realities for which they stand. The psychiatric profession classifies this retreat as schizophrenia, but that does not prevent it from being the theme of a popular song:

I'm going to buy a paper doll that I can call my own,
A doll that other fellows cannot steal. . . .
I'd rather have a paper doll to call my own
Than a fickle-minded real live girl.[18]

This, then, is the picture of love's unhappy progress, as presented by the song writers of the commercial song-publishing world. The unrealistic emotions and the bathos of popular songs have, of course, long been notorious. It

[15] "I Need You Now," by Jimmy Crane and Al Jacobs. Copyright, 1953, by Miller Music Corp.

[16] "I'll Never Smile Again," with words and music by Ruth Lowe. Copyright, 1939, by Pickwick Music Corp.

[17] "I'm Gonna Lock My Heart," by Jimmy Eaton and Terry Shand. Copyright, 1938, by Shapiro, Bernstein & Co., Inc.

[18] "Paper Doll," by Johnny Black. Copyright, 1915, by E. B. Marks.

may well be asked if songs can be otherwise and yet be popular.

In answer to this question, let me next present the problems of love as seen by the writers of blues songs, such as are the basis of jazz. The first thing to be noticed is that the object of love is not idealized, but is looked at fairly realistically. It is one thing to call a pretty girl an angel, but quite another to look at angels as they are seen in "Harlem Blues":

Now you can have your Broadway, give me Lenox Avenue,
Angels from the skies stroll Seventh, and for that thanks are due
To Madam Walker's Beauty Shops and the Poro System too. . . .[19]

Shortcomings of character or appearance in the object of one's love are candidly acknowledged:

The man I love's got lowdown ways for true,
Well, I am hinkty and I'm lowdown too.[20]

You're so mean and evil, you do things you ought not to do,
But you've got my brand of honey, so I guess I'll have to put up with you.[21]

In other words, there is no to-do made about looking and looking for an ideal girl or man—one adjusts oneself to the kind of women and men that actually exist. Refraining from "always chasing rainbows," the people depicted in the blues appear to save themselves a vast amount of emotional energy.

The loved one's imperfections, however, do not appear to stand in the way either of the intensity or durability of one's affections, as is indicated in this lament over a woman's death:

I tried to keep from cryin',
My heart felt just like lead.
She was all I had to live for,
I wish that it was me instead. . . .[22]

[19] "Harlem Blues," by W. C. Handy. Copyright, 1922, by W. C. Handy; copyright renewed. Included in *A Treasury of the Blues*, ed. W. C. Handy (New York: Simon and Schuster, 1949).
[20] "The Basement Blues," by W. C. Handy. Copyright, 1924, by Handy Bros. Music Co., Inc.
[21] "Goin' to Chicago Blues," by Jimmy Rushing and Count Basie. Copyright, 1941, by Bregman, Vocco and Conn, Inc.
[22] "St. James Infirmary," by Joe Primrose. Copyright, 1930, by Gotham Music Co.

Furthermore, there is no magical attitude toward love indicated in the blues. Love means a mutual human relationship, and therefore there are duties and responsibilities, no less than there are rewards. In its crudest and most elementary statement, the duty is financial:

You want to be my man you got to give me $40 down,
If you don't be my man, your baby's gonna shake this town.[23]

You sittin' down wonderin' what it's all about,
If you ain't got no money, they will put you out,
Why don't you do right, like some other men do?
Get out of here, and get me some money too.[24]

In general the duties described are those of living up to one's obligations as a mate, of providing that minimum of dependability that makes, as they say, a house a home:

Kind treatment make me love you, be mean and you'll drive me away,
You're gonna long for me, baby, one of these old rainy days.
Yes, I love you, baby, but you don't treat me right,
Walk the streets all day, baby, and never come home at night.[25]

And the famous blues singer, Bessie Smith, gives the

[23] "The Memphis Blues," by W. C. Handy. Copyright, 1912, by W. C. Handy. (Included in *A Treasury of the Blues.*) When the lecture on which this paper was based was delivered in San Francisco, it was extensively reported in the San Francisco *News*. In the correspondence columns of the *News* a few days later, there appeared a protest from a reader who remarked regarding my quotation of these lines, "It is good to know that our future teachers [at San Francisco State College] are acquiring moral and spiritual values by getting the good honest feel of the brothel." Mr. Ralph Gleason, writing in the musicians' magazine, *Down Beat*, and taking his interpretation of my lecture from the letter writer in the *News*, worked himself up into quite a moralistic lather against what he imagined to be my recommendation of love on a cash-down basis over white middle-class morality. I trust it is not necessary to explain that what I am doing here is attempting to draw a humorous contrast between love regarded *as magic* and love (including facsimiles thereof) regarded as *involving mutual obligations.* The statement that love involves obligations is not entirely absent, of course, from popular songs. A recent example is "Little Things Mean a Lot," by Edith Lindeman and Carl Stutz (New York: Leo Feist, 1954), which, as sung by Kitty Kallen, a few years ago enjoyed vast popularity.

[24] "Why Don't You Do Right?" by Joe McCoy. Copyright, 1942, by Mayfair Music Corp.

[25] "Blues in the Dark," by Jimmy Rushing and Count Basie. Copyright, 1943, by Bregman, Vocco and Conn, Inc.

following advice to girls—advice which is full of the sense of one's own responsibility in a love situation:

So if your man is nice, take my advice,
Hug him in the morning, kiss him every night,
Give him plenty loving, treat him right,
For a good man nowadays is hard to find.[26]

The physical basis of love is more candidly acknowledged in the blues than in most popular songs. I am indebted to Dr. Russell Meyers of the University of Iowa Hospitals for the following observation about Jelly Roll Morton's "Winin' Boy Blues," in which there occurs the line, "Pick it up and shake it, life's sweet stavin' chain."[27] Dr. Meyers equates this line to Herrick's "Gather ye rosebuds while ye may," translating thus: "A 'stavin' chain' is the heavy chain used by loggers to bind together logs to be floated down river, so that it is metaphorically that which binds together, i.e., sexuality; the idea is, as in Herrick, that you shake it now, while you are still able."

Popular songs, to be sure, also refer to the physical basis of love, but usually in extremely abstract periphrasis, as in "All of me, why not take all of me?" In the blues, however, as in the Elizabethan lyric, the subject is treated metaphorically. The following is from a song made famous by Bessie Smith:

You better get yourself to a blacksmith shop to get yourself overhauled,
There ain't nothing about you to make a good woman bawl.
Nobody wants a baby when a real man can be found,
You been a good ol' wagon, daddy, but you done broke down.[28]

So there are disappointments in love in the blues, no less than in popular songs. But the quality of disappointment is different. The inevitability of change in a changing world appears to be accepted. Conditions change, people change,

[26] "A Good Man Is Hard to Find," by Eddie Green. Copyright, 1917, by Mayfair Music Corp. This song is not of Negro composition and is not, strictly speaking, a blues. However, ever since its famous rendition by Bessie Smith (Columbia 14250-D), it has been part of the blues repertory.

[27] See General 4004-A, in the album *New Orleans Memories* by Jelly Roll Morton.

[28] "You've Been a Good Ole Wagon" (Smith-Balcom), sung by Bessie Smith (Columbia 14079-D; re-issue, Columbia 35672). Copyright by Leeds Music Corporation, 322 W. 48th St., New York, N.Y.

and in spite of all one can do to preserve a valued relationship, failure may result:

Folks I love my man, I kiss him morning, noon and night,
I wash his clothes and keep him dry and try to treat him right.
Now he's gone and left me. . . .[29]

I've got a hard-working man,
The way he treats me I can't understand,
He works hard every day,
And on Sat'day he throws away his pay.
Now I don't want that man,
Because he's done gone cold in hand.

Now I've tried hard to treat him kind,
But it seems to me his love has gone blind.
The man I've got must have lost his mind,
The way he treats me I can't understand.
I'm gonna get myself another man,
Because the one I've got done gone cold in hand.[30]

The most vivid statement of a sudden change of situation, involving desertion and heartbreak, is made in "Young Woman's Blues," by Bessie Smith:

Woke up this mornin' when the chickens were crowin' for day,
Felt on the right side of my pilla, my man has gone away.

Her reaction to this blow, however, is not, as in popular songs, any giving away to self-pity. The song continues:

I'm a young woman, and I ain't done running round.[31]

In other words, she may be hurt, but she is far from demoralized. This refusal to be demoralized under conditions which in popular songs call for the utmost in wailing and self-commiseration is repeatedly to be found in the blues. Instead of the self-abasement that we find in the "kick-

[29] For this and several other quotations from blues songs in this paper, I am indebted to Professor John Ball of the Department of English, Miami University, Oxford, Ohio, who, as a student of jazz, has transcribed from his record collection the words of many blues songs, including many which have never appeared in print.

[30] "Cold in Hand Blues" (Gee-Longshaw), sung by Bessie Smith (Columbia 14064-D; re-issue, Columbia 35672). Copyright by C-R Publishing Co., 2908 Americas Bldg., Rockefeller Center, New York.

[31] "Young Woman's Blues" (Bessie Smith), copyright, 1927, by Bessie Smith; copyright renewed, 1954, by Empress Music, Inc., 119 W. 57th St., New York 19, N.Y.

me-in-the-face-again-because-I-love-you" school of thought, the heartbroken men and women of the blues songs regroup their emotional forces and carry on without breakdown of morale. The end of a love relationship is by no means the end of life. As Pearl Bailey has sung:

Gonna truck downtown and spend my moo,
Get some short-vamp shoes and a new guy too . . .
Cause I'm tired, mighty tired, of you.[32]

There is, then, considerable tough-mindedness in the blues—a willingness, often absent in popular songs, to acknowledge the facts of life. Consequently, one finds in the blues comments on many problems other than those of love, for example, the problem of urban congestion, as in "I'm going to move to the outskirts of town," or of alcoholism, as in the song, "Ignorant Oil." There is also much folk wisdom in the blues, as in "Nobody knows you when you're down and out," or in such observations as:

Now if a woman gets the blues, Lawd, she hangs her head and cries,
But if a man gets the blues, Lawd, he grabs a train and and rides.[33]

I am often reminded by the words of blues songs of Kenneth Burke's famous description of poetry as "equipment for living." In the form in which they developed in Negro communities, the blues are equipment for living humble, laborious, and precarious lives of low social status or no status at all—nevertheless, they are valid equipment, in the sense that they are the opposite of escape literature. "Rock Pile Blues" states explicitly what the blues are for:

My hammer's heavy, feels just like a ton of lead,
If they keeps me slaving someone's gonna find me dead.
Don't mind the rock pile, but the days are oh so long,
Ain't no end of misery, that is why I sing this song.[34]

As a student of general semantics, I am concerned here with two functions which literary and poetic symbols perform

[32] "Tired" (Roberts and Fisher), sung by Pearl Bailey (Columbia 36837).

[33] See note 29. Memo to Professor Ball: Where on earth did you find this, John?

[34] "Rock Pile Blues," by Spencer Williams. Copyright, 1925, by Lincoln Music Co. (Included in *A Treasury of the Blues.*)

with respect to our emotional life. First, by means of literary symbols we may be introduced vicariously to the emotions and situations which we have not yet had occasion to experience; in this sense, literature is preparation. Secondly, symbols enable us to organize the experiences we have had, make us aware of them, and therefore help us to come to terms with them; in this sense, literature is learning.

If our symbolic representations give a false or misleading impression of what life is likely to be, we are *worse* prepared for life than we would have been had we not been exposed to them at all. The frustration and demoralization of which Wendell Johnson writes are of necessity preceded by the expectations created by unrealistic idealizations. This is not to say, of course, that idealizations are in themselves unhealthy; they are a necessary and inescapable product of the human processes of abstraction and symbolization, and without idealizations we should be swine indeed. But there is a world of difference in the semantogenic effects of *possible* and *impossible* ideals. The ideals of love, as depicted in popular songs, are usually impossible ideals.

Hence the question arises: do popular songs, listened to, often memorized and sung in the course of adolescent and youthful courtship, make the attainment of emotional maturity more difficult than it need be? It is almost impossible to resist having an opinion on this question, although it would be hard to substantiate one's opinion except on the basis of considerable experience in contact with the emotional problems of young people. Mr. Roy E. Dickerson, executive secretary of the Cincinnati Social Hygiene Society, who has had this experience, has offered the following comment on the thesis of this paper:

> In my judgment there is no doubt about the unfortunate influence of IFD upon the younger generation today. I detected it, I think, in even such a highly selected group as the delegates to the Seventh National Hi-Y-Tri-Hi-Y Congress held under the auspices of the National Council of YMCA's at Miami University recently. I had the pleasure of handling the group of the section of the Congress which gave attention to courtship and marriage. It was still necessary to debunk some super-romantic concepts.
>
> I am up to my eyes in marriage counseling. I feel that I am consulted again and again about ill-considered marriages based upon very superficial and inadequate ideas regarding the nature of love and how it is recognized.

The existence of the blues, like the existence of occasional popular songs with love themes which do not exhibit the IFD pattern, demonstrates that it is at least possible for songs to be *both* reasonably healthy in psychological content *and* widely sung and enjoyed. But the blues cannot, of course, take over the entire domain of popular song because, as widely known as some of them have been, their chief appeal, for cultural reasons, has been to Negro audiences—and even these audiences have been diminishing with the progressive advancement of Negroes and their assimilation of values and tastes in common with the white, middle-class majority. Furthermore, while there is lyricism to be found in blues *tunes* and their musical treatment, the *words* of blues songs are notoriously lacking in either lyricism or delicacy of sentiment—and it would seem that popular songs must, to some degree, supply the need for lyrical expression, especially about matters of love.

With all their limitations, however, the blues demonstrate that a popular art can function as "equipment for living." Cannot our poets and our song writers try to do at least as much for our young people as Bessie Smith did for her audiences, namely, provide them with symbolic experiences which will help them understand, organize, and better cope with their problems? Or, if that is too much to ask (and perhaps it is, since Bessie Smith was, in her own way, an authentic genius), can they not at least cease and desist from further spreading the all-too-prevalent IFD disease?

Originally presented at the Conference on General Semantics, Washington University, St. Louis, Missouri, June 12, 1954. It was also given as a lecture-recital before the Associated Students of San Francisco State College, July 8, 1954, at which time the musical illustrations were provided by the blues singer, Claire Austin, Bob Scobey's Frisco Band, and Clancy Hayes.

The materials of this paper were again presented at the Folk and Jazz Festival at Music Inn, Lenox, Massachusetts, September 5, 1954. Music on this occasion was provided by the Sammy Price Trio, with blues-singing by Jimmy Rushing and Myra Johnson. They were also presented, with the assistance of the Bob Scobey Frisco Band and Lizzie Miles, blues singer, before audiences at the University of California at Davis, San Jose State College, Beloit College, Northwestern University, University of Chicago, and Purdue University, in 1955 and 1956. In August, 1961, they were presented again before a seminar on communication from the Stanford University Institute of Communication Research, meeting at the Sugar Hill night club in San Francisco, with musical illustrations provided by Barbara Dane, blues singer, with Kenneth "Goodnews" Whitson on piano, Brownie McGhee on guitar, and Sonny Terry on harmonica.

Sexual Fantasy and the 1957 Car

S. I. HAYAKAWA

AMERICAN males, according to a point of view widely held among Freudian critics of our culture, are afraid of sex. If a woman indicates to a man that she loves him and desires him, the chances are that she will scare him away. Her open manifestation of desire is likely to arouse, not his enthusiastic response, but his underlying anxieties. For endemic among American males, so the argument goes, is, if not impotence, the fear of impotence. Behind the masculine front lies the anxious question, "Am I really male?"

Such critics of the culture point to the American form of stag party, which has superficially the comforting implication of men being he-men together, as but one of a number of disguises which sexual anxiety can take. The implication of stag parties that stags don't think about is that it is an institutionalized way of running away from women—running away from the real tests of being a lover, husband, father, and a man. But sex is not too far away from any stag party—a sniggering, surreptitious sex interest such as is shown in a news story like the following:

HOLLYWOOD, FEB. 9 (UP)—Police today released several husbands who were arrested while allegedly watching a lewd movie at a lodge hall while their wives played bridge in a room next door. Officers said 62 men were arrested last night after a policeman climbed a telephone pole and watched the movie through a window. Detectives said the hall had been rented by a Knights of Pythias group for a "business meeting."

The real giveaway as to the psychology of the men in this situation is contained in the last paragraph of the story:

On the way to jail, one suspect said, "Boy, a life sentence isn't going to be nearly long enough." Another asked, "Where do you join the Foreign Legion?"

And well they might join the Foreign Legion. For they insult their wives doubly, first by declining or fearing to respond fully and joyfully to their wives' sexuality, and secondly by gratifying themselves instead with the mental masturbation of obscene movies. For all too many American men a wife is not a wife but a mother substitute, alternatively loving and punitive, someone to run away from when one wants to be naughty, and then returns to, to be spanked and forgiven.

Such assertions as the foregoing about American men are familiar enough in the writings of Karl Menninger, Franz Alexander, Karen Horney, and others with a psychoanalytic orientation. They are also familiar through the writings of nonpsychiatrists like Philip Wylie, with his diatribe against momism. I myself have been tempted to dismiss these charges as unfair generalizations, based too much on experiences with patients, and not enough on observations of the majority. All American men aren't like that—I have argued—not even most of them.

But in 1957 I am being contradicted. I am being contradicted by perhaps the most powerful voice in America—the voice of that industry upon whose prosperity rests, we are told, the prosperity of the nation, namely, the automobile industry, which appears to have decided that the supplying of means of transportation is but a secondary reason for its existence, and that its primary function is the allaying of men's sexual anxieties. As if to back up with a fifty-million-dollar bang what psychoanalytic critics have been saying about the American male, the automobile industry is saying in 1957: "The fundamental fact about American male psychology is the fear of impotence. Let's give the men, therefore, the One Big Symbol that will make them feel that they are *not* impotent. Let's give them great big cars, glittering all over and pointed at the ends, with 275 h.p. under the hood, so that they can feel like men!" For, as the consumer motivational research people must have told the powers-that-be in the industry, this is what will make men trade in their present cars and put themselves into hock for 1957 models. The motivational research people do not survey merely the patients of psychoanalysts; they survey the entire buying public. And what most of the public wants, it appears, is a potency symbol.

Granted that a car is transportation. Granted that restless annual style changes and the quest for novelty are necessitated by business competition. Granted that a car is a prestige symbol, a personal symbol, or what you will. Granted even that many cars have always been for many men unconscious symbols of potency. The 1957 cars are nevertheless unique in sacrificing *all* else—common sense, efficiency, economy, safety, dignity, and especially beauty—to psychosexual wish fulfillment.

Few people actually need more than 40 h.p.—the Volkswagen has only 36 h.p. and is still capable of violating the top speed limit in practically any state of the union. But since the U.S. is a lavish economy, let us say that the average buyer of an American automobile is entitled to at least 85 h.p., and for a luxury car with power-driven accessories, he is entitled to 160 h.p.—the rating of the 1951 Cadillac.

What about the horsepower above 160? I believe it can be

safely said that every single horsepower above that figure is purely symbolic, and has *nothing* to do with transportation except to make it more hazardous. The 160 h.p. car can provide more than enough size, speed, and power to serve not only all conceivable practical purposes to which a passenger car can be put, but also to gratify the normal amount of will to aggression.

The argument that horsepower above that figure can contribute to safety because it enables you to pull ahead in passing is convincing only to those whose personal inadequacies leave them wanting to be convinced. No sensible driver ever finds himself in this most easily avoided of avoidable dangers. (If you find yourself in a tight situation where you need this extra "pull ahead" power, it's time you pulled over to the side of the road to sober up before proceeding.) Hence I repeat, every horsepower above 160 is purely for the gratification of one's fantasy life—in the psychiatric sense.

The bolt-out-of-the-blue performance that enables most

V-8's these days to accelerate from a standing start to 60 m.p.h. in eleven seconds or less is again purely symbolic. If you are not a bank robber (and most of us are not), what's this unused and unusable acceleration for, if not for psychological satisfactions? And the ability of most cars nowadays (even including what used to be called the "economy" Big Three) to attain speeds of 125 m.p.h. and over again has no function other than to say to the buyer, who even on the open road rarely gets a chance to do 80, "Don't feel badly because you are a dubiously satisfactory bedmate. You're a *mighty* potent fellow. You are Captain Midnight! You are Buck Rogers!"

Even more revealing than horsepower or acceleration is design. First of all there is, of course, the rocket ship motif. As Freudian students of spaceship and rocket-travel literature have pointed out—I think especially of such students of

the subject as the late Dr. Robert Lindner of "The Jet-Propelled Couch," Dr. Rudolph Ekstein of the Menninger Foundation, and Dr. Robert Plank of Cleveland Heights—spaceship fantasies are deeply related to difficulties in interpersonal relations. As the individual retreats into himself because he feels powerless to deal effectively with the living men and women around him, he often lives increasingly in a fantasy world of power and heroic action in distant, interplanetary spaces. The seven-year-old cuts box tops from cereal packages and gets himself a space helmet to act out his fantasies. The thirty-five-year-old buys a Plymouth Fury. Both reveal themselves to be in their sexual latency period, which is all right, of course—for the seven-year-old.

And to continue on the subject of design, there are the protuberances, the knifelike projections, the gashes, the humps—all dazzingly colored and outlined in strips of chrome. The symbolism of these is enough to make Dr. Freida Fromm-Reichmann blush—and she doesn't blush easily.

Once, a score or more years ago in Kobe, Japan, I saw in the foreign section a "sex store"—a place where sexual curiosities could be bought—erotic art, indecent appliances of various kinds, all apparently calculated to awaken sexual interest in those whom age or dissipation had enfeebled, or to serve as collectors' items for those whose sexual life was mostly at the imaginative or symbolic level. Among the items on display was a collection of rubber contraceptives fantastically designed. Some were surrounded with knifelike or

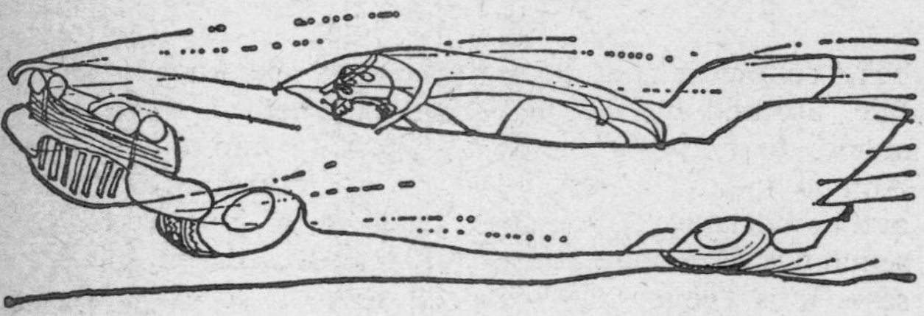

"The seven-year-old gets himself a space-helmet to act out his fantasies. The thirty-five-year-old buys a Plymouth Fury."

sawlike rubber fins, others were covered with big rubber spikes, some were fringed with tassels, some were ornamented like the noses of fighter planes with fierce bird and animal heads.

These pathetic potency symbols for the impotent and near-impotent come to mind as I contemplate such monstrosities as the 290 h.p. Mercury Turnpike Cruiser, the 345 h.p. De Soto Adventurer, and the 375 h.p. Chrysler 300-C.

The cars of 1957 have two disadvantages when compared with the obscene little objects in that store in Kobe. First, they are a menace to public safety—and quadruply so when their possessors are under the influence of liquor. Secondly, how can they serve as fetishes to be collected when you can't even get them into your garage?

This article was reprinted in the November, 1957 issue of Car Life. *A reading by the author of this article and "Why the Edsel Laid an Egg" was issued as a phonograph record distributed by the International Society for General Semantics.*

Why the Edsel Laid an Egg: Motivational Research vs. the Reality Principle

S. I. HAYAKAWA

THE following are later reflections on the American automobile, aroused by the many letters which I received in response to my article, "Sexual Fantasy and the 1957 Car." Among the questions raised by my correspondents is why automobiles are discussed at all in a journal of general semantics. This question is easily answered. As *ETC*'s cover says, it is "concerned with the role of language and other symbols in human behavior and human affairs."

The automobile is certainly one of the most important nonlinguistic symbols in American culture. As the advertisements keep telling us, it is one of our ways of telling others who we are, from Cadillac as a "symbol of achievement," to Ford as a symbol of "young-mindedness," to Plymouth, which says, according to a recent ad, "We're not the richest people in town, but we're the proudest. We're the kind of family that gets a big bang out of living." Even those who simply want transportation, with no fads or frills or nonsense, can buy a Jeep and "say" so. The automakers are therefore the grammarians of this nonverbal "language," and shortcomings in the "language" are necessarily shortcomings in the range of expression available to the consumer.

Different people have different needs, with respect both to transportation and self-expression. Hence there should be, in a rich economy like that of the United States, variety in automobiles no less than in other facets of life. Hence I believe that manufacturers should build *some* cars of very high horsepower for those who need such cars, whether for practical or psychological reasons. I do not object to *some* cars being styled to allay unconscious sexual anxieties or to provoke spaceship fantasies, if people want such cars. *Some* cars should be little and unpretentious, because there are many modest, unassuming people in the U. S., hard as this may be to believe on the basis of car ads. And since, as one obscene cigarette ad puts it, some people "like their pleasure BIG,"[1] *some* cars, whether for practical or psychological reasons, should be big. Some people love ostentation; hence it is inevitable and necessary in a free economy that manufacturers produce for their benefit *some* huge and suitably dazzling ostentation wagons.

My quarrel with the American automobile industry in 1957 was not that it produces overpriced, overpowered, oversized, and overelaborate cars, but that it produces them almost to the exclusion of all other kinds. Except for some interesting experiments at the fringes of the market by American Motors and Studebaker, the dominating forces in the

industry—General Motors, Ford, and Chrysler—are still carrying on in 1958 their assault on consumer intelligence. The "Big Three" are producing no cars that are not expensive, hideous, and (except for a few sixes) costly to operate and powered far beyond the needs of the ordinary motorist.

The Chevrolet, already too long, low, and broad in 1957 for the practical, day-to-day chores to which Chevrolets have been put ever since I can recall, is 9″ longer, 2½″ lower, and 4″ broader in 1958. Mercury ("The big M"—for masculinity?) offers engines from 312 to 400 h.p. in its "Marauder" line.[2] Again we are being told that what we need is power

[1] See Vance Packard, *The Hidden Persuaders* (New York, David McKay, 1957), pp. 127-129; also Chapter VIII, "The Built-in Sexual Overtone."

[2] "After psychiatric probing a Midwestern ad agency concluded that a major appeal of buying a shiny new and more powerful car every couple of years is that 'it gives him (the buyer) a renewed sense of power and reassures him of his masculinity.'" Packard p. 79.

("Try the B-12,000 engine. It puts 12,000 pounds of thrust behind every engine stroke!"), Gull-Wing fenders, Swept-Wing styling, with Turbo-Flash performance, in Firesweep Corsair Star Chief hardtops with that Bold New Look. Again the explicit statement of the sex theme, "Hot, Handsome, a Honey to Handle."

For what? For Father to commute seventeen miles to work —a distance which, with favorable traffic conditions (and they are not always favorable), he will cover at an average rate of 30 m.p.h. For Mother to drop Chrissie off at dancing school, stopping at the supermarket and the public library on the way back. For Doug, the candy salesman, to make his calls on neighborhood stores. For Florence, the social caseworker, to visit her clients. For Pete, the insurance adjuster; for Stanley, the instructor at the university extension center; for Andy, the television repair man—all of whom need their cars for their work and their occasional holiday week-ends.

It does not come altogether as a surprise, therefore, that in the spring of 1958 the volume of new automobiles sales was crushingly disappointing to the trade. The Edsel laid a colossal egg. *Time* (March 31, 1958) reported that the sale of "medium-priced" cars fell disastrously. The manufacturers blamed the recession.

One wonders, however, whether the recession itself is not partly to be blamed on the carmakers who, in defiance of all rational consumer interests—economy, convenience, safety, maneuverability, and beauty—have been trying to foist upon the *majority* of the public fabulously overpriced jukeboxes such as only people of deprived origins or the neurotic would want to buy and only the prosperous can afford to maintain. What I objected to in the cars of 1957, and what I still object to in 1958 is the assumption apparently held by carmakers—an assumption revealed in the 200-plus h.p. engines and the tailfins and the spaceship platforms with which they equipped the lowest-priced and most popular cars, the Ford, Plymouth, and Chevrolet—that *the majority of the population is mentally ill.*

The trouble with car manufacturers (who, like other isolated people in underdeveloped areas, are devout believers in voodoo) is that they have been listening too long to the motivation research people. Motivation researchers are those harlot social scientists who, in impressive psychoanalytic and/or sociological jargon, tell their clients what their clients want to hear, namely, that *appeals to human irrationality are likely to be far more profitable than appeals to rationality.* This doctrine appeals to moguls and would-be moguls of all times and places, because it implies that if you hold the key to people's irrationality, you can exploit and diddle them to your heart's content and be loved for it.

The Great Gimmick of the motivation researchers, therefore, is the investigation of irrationality, of which we all have, goodness knows, an abundance. Many people (perhaps most) have sexual anxieties and fears of impotence, as the motivation researchers say. Many upward-strivers (most, I am sure) like to impress their neighbors with the display of costly status symbols. Many people (surely not most!) allay their feelings of inadequacy with spaceship fantasies.

But what the motivation researchers, many of whom call themselves Freudians, do not bother to investigate, since it is too obvious, is rationality—or what Freud called the reality principle.[3] Father may indeed see a bright-red convertible as a surrogate mistress and the hardtop as a combination wife-and-mistress, but he settles for a lesser car than either because Chrissie is going to an orthodontist. Doug, in his secret fantasies, screams along the track of the Mille Miglia at 200 m.p.h., but in actuality, especially when his wife and children are with him, he never drives above fifty-five. Andy's dreams are crowded with jet-propulsion themes which clearly mark him as haunted by feelings of sexual inadequacy, but on his eighty-five dollar-a-week salary he cannot be snow-jobbed into a conviction that his self-respect requires him to maintain a car that swallows six dollars' worth of gasoline every two hundred miles and costs a hundred dollars to repair every time his fender is dented.

What the motivation researchers failed to tell their clients (perhaps because they hadn't thought of it themselves) is that *only* the psychotic and the gravely neurotic *act out* their irrationalities and their compensatory fantasies—and it is because they act them out that we classify them as mentally ill. The rest of us—the mildly neurotic and the mature, who together constitute the majority (among whom I make bold to include myself)—are reasonably well oriented to reality. We do not indulge our fantasies unless it is socially and psychologically safe to do so (as in taking fencing lessons or marching in

[3] "But what about those consumer-motivation studies . . . ? The trouble here seems to have been the elemental mistake on which research can founder–failure to ask questions which elicit meaningful replies. For example, the Ford Motor Company asked no questions at all about: car prices, cost of upkeep, cost of operation, rising insurance rates, growing difficulty in parking, irritation at cars too long for garages, etc. In fact, the consumer research program . . . completely ignored automobiles as functioning machines of transportation." *Consumer Reports,* April, 1958, p. 218.

regalia in a Shriners' parade) and within our financial means (as in reading paperback murder mysteries).

Motivation researchers seem not to know the difference between the sane and the unsane. Having learned through their "depth" techniques that we all have our irrationalities (no great discovery at this date), they fatuously conclude that we are equally governed by those irrationalities at *all* levels of consumer expenditure—although it doesn't take a social science genius to point out that the more expensive an object is, the more its purchase compels the recognition of reality. The fact that irrationalities may drive people from Pall Mall cigarettes to Marlboro or vice versa proves little about what the average person is likely to do in selecting the most expensive object (other than a house) that he ever buys.

The trouble with selling symbolic gratification via such expensive items as the Phallic Ford, the Edsel Hermaphrodite, and the Plymouth with the Rear-End Invitation is the competition offered by much cheaper forms of symbolic gratification, such as *Playboy* (fifty cents a copy), *Astounding Science Fiction* (thirty-five cents a copy), and television (free). When, on the advice of their voodoo men, automakers abandon their basic social function of providing better, safer, and more efficient means of transportation in favor of entering the business of selling dreams (in which the literary and entertainment industries have far more experience and resources), they cannot but encounter competition which they are not equipped to meet.

The consumer rush to the little foreign cars does not appear to me a passing fad, although Detroit is trying to reassure itself by saying that the foreign-car trend has reached its peak. The Morris Minor, the English Fords, the Hillman, the Simca, the Volkswagen, the Volvo, the Fiat, and all the other lovely little bugs that we see today in increasing numbers are cheap to operate. As for what they "communicate," they give out simple, unassuming messages devoid of delusions of grandeur. Their popularity indicates a widespread reassertion of an orientation toward reality, which says that $1,600 is less than $2,800, that 30 miles per gallon is cheaper transportation than 8 to 13 miles per gallon, that a 155″ Renault is easier to park than a 214″ Dodge. The very people who are writing the ads for Plymouth, Ford, Chevrolet are driving DKW's, MG's, and Triumphs, while their bosses, the agency heads, ride around in Jaguars and Bentleys. It will take the American auto industry five years, if not a decade or two, to regain the respect and confidence of its friend, the American consumer.

Now that American automakers, with hundreds of thousands of unsold cars on their hands, are in such deep trouble, you would think that they would turn away in disgust from the voodoo men who gave them such a bum steer. But they are slow to learn. *Consumer Reports* (April, 1958) quoted as follows from *The Wall Street Journal:* "Ford Motor has called on the Institute for Motivational Research to find out why Americans buy foreign economy cars."

Although the answer is right there in the question, I am sure that the Institute for Motivational Research is not so stupid as to point out this fact to the Ford Motor Company. I foresee, therefore, years of prosperity ahead for the Institute for Motivational Research, for Social Research, Inc., and all the other Shamans of the Hard Sell. But will Ford be able to survive another round of good advice such as they got on the Edsel?

This article was reprinted in the trade journals, Advertising Age *and* Madison Avenue, *where it aroused considerable controversy in advertising circles. Since many people have inquired, it should be reported that the author was driving a 1952 Nash Ambassador and a 1954 Hillman at the time his articles on the automobile were written. In 1959 he acquired a Citroën ID-19.*

The Language of Pictures

PAUL R. WENDT

MAN has been communicating by pictures longer than he has been using words. With the development of photography in this century we are using pictures as a means of communication to such an extent that in some areas they overshadow verbal language. The science of semantics has studied the conveyance of meaning by language in considerable detail. Yet very little is known as to how pictures convey meaning and what their place is in the life of man.

Perhaps this neglect may be due to the poor repute pictures have in our society as a means of communication. For example, in the field of education, pictures, as a part of the group of audio-visual materials available to teachers, are still considered supplementary rather than complementary to other teaching materials such as textbooks or other purely verbal materials. The term audio-visual "aids" persists, although a number of educators have tried for a decade to persuade their colleagues to discontinue its use on the basis of its connotation of (1) something used by poor teachers who cannot teach without gadgets, (2) a luxury to be trimmed off the budget in hard times, and (3) a mental crutch for backward pupils.

Pictures are of course surrogates for experience. As such they may be said to be closer to extensional meaning than to intensional meaning. At least their position lies in between these two. They are not always close to the actual experience even though the school of "you press the button and we do the rest" implies that merely pointing the camera at Aunt Minnie results in a good likeness to cherish when she is not around. Neither are pictures symbols as words are symbols, since even Aunt Minnie's nephew, age four, can recognize her snapshot though he cannot read.

Pictures are a language in themselves. They are not merely limited representations of reality operating within narrow limits of expression. On the contrary photography is a very flexible medium with a wide range whose limits have not yet been sighted. The range extends from absorbing realism to a fairly high level of abstraction. Let us consider the realistic end of the scale.

The tendency today is to say that the heyday of the movies is over. Television is gnawing at the vitals of Hollywood. But the powerfully realistic effect of the film remains. The other day the writer showed to one of his classes a film, *The Cinematographer,* which purports to show the work of the director of photography in a large studio. Excerpts from several dramatic films were shown to illustrate the different types of sciences a cinematographer encounters. None of these excerpts was longer than one minute. After the film ended some members of the class complained that the excerpts were so realistic and exciting that they "lost" themselves in the content of the episodes and completely forgot that the purpose of the film showing was to study cinematography. Each episode in turn caught these students up in a rich representation of reality. The excerpts were very dissimilar in content so that it was a wrench to change from one scene to another. Nevertheless the students were deeply involved in each excerpt in turn, and only when the lights came on in the classroom did they remember where they were.

Motion pictures are a powerful medium of persuasion. Hitler's films of the bombing of Warsaw were such terribly realistic records that they could be used as a tool of conquest. At times a motion picture may seem even more realistic than the real experience.

At the other end of the scale from realism to abstraction, pictures have many qualities of language. Like words every picture has a content of meaning partly intensional, partly extensional. Whether this meaning is more or less extensionally clear or abstractly difficult to understand depends of course on many factors inherent in the viewer, such as his past experience. But it also is dependent on factors in the picture itself which we might call the grammar of photography.

Composition is all important. In chirographic, or handmade pictures, composition is achieved sometimes by selection of the point of view but more often by manipulation of space relationships of objects perceived or imagined. The still photographer, unless he is using techniques which are essentially chirographic, such as retouching, montage, or collage, is bound by the objects of reality as the eye of his camera sees them. He achieves composition by painstaking selection of the camera angle, by using a variety of lenses, by choice of filters and emulsions, and by controlling lighting on the subject or scene. Choosing a camera angle may take a professional photographer days of continuous effort, even though television camera operators may be forced to do it in seconds. The angle and the lens used for the shot determine the basic composition. The lighting, however, gives the photographer an enormous range of control over the representation of reality. High key photography in which all the values are crowded toward the whites and light grays, gives the impressions of light, of lightness, or happiness, or innocent pleasures. Low key photography with many shadows and low values is appropriate for mystery, danger, depression. Every textbook in photography contains the series of portraits of a model taken with different lighting effects, showing how one face can be made to look like many strange people. Pictures have affective connotations.

These constitute the grammar of photographs. The analogy holds even down to details such as synizesis. Two crucial objects in a picture, like two syllables, can be blended and not discriminated from each other, thereby changing the meaning entirely. Even though the photographer uses lighting and other techniques to separate the two objects, the viewer may still misread the picture because of lack of experience or poor viewing conditions. Always it is important to remember that pictures, like words, are merely surrogates for reality, not reality itself.

In motion pictures we find the syntax of photography. Motion pictures present a flowing discourse in picture surrogates. Like a paragraph, a motion picture sequence is a highly structured time-space analysis and synthesis of reality. Using individual "shots" like words, the sequence inflects the static frame of film by motion. One scene with motion by actors or by the camera resembles a sentence. Short dynamic scenes have the same effect as blunt statements. Longer scenes with complicated changes in composition created by camera movement have somewhat the effect of compound sentences.

Pictures, like words, must make a logical continuity, according to accepted rules. For example, a motion picture showing two people conversing must first show them more or less side-to, to establish their relative positions. Then as each speaks he is shown over the other's shoulder. This is the familiar "reverse-angle" shot. That this is a culturally based convention of film syntax is shown by the experience of representatives of the U. S. Office of Information who have found that natives of foreign countries who have not seen motion pictures cannot "understand" the reverse-angle shot. They cannot adjust to our stereotyped representations of reality. They don't understand our language of pictures. Similarly, most of the action in a motion picture must be "matched." That is, if an actor is shown walking up to a door in a distant shot, the following close-up should show him approximately in the same position as he was in the last frame of the long shot. "Matching the action" is a convention in cinematography, part of the film language. It is not always used. When the tempo of the film is fast it is common practice for the editor to elide some of the action, as an author does when he wants the same effect. And of course films *can* compress time dramatically.

Paragraphing is accomplished by the traditional fade-out and fade-in, or by the dissolve or optical effect as soft or hard "wipes." The pace of the narrative is determined more by the film editor than by the script. The editor of words clarifies the presentation of content by eliminating words, sentences, paragraphs, and even chapters. The film editor clips out frames, scenes, sequences, and even large parts of a film (resulting sometimes in "the face on the cutting room floor"). The book editor may achieve lucidity by rearranging the author's text, moving paragraphs and chapters. The film editor boldly changes the order of film sequences. Both the book editor and the film editor can have a decisive influence on the style of the finished work. Both can call for rewriting or new photography. Both can affect the pace of the manuscript or the "rough cut." Both are experts in grammar, syntax, and style.

More important than the mechanical analogy to words are the semantic dimensions of pictures. Every photograph is an abstraction of an object or an event. Even the amateur, ignorant of the plasticity of the medium, makes an abstraction of Aunt Minnie when he presses the button. Only a few of Aunt Minnie's characteristics are recorded on the film.

The professional photographer in control of his medium knows he is abstracting. If he is competent he abstracts to a purpose. Knowing he cannot possibly record the whole event, he sees to it that the abstracting preserves those features he wants to present to the picture-reader. By manipulation of the variables at his command, he lets us "see" the event as he thinks it should be "seen." If he is a news photographer he probably wants to present a "realistic" event, full of details, although often he is working under such handicaps of haste that the picture as we see it in the newspaper has become simplified and perhaps indistinct. Then it lacks background or environment, it lacks the richness and crispness which a realistic picture must have. Some news pictures are so simplified that they look like symbolizations. They fit the definition of a symbol as "that which suggests something else by convention."

The fashion photographer, however, preparing for an advertisement in *The New Yorker*, controls the photographic medium to produce a simple, stylized figure, often against a blank background. This picture is realistic only to a limited extent and approaches the characteristics of a symbol. Carried even further a photograph can be almost purely symbolic, devoid of the very characteristics that are usually associated with photography. Take as an example the famous combat photo of the planting of the American flag by Marines on the summit of Mount Suribachi. There is nothing in the frame but the men struggling to raise the flag and a few rocks of the mountain top. This picture has been accepted as a symbol. It has even been reproduced in bronze in Washington, D. C., as a memorial to the Marines. We accept a statue as a symbol. But here is a case where the statue was copied directly *with little change* from a press shot.

At this point we may consider a paradox. *Life* magazine a few years ago ran a series of photographs called "What's in a Picture." One showed a tired interne in a hospital having a quick cup of coffee while still in his surgical gown. Another showed a boy and his dog walking the railroad track. In a third Cardinal Mindszenty was on trial in Hungary. A fourth showed the exhaustion in the face of a combat Marine. There is no doubt that these pictures rate among the most graphic that have ever been taken. In fact, this is why *Life* ran them as a separate series, to show that some of the best pictures need no explanation. This, however, is a characteristic of symbols, and these pictures achieve their greatness because they present symbols—the American doctor, a typical boy, the horror of brain-washing behind the Iron Curtain, and the life of a front-line soldier. It is a paradox that these most graphic pictures are symbolic. They are *at the same time* very real and very symbolic.

A picture is a map, since there is not a one-to-one correspondence between elements of the picture and elements of the event. We might say, as J. J. Gibson says about the retinal image, that a picture is a good correlate *but not a copy* of the scene photographed. A picture definitely has structure. It is a configuration of symbols which make it possible for us to interpret the picture, provided that we have enough experience with these symbols to read the picture.

Pictures can be manipulated like words so as to seem to change their referents. The motion picture editor can lengthen and shorten individual scenes and place them in such a juxtaposition in a carefully planned tempo as to create an impression foreign to the events photographed. It would be possible to assemble a number of pictures of active American businessmen and cut them together to give the impression of frantic competition for money when this did not exist in the actual situations.

Once we have established the fact that photographs of events are *not* the events, that they show by intent or accident only a few characteristics of events, we have the perspective to question some reactions of people to pictures. In spite of

The Map Is Not the Territory

decades of visual education there still are teachers who will not use teaching films when they are easily available. This refusal has been dismissed as conservatism, laziness, and poor teaching. Could it be that some of these teachers, projecting films in undarkened rooms on a wall (for want of a proper screen) and with a screen image not large enough to give a realistic effect, have unconsciously concluded that motion pictures are not enough different from words to bother with? Obviously the great asset of films is realism, which gives the pupils a chance to identify with characters on the screen and "lose" themselves in the picture. When this realism is wiped out by poor reproduction or poor projection, the faint images on the wall lose details, become more outlined and stylized, and have little advantage, if any, over words. Like words they are so vague that they can be interpreted individually by each viewer. Pictures, unlike words, depend very much indeed on the quality of their reproduction for the kind and amount of meaning the picture-reader gets from them.

Because of the plasticity of the photographic medium it is well that there are few pictures that do not have captions. In a sense these are indices like $Interne_1$, $Interne_2$. We feel the need of captions on pictures as we do not feel the need for indices on words. Yet we usually feel that pictures are much more likely to be completely self-explanatory than words.

General semanticists know it is hard to make the average person realize that he brings meaning to the word, that the word does *not* contain any meaning. A word is just a series of hen tracks which we are told authoritatively stands for a certain concept.

It is still harder to convince anyone that we also bring meaning to a picture. If the picture is well within our previous experience it means something. What it means depends on the kind of our experience. The picture of any political figure is interpreted in radically different manner by opposing parties. City children react differently to a picture of a cow than do farm children. Thus pictures can reinforce stereotypes because the characteristics of people or events which the photographer presents through the medium are not strong enough to overcome the "embedded canalizations" in the reader.

When the picture is not within the range of our experience we react to it almost as little as to an unknown word. Scenes of mass calisthenics performed by ten thousand Russians mean to us little more than "mass conformity," whereas they may originally have been meant to express "ideals." Strange animals are to us just configurations of light and shade on paper. If they moved on the screen we can apply more of our experience to understanding what we see. Professional photographers, like teachers, have their readers carefully estimated. Like teachers, they see to it that their pictures contain plenty of the familiar (to their particular reader) and some of the unusual. We are able to reach out a short distance into the unknown from the solid base of our own experience. The difference here between words and pictures is that the distinction between the known and the unknown is sharpened by pictures. If we read that an emu is like an ostrich, only larger, we have a vague idea about it. If we see a picture of an emu we remember more clearly the features similar to an ostrich and perhaps notice how the emu is different and new.

Pictures are multiordinal. They are interpreted on different levels of abstraction. We have seen this happen in the *Life* series mentioned above. Our Aunt Minnie is just another aunt to strangers; they think she looks like the Genus Aunt. The fact that pictures are interpreted on different levels is the basis for some items in some common intelligence scales. The lowest level is that in which the child merely enumerates objects and people: "I see a woman and a girl and a stove," etc. This is analogous to the descriptive level of words. A higher level of reaction would be description and interpretation such as, "The woman is probably the girl's mother and she is cooking her supper."

A picture causing a semantic disturbance is familiar to everyone. "Oh, that doesn't look like me at all. What a terrible picture!" Or the vacationers who have rented a lake cottage on the basis of glamorous pictures in an advertising folder get a shock when they find that the lake is much smaller than they thought, that the trees are scrubby, and that the cottage is in disrepair. Visitors to California complain that the "blue Pacific" is not always blue, as the postcards invariably show it. Or they say, "Is *that* Velma Blank, the great movie star?" It is in situations like these that we can best realize that pictures, although somewhat better than words, are only maps of the territory they represent.

Pictures can be self-reflexive. A photograph of a photograph is a standard method of reproduction, for example, in the making of filmstrips. It is by such reproduction that it is possible to present to congressional committees photographs which seem to show members of the cabinet or senators in conversation with persons with whom they never exchanged more than a word.

Pictures, then, have many of the characteristics of language, not in the figurative sense of "the language of flowers" but in the very real characteristics of structure (syntax, grammar, style) and of semantics. The most crucial characteristic is that pictures are abstractions of reality. A picture can present only a few of the aspects of the event. It may, under the strict control of the photographer, become as abstract as a symbol.

It is most urgent that there should be more awareness of the abstracting power of photography, that pictures *do lie*. Instead we find great naïveté. People believe what they see in pictures. "One picture is worth a thousand words" not only because it is more graphic but because it is believed to be the gospel truth, an incontrovertible fact. A teacher may present her pupils in a big city with a side view of a cow. They should then know what a cow is! Little do they dream that to a farm boy a cow is a complex of associations which even four hours of movies could not present. We find pictures used as "illustrations." They are inserted in textbooks as a last resort to relieve the copy. One picture of Iowa in the geography text must suffice for Iowa. The author says, "This is Iowa." The general semanticists would recognize this as the error of "allness," ascribing to a word all the characteristics of the thing abstracted from. The danger of "allness" is so much more lively in the case of pictures than in the case of words because everyone assumes pictures *are* reality.

Of course pictures provide us with more cues from reality itself (cues for eliciting the meaning we bring to the picture) than the arbitrary hen tracks we call "words." But the basic error is to fail to realize that the meanings of pictures are not in the pictures, but rather in what we bring to them.

Dr. Wendt is associate professor of education at Southern Illinois University, Carbondale, Illinois.

HUMAN INSIGHT

Why Do Frenchmen?

GREGORY BATESON

DAUGHTER: Daddy, why do Frenchmen wave their arms about?

FATHER: What do you mean?

D: I mean when they talk. Why do their wave their arms and all that?

F: Well, why do you smile? Or why do you stamp your foot sometimes?

D: But that's not the same thing, Daddy. I don't wave my arms about like a Frenchman does. I don't believe they can stop doing it, Daddy. Can they?

F: I don't know. They might find it hard to stop. Can you stop smiling?

D: But, Daddy, I don't smile *all* the time. It's hard to stop when I feel like smiling. But I don't feel like it all the time. And then I stop.

F: That's true—but then a Frenchman doesn't wave his arms in the same way all the time. Sometimes he waves them in one way and sometimes in another—and sometimes, I think, he stops waving them.

* * *

F: What do you think? I mean, what does it make you think when a Frenchman waves his arms?

D: I think it looks silly, Daddy. But I don't suppose it looks like that to another Frenchman. They cannot all look silly to each other. Because if they did they would stop it, wouldn't they?

F: Perhaps—but that is not a very simple question. What else do they make you think?

D: Well—they look all excited . . .

F: All right—"silly" and "excited."

D: But are they *really* as excited as they look? If I were as excited as that, I would want to dance or sing or hit somebody on the nose . . . but they just go on waving their arms. They can't be really excited.

F: Well, are they really as silly as they look to you? And anyhow, why do you sometimes want to dance and sing and punch somebody on the nose?

D: Oh, sometimes I just feel like that.

F: Perhaps a Frenchman just feels "like that" when he waves his arms about.

D: But he couldn't feel like that *all* the time, Daddy, he just couldn't.

F: You mean—the Frenchman surely does not feel when he waves his arms exactly as you would feel if you waved yours. And surely you are right.

D: But, then, how *does* he feel?

F: Well, let us suppose you are talking to a Frenchman and he is waving his arms about, and then in the middle of the conversation, after something that you have said, he suddenly stops waving his arms, and just talks. What would you think then? That he had just stopped being silly and excited?

D: No . . . I'd be frightened. I'd think I had said something that hurt his feelings and perhaps he might be really angry.

F: Yes, and you might be right.

* * *

D: All right—so they stop waving their arms when they start being angry.

F: Wait a minute. The question, after all, is what does one Frenchman tell another Frenchman by waving his arms? And we have part of an answer—he tells him something about how he feels about the other guy. He tells him he is not seriously angry—that he is willing and able to be what you call "silly."

D: But, no—that's not sensible. He cannot do all that work so that *later* he will be able to tell the other guy that he *is* angry by just keeping his own arms still. How does he know he is going to be angry later on?

F: He doesn't know. But, just in case . . .

D: No, Daddy, it doesn't make sense. I don't smile so as

to be able to tell you I am angry by not smiling later on.

F: Yes, I think that that *is* part of the reason for smiling. And there are lots of people who smile in order to tell you that they are *not angry*—when they really are.

D: But that's different, Daddy. That's a sort of telling lies with one's face. Like playing poker.

F: Yes.

* * *

F: Now where are we? You don't think it sensible for Frenchmen to work so hard to tell each other that they are not angry or hurt. But after all, what is most conversation about? I mean, among Americans?

D: But, Daddy, it's about all sorts of things—baseball and ice cream and gardens and games. And people talk about other people and about themselves and about what they got for Christmas.

F: Yes, yes—but who listens? I mean—all right, so they talk about baseball and gardens. But are they exchanging information? And, if so, *what* information?

D: Sure—when you come in from fishing, and I ask you, "Did you catch anything?" and you say, "Nothing," I didn't *know* that you wouldn't catch anything till you told me.

F: Hmm.

* * *

F: All right—so you mention my fishing, a matter about which I am sensitive—and then there is a gap, a silence in the conversation—and that silence tells you that I don't like cracks about how many fish I didn't catch. It's just like the Frenchman who stops waving his arms about when he is hurt.

D: I'm sorry, Daddy, but you *did* say . . .

F: No, wait a minute—let's not get confused by being sorry. I shall go out fishing again tomorrow and I shall still know that I am unlikely to catch a fish . . .

D: But, Daddy, you said all conversation is only telling other people that you are not angry with them.

F: Did I? No—not *all* conversation but much of it. Sometimes if both people are willing to listen carefully it is possible to do more than exchange greetings and good wishes. Even to do more than exchange information. The two people may even find out something which neither of them knew before.

* * *

F: Anyhow, most conversations are only about whether people are angry or something. They are busy telling each other that they are friendly—which is sometimes a lie. After all, what happens when they cannot think of anything to say? They all feel uncomfortable.

D: But wouldn't that be information, Daddy? I mean—information that they are not cross?

F: Surely yes. But it's a different sort of information from "the cat is on the mat."

* * *

D: Daddy, why cannot people just *say,* "I am not cross at you" and let it go at that?

F: Ah, now we are getting to the real problem. The point is that the messages which we exchange in gestures are really not the same as any translation of those gestures into words.

D: I don't understand.

F: I mean—that no amount of telling somebody in mere words that one is or is not angry is the same as what one might tell them by gesture or tone of voice.

D: But, Daddy, you cannot have words without some tone of voice, can you? Even if somebody uses as little tone as he can, the other people will hear that he is holding himself back—and that will be a sort of tone, won't it?

F: Yes, I suppose so. After all, that's what I said just now about gestures—that the Frenchman can say something special by *stopping* his gestures.

* * *

F: But then, what do I mean by saying that "mere words" can never convey the same message as gestures—if there are no "mere words"?

D: Well, the words might be written.

F: No—that won't let me out of the difficulty. Because written words still have some sort of rhythm and they still have overtones. The point is that *no* mere words exist. There are *only* words with either gesture or tone of voice or something of the sort. But, of course, gestures without words are common enough.

* * *

D: Daddy, when they teach us French at school, why don't they teach us to wave our hands?

F: I don't know. I'm sure I don't know. That is probably one of the reasons why people find learning languages so difficult.

* * *

F: Anyhow, it is all nonsense. I mean, the notion that language is made of words is all nonsense—and when I said that gestures could not be translated into "mere words," I was talking nonsense, because there is no such thing as "mere words." And all the syntax and grammar and all that stuff is nonsense. It's all based on the idea that "mere words" exist—and there are none.

D: But, Daddy . . .

F: I tell you—we have to start all over again from the beginning and assume that language is first and foremost a system of gestures. Animals after all have *only* gestures and tones of voice—and words were invented later. Much later. And after that they invented schoolmasters.

D: Daddy?

F: Yes.

D: Would it be a good thing if people gave up words and went back to only using gestures?

F: Hmm. I don't know. Of course we would not be able to have any conversations like this. We could only bark, or mew, and wave our arms about, and laugh and grunt and weep. But it might be fun—it would make life into a sort of ballet—with the dancers making their own music.

Gregory Bateson, who has done anthropological field work in New Guinea and Bali, is co-author (with Jurgen Ruesch) of Communication: The Social Matrix of Psychiatry *(1951). As senior co-author of the famous paper, "Toward a Theory of Schizophrenia"* (Behavioral Science, *October 1956), he made a significant contribution to the understanding of that illness. He is ethnologist at the Veterans Administration Hospital, Palo Alto, California.*

How Sane Is "Sane"?

ADRIAN YOUNG

SOME of the patients had been acting as if unaware of what was happening around them; and some were aware of things that weren't happening. And then it came to me. Suddenly, "That's the sort of thing I do myself," I said. Not so often or in ways as easily seen, nor do I ever do it with important acquaintances, when I keep guard on myself with a critical eye. But in my off moments, every now and then, I do it.

I

What sort of thing? The sort Matthew Prin does. He seldom hears me when first I speak to him, and I expect my opening sentence to be broken by a "What do you say?" that springs to his lips on a sudden effort of attention. My voice must first find him in the soundless carapace that all but seals him and pull him to a chink in it. He will ask me for the soap when it lies white on the red squares by his feet. He will set things down with a bang, for he is so absorbed he is never quite aware where the floor is. I saw him dumping dead flowers into a waste basket, and although a quarter of them fell on the floor he rushed away without seeing them, anxious to return to his chair and to whatever is going on within him as he sits. Matthew is a schizophrenic, just eighteen years.

But it wasn't he, it was I, who before mounting my bicycle to ride it home, took my keys out and locked the wheel—only yesterday.

II

And the sort of thing I have seen in Peter Ylonen. I find myself in agreement with many of his remarks, for he is well informed, an acute observer, and an infectious enthusiast. He will sweep, wash and polish around the ward, not only with willingness but with gusto. In the crowded morning washroom he will do his chinning the bar and his presses, conscious that he is a good example. He must have his exercise to keep his bowels and his muscles fit (flexing his right arm as he tells me so). He will give us a lecture on cabinetmaking, diet, or the sex life with fluency, animation, assurance, and, it must be admitted, sense and persuasiveness. He sometimes hustles an unresisting depression patient into doing something that seems to him good for the patient (and often he's right). With nurses and attendants he will wrangle violently and at length—to the point of almost blows—on some point of another patient's treatment on which he differs. A manic-reaction type.

And the chief distinction between me and Peter is chinning the bar. I never do it. Apart from that, I give as many lectures, but none on cabinetmaking. My friends tell me I act as one who believes he knows better than they what is good for them. And I seem to impress others as living in a permanent emergency, judging by the number of times I am asked, "Where's the fire?"

III

Stephen Old is a depressed case. He started with nothing as an orphan. He spent an exploited youth on a farm. He was discharged from the army with a stomach ulcer (often a companion of anxiety). He was out of work for ten years of depression but raised five children (something to worry about). Three years ago he found a job he liked and that paid well. He worked long hours and with great energy. His employers considered him scrupulously honest and highly conscientious. He began accusing himself of taking ten dollars out of the receipts. Perhaps he was tired out, perhaps distrustful of his good fortune, worried that no longer he had anything to worry him. But his habit of anxiety had to have stones for its tendrils. Of his theft there was no proof, and no one believed him. He then said he had carnally known a cow at the age of eight. And this sin he has committed, he declares, has brought retribution forty years after, and the world is at a standstill. "You see, Adrian, there's no lights in the windows. I don't hear the streetcars. They didn't have the radio on tonight. Was there a paper today? And it's all on account of me. Children are dying out there." So he cut his throat.

Not that I ever got as far as the razor. But there are times that my past appalls me. All I can remember of it are things I didn't say, the clever things, the manly things, the things that would have made someone happier. I remember the careless deed and the clumsy phrase that cost me a friend. And with scrutiny the small becomes great. Every inventory shows only debits—in appearance, manner, livelihood, knowledge, religion. How can anyone like me? But they don't. And I can't vary the pattern—my tomorrows are my yesterdays. I have no desire for more, if this is my life. But I have never taken the next logical step—the rope, the razor, or the overdose. Life still is pleasanter than that for me. I write a poem or a letter to a woman, I trudge in the rain, or play some *chanson triste* with my toneless fingers. If I had lived Stephen's life, if I had no one to write or talk to, if I couldn't play at all—but that's only speculation.

IV

Basil Spring is paranoid. After his father had run away from his mother, he was ashamed that at nine or ten he should be sleeping with his mother. Later he quit several jobs for he knew there were men there that were saying he was going crazy. They laughed at him. "It won't be long now," they said. It was a girl, the girl in the Salvation Army hostel who told them. She was after him to marry him. Down south she followed him, five hundred miles, and when he moved east, four hundred more. He saw her on the street car, heard her talking on the street behind him: "Sure he's going crazy. He's going to lose his hair first, and then he's going crazy."

Oh no. I'm not as bad as that. But I have wondered whether the girls on the street car who whispered and laughed and looked in my direction were laughing at me. Had I tied my tie outside my collar? Was the fly of my trousers open? And perhaps I was wrong. Perhaps they weren't speaking of me. When Basil thinks this, he's wrong —nearly always.

By finding in myself symptoms displayed by the patients, I came to understand the meaning of them. Their charts or versions of the outer world were falser than mine, and more than with me the things they did led them further from their desire. In some part of their relations to the outer world they were self-thwarting, maladjusted, sick—just a trifle more than I was. So I had the key to the door, but they hadn't.

To react in any other way—to be annoyed or impatient, say, at a mentally ill person—is itself maladjusted. One day when Basil's treatment had been terminated, and he was resting, one of the other patients was talking to the nurse and me. Cheerful, a little boisterous, his voice rose, and mine rose too. "What do you think this is anyway?" said Basil, sitting up. "A beer parlor? Am I supposed to have quiet or am I not, nurse?" He was right, of course, and I've often put things myself just as bluntly. But the nurse complained that he was always "crabby" and "mean." Another morning he was changing when he suddenly paused and glared at me. "I hope you've found something interesting to look at," he said. I wasn't specially aware of him. I was just there and I was supposed to be there. One night the nurse and I were exchanging whispers. The day before she had left her key at home. With much trouble, she was telling me, she had entered by the window to find that her husband had left the door open. It was amusing. Suddenly Basil was in front of me. "Are you a man?" he said. "If you are, stand up and put up your fists." He had recently passed us on the way to the toilet, and I knew he believed we'd been laughing at him. Typically paranoid. An overanxious assertion of the self that at last leads to its thwarting. Not "nasty"; not "crabby"; just sick.

V

And there is conduct apparently praiseworthy. Carl has always to be reassured that there is food for all the patients before he will eat. But it is hardly safer to judge by the surface here. Carl had no reason to assume that others had less food. He was expressing, not at all to the advantage of others, a feeling of unworthiness. Carl's capacious and volatile sympathy is constantly engaged for others; for one of his fellow patients, for instance, who before smoked a couple of packages of cigarettes a day, and frets now on four; for his brother, also in hospital, who he said was a fine boxer but failed in a bout with the lightweight champion because he wouldn't agree to dishonest fighting; for the moneyless patients who were not understood, he said, by doctors, who came from well-to-do homes; and for himself, as he told his history of sleeping behind log piles, living for days on dry bread, excited beyond control by the woman he lived with who drank his money and bedded with other men. But the number and frequency of his causes, and his occasional want of judgment in choosing them, suggests that he is moved as much by his need for vehement expression as concern for others.

And among those who glory in the name of sane, the gestures of love and hate are open to question. There is the kiss of habit and the blow of the lifesaver. But apart from these, they may express a compulsion to kiss or hit, not a desire to kiss or hit *me*. What is expressed is an inner state, never any relation to me at all. How maladjusted then to resent or enjoy the blow where there is no hate and the kiss that expresses no love, me-wards.

The perfectly sane, perfectly adjusted man likely couldn't be found. For who never has anything wrong with his body? So "mental" (psychosomatic) illness is also liable to be found, acute or mild, anywhere. Indeed, where there is a full history, illness can be seen as the slow hardening over the course of years of habits of response, habits that hinder a person's adequately knowing or dealing with his world. Mental illness doesn't suddenly appear where there was none before. Nor does a vessel sink without a plank being sprung or stove in, or without a slow rising of water to the gunwale. Nor is a person once ill ever more to be shunned, any more than if he had suffered from syphilis or cholera. Illness of any kind comes and goes, and fixing a date for either the coming or the going is neither useful nor possible.

VI

When I visited Bob Smart, he lay grimacing, winking, waving his arms; and continuously talking: ". . . This is Sir Robert Smart. We are standing by for Bob Smart speaking from London. Take it away, Bob Smart . . . This is GSE, E for Extra, broadcasting on 2.916 meters; GSB for broadcasting on 9.51 meters, and GSD for Daventry broadcasting on 11.25 meters . . . I have three questions to ask the radio audience: who succeeded Pope Pius the 12th; secondly, who succeeded Edward the Eighth; thirdly, where was Mr. Henry Smart at three minutes from yesterday . . . Is that Robert Smart's body or Robert Smart's bier? Do you know that bier besides being something to drink is something George the Fifth knows about . . . (laughing to himself). Cut it out, Bob, you fool—I can't stop it . . . anxious son desires to communicate with anxious father. Hello, anxious, this is anxious speaking . . . Hello, Leningrad, Hello, Lenin, how's grad? Sure I'll smoke Grads. How's grads? . . . I have no faith in anybody, not even in my own dead body . . . This is the voice of the Andes in Quito Ecuador South America, heralding Christ Jesus' blessings . . . Clear the channel for Bob Smart, official representative of Radex . . . Go ahead, Bob . . . You're a dead man, Bob Smart . . . Make up your mind, Bob Smart; if not, we'll have to call in our friend Pope Pius the Seventh; who will declare that the time is up, for it's either up or down, Bob Smart . . . Robert Smart was born of the Virgin Mary, suffered under Pontius Pilate, was crucified, dead, and was buried, and on the third day of our Lord, rose again . . . You, Harriet Cole, shall be called upon to justify before God that Robert Smart never existed upon the earth . . . Harriet Cole, swear by Almighty God, that you know not the whereabouts of Robert Smart . . . On the eighth day of June last, Mr. Henry Smart had driven us home in his car, and had stopped on Riverside Boulevard. As the door closed, it caught the thumb of Mr. Robert Smart, causing it to bleed, and we had to proceed to a druggist's to get it dressed . . . It was a warm moonlight night, and Miss Harriet Cole was with us . . ."

His grimaces were knowing and ingratiating: "You and I know what it's all about"; or debonair: "You can't help liking me for I am gay and witty"; or childlike: "I am helpless, I need you, so you have to help me and like me." These grimaces I could have said were smiles, but that moment when the wind of his malady had ceased moving, his face hung as a cloth mask with blank eye sockets. They hardly expressed a continuous personality more than his talk did. Like flotsam from a wreck, they seemed as if dissevered, unexpected, illogical; yet in their own frame of reference had logic and meaning.

The boy was sixteen. A few months before he had stood first or second in a class of forty; and the Stanford-Binet test had placed him as a superior adult. Several had remarked in him a vein of humor. He had been commended for his care in collecting and accounting for subscriptions to the school paper. One day he went "insane" and flung himself down the cellar steps. Ridiculous. It was the present stage of a process that sixteen years before had started.

His mother was only happy in the focus of attention. Her pabulum was parties. She invited her friends to affairs at home, but she discouraged her husband from inviting home his. She was not pleased when her child was born and from his birth showed him no love. "Take him away from me," she was often saying. Red marks appeared on the child's body in his early weeks. His father couldn't account for them; but he had no sooner said he was going to consult a child specialist than the marks vanished and he never saw them again. He later believed them to come from the mother's pinchings.

The things he never spoke Bob confided in a notebook. His relations with his mother appear not only in his resentment of her telling people, "I shall send my son on an errand"; and in saying, "I like evil. My mother and all her family liked evil and I have imitated her." They appear also when he writes, "Here are some necessary qualities of a good mother: honesty, courtesy, motherliness, modesty, honesty: christian, friendly with everybody as far as possible, proper disciplination of children," of which I inferred he had found the antithesis in his mother.

His teachers observed that he didn't mix with other pupils, and walked the way between school and home alone. In sports and games he took no part, and at the boys' camp he went to at his father's urging, he felt out of place. In the past year or two he had been keeping more and more to himself. He had few boy friends and none among girls. His boy friends he had lately been avoiding, sensitive to things they had said about him, it seemed. Radio was his chief interest, and his father had bought him a strong receiver. Since he would be alone, his father encouraged him in the systematic logging of stations.

He had, his teachers noticed, a tendency to brood and to take himself too seriously. In his notes, he says, "I dislike showing ignorance but I stopped voluntarily answering questions in class because it looks as if I were showing off. I lost my interest in Latin when the teacher stopped asking me questions, I believe, because she thought I was learning the subject. Result—I got 81% in Latin, 19% short of what I should have made." "I always do my calculations in geometry differently to others, reaching a wrong conclusion, so that I will be able to explain my method. Some of the other students have noticed this." "Sarcasm gets me down, teasing gets me down, a joke on me gets me down, even though I may laugh at the time, I worry later." "I seem to eat more when I am upset."

Self-conscious as he was, he was driven to impress his viewpoint on others—groping for a cause, perhaps, to which he could give himself. To one of the teachers he proposed organizing the class for a salvage drive. The teacher suggested the matter be discussed by the class, and heard no more of it. His father sent Bob to a farm last summer. The farmer was an opponent of the government, and Bob returned fervidly of the opposition, projecting a book on the principles of national planning. He read some papal pronouncements on economics and in a letter to a friend expressed much interest in Pope and Cardinals. Latterly inattentive at school he fell to 26th. And in his notes he wrote: "I did want to be a leader among men, but now I am puzzled."

With Harriet Cole I sat beside him for an hour. She was his only other visitor apart from his father. She was a nurse and her mother had boarded Bob for his last few months at school, for his father had hoped that getting him away from home would improve his condition. Only now and then did his talk recognize her. He would sing a theme from Beethoven. He was very fond of music, she said.

Well, there is the pattern. When the person nearest a child is wanting in love, doubt grows whether anyone loves him. Fear of hurt finds it where none is intended, and is a bar to friendship. If not love—respect perhaps: he studies and in class tries to show his attainments.

This (for the mentally ill are often more than commonly sensitive) he feels is resented. And as with all for whom a 100 per cent is an inner need, second place failure, he was often thwarted. Respect—if not from knowing more, from doing more: he has a plan for the classes, increasing the flow of salvage, but proposing it to the class, as the teacher advised, for one as diffident as he, is not to be thought of. He plans a book on economics, and is not encouraged.

His doubts crumble the self-assertion demanded in approaching girls. He masturbates and feels remorse for it. He overeats—not so much for the food, but food as a symbol—reassurance at least on one level. He speaks much of religion—last haven of the unloved. Once he goes to an Episcopalian Church, and, in his illness after many months, recites the liturgy. But he speaks most of the Pope, who proffers a strong staff to doubters of themselves.

His endless talk and his grimaces that strive to pose an all but impossible bar to the world that hurt him, these tell the story. His grimaces reach for affection. The warp of his talk is radio, which in more than common measure he had mastered; stretched across it a weft of thwartings and wishes. For him the channels are cleared; knighted and a great wit; it is he puts the questions; it is he was crucified, dead and was buried; he has no faith in anybody; and a torn thumb is a sweet recall for it had gained him a charming girl's compassionate attention. And flecking bold the web's whole width—death.

Schizophrenic reaction type with a manic trend: poor prognosis. Patients requiring lengthy treatments are taken to a larger center, so after a time Bob was transferred. For the few minutes before the attendant came for him, Bob and I were alone. After he was dressed, I sat down and ignoring his verbal vagaries, told him this: "You are sick, Bob, for you believe the world has no love, no place for you. But you are going to be well again. Your father wants you to be well. So do I. And when you're well once more, you can help those who are sick, for you have the capacity, and he can best feel for the sick who has been sick himself." It was not much of a gift, but it was the best I could offer; and from what I know of such cases, I felt that for all the interference that poured unceasing from his lips, he was likely receiving.

And where in the sixteen years did Bob cease to be sane? At as many different places as there are definitions of "insane." Doctors don't use the word but many quaint notions of its meaning can be found among laymen. Such a definition or notion is a glass window that stands between me and the patient. Whatever kind of glass I put in the window the patient is unchanged; but if the glass colors or distorts him it will greatly alter the relation between him and me—to the damage of both of us. "Insane" suggests Bela Lugosi, monsters, and sudden death, something otherworldly and fearful (and in fearing we cease to understand and are cruel).

And our definitions are so framed as to exclude ourselves. But in a world of imperfect people, few can escape false evaluations, acquiring them by contagion from the maladjustments of parents, teachers, leaders. It becomes none of us to assume ourselves better than those in hospital—they were perhaps more sensitive, had it a little tougher. Time and again, as patients have told me their stories, I have lived again young agonies of mine. Why am I not, I wonder, in the next bed? I wrote, like Bob, many pages of diary; studied for the first places; played no games; feared, yet fretted away from, girls; walked alone in the rain. Histories like this are viewed gravely. But through many differences of opinion, clashes of will, I never had cause to doubt that my parents loved me. And I was lucky never to meet a problem past my strength at the time it was necessary to meet it. And I somehow broke through the schizophrenic shell that slowly was encasing me, and my relations with others came to be tolerably objective. But it's hardly a thing to claim credit for.

For most people, the matter is extremely simple: the "nuts" are behind walls, and the "sane" (including themselves) are outside. But you and I are outside not so much because we are "sane," but because we are still able to earn a living, or because our neighbors haven't found us too unbearable a nuisance, or because mental hospitals are very overcrowded and there isn't room for us, or mostly because we haven't the sense to know when we're "mentally" sick, and to go to the proper place for advice or treatment. So let's banish the word "insane" before somebody tumbles and labels us with it.

More important than labeling people is to do what we can to prevent mental illness or cure it when it happens. What can a person with no training do? But before that, what is important in a psychiatric nurse's approach to a patient? According to Miss Ingram, it includes politeness, warm and welcoming; the listening that is a compliment and the patience that is a disguise for interest in another person; even temper, never upset by emotional disturbances in others; an absence of criticism, in tone, word or gesture; and poise—for embarrassment leads to inappropriate behavior, to assumptions of superiority, or to withdrawal from a situation where we are not at ease. It is good nursing, but there's none of it that wouldn't pass for good manners, manners that in charming, heal.

And much of our child lore is good psychiatry. It is not well to talk down to child or psychotic, for it is recognized and resented. His evaluations may be falser than usual for adults of our culture, and yet his perception and reasoning be quite acute. Hasty conversations, reluctantly spared from other tasks we are agog to be away to—their effect is alike on children and on patients whose response is tardy and effortful; discouraging, confirming feelings of neglect or unworthiness. We try to arrange our work that our meetings may be leisurely. Sick people readily take talk as being of them, even when it isn't; and if they are discussed in their hearing they will not unreasonably take it for slighting or discourteous. (Even when seeming to be stuporous, they may be alertly aware of what is passing.) And in a sick person the objective reference of words has paled, and they are little more than symptoms of inner states. We neither let their flattery gratify us, nor their obscenity disturb. The words haven't the meanings they would have in the mouths of the relatively well. Parallels like these are not surprising, for in many reactions mentally ill persons are still children; or failing to meet their adult problems, fall back to the child, for as children they had adjusted themselves well and quickly. The same fears, the same tantrums, the bed-wettings, the using food for meanings besides nourishment, the unexpected remembering of things not seemingly noticed—these can be observed as well in the ward as the nursery.

None who reads this will deny himself capable of good manners or of raising children; and with a little reflection on the meaning of these and a firm will to apply them, we are equipped for the furtherance of mental hygiene in ourselves and our neighbors—and we needn't be on the Nurses' Registry to do it. A person who speaks to hurt us, or loses his temper or swears is obviously ill: his conduct is no step to the solution of the problem facing him; it is the opposite—for his neighbors who are with him are less likely to help him now than before. How well then for our own peace to treat him thus: "The meaning of his doings is not hatred for me, but sickness in him; and what *I* do must help him get better."

VII

It was meeting Ann last week that made me sure of it. Not for months had I seen her, and as we sipped our coffee she told me of Stephanie. Ann and Pearl share the same flat. Pearl has a sister, Stephanie. For a year she had been in a "mental hospital." There was nothing they could do for her, said the doctors; Pearl therefore took Stephanie to stay with her.

The mother of Stephanie and Pearl appears to have been capricious. At one moment she was doing things that Stephanie should have been doing for herself; and at another she was critical and unfriendly. She could be both at once: "It takes you so long," she would say, "I'd rather do it myself." Once, on her own, Stephanie with care did her lank hair up in a way that suited her better. "You look half decent today," was her mother's response. "I don't know why you can't do it all the time." And Stephanie pulled her hair down as it had been.

Feelings of insecurity would normally follow in the absence of other factors; and their expression in Stephanie was demands on the attention, the property, and the time of others. She would finish nothing she began. Brushes and other toilet articles belonging to the other girls, as she needed she took. She spoke in self-pity; she was uncouth in her table manners and careless in her appearance, letting her hair hang lank and unpinned. And sometimes when alone she would break into laughter.

Not comfortable living with her, especially when you aren't her sister. And Ann (who isn't) is a salesgirl; she doesn't read widely; she enjoys company. At first she closed her door, and tried keeping Stephanie out of awareness. But Stephanie, loudly awake, reached her (and the adjoining flats) doors or no doors. So every night she had to be given a sedative. During the day she couldn't be let out, so two of the neighbors upstairs took turns in staying with her. Ann would often have Pearl to sleep with her when her sister was making rest impossible. And one very important night, when Pearl was depressed and weary, Ann said to her, "Now don't worry. You're not alone in this. We're both in it."

Ann concluded Pearl to be soft, selfless but soft, and she adopted a manner to Stephanie that was friendly but firm. In living with other people, she told Stephanie, some things had to be given up, however satisfying, and if she chose not to give them up, off she must go. This was a strong motive to improvement, for she much preferred staying there to living in hospital.

She used all the hot water in the block one night, by lying in the bath, tap on full, and the drain open. The caretaker came inquiring for the wastrel. "You're living in the same house as a whole lot of other people," said Ann to Stephanie, "and you wouldn't want to start off by having them dislike you."

Another night they heard her going out. Through the window they saw her cross the lawn with her coat on. Pearl was for following her. "It's that sort of thing you've done too much of," said Ann. "It's the sort of attention Stephanie wants but shouldn't get." Stephanie had gone for a swim in the lake naked, and wakened up an annoyed caretaker to let her in. When she came in, Ann told her, "If ever you do that again, I won't wait till morning. I'll get a cab and you'll go right away, and I don't care where."

Stephanie exploited Pearl. She could wheedle, sulk, or wear Pearl night after another into going out with her. One week Pearl had been out with her three successive nights. On the fourth Pearl refused and Stephanie was angry. "Pearl works all day," said Ann, "and she is much too tired. It is very thoughtless of you to ask her." No longer a squabble for two—there was what stays the blows and words of contenders: the desire to be respected by the onlooker.

Instead of merely denying irresponsible demands, Ann tries to set Stephanie on her own feet. "Give me a cigaret," she asked once. Though Stephanie is thirty, Pearl said, "I don't think you should smoke, honey"; and though Stephanie is thirty, she sulked. Ann said to her sharply, "You smoke when you can afford to buy your own—we can't keep you in cigarets."

After a while she began to clean the silver and wash the floors, though she didn't like it, and usually left spots that hadn't been cleaned. She began to crochet. Ann, who works in a lingerie shop, had brought home two blouses for a friend. Stephanie was taken by one of them the moment she saw it. Was it her size, could she try it on? She liked it even better when it was on her, "but I can't pay for it," she said. "You're doing crocheting for Claire—you can pay for it out of that," said Ann.

"Every day," said Ann, "I see a change in that girl. If you came in, you wouldn't notice a difference between the three of us. At night she used always to wait for someone to make her Postum for her. Last night I was making tea. I asked each of the girls if she wanted any. Stephanie said 'I'll have Postum,' took the tin down and made it herself.

"I always talk to her as one girl to another, just as I should with anyone else, never talking down to her; and—especially when I have to step on her—treating her as an equal. I make a point of noticing any pains she takes with her appearance, telling her she looks nice, and that to get a job she must be careful of her looks. And I have had to train her in table manners like a child.

"And her morbid gloomy thoughts! One day she told me of a hospital of two hundred lepers, and kept saying how dreadful leprosy must be. Then she'll complain how hard her life is. I don't even reply to things like this, or I say how lucky we are to have an apartment like ours when places are scarce, or how late in the fall the warm weather has lasted. 'Look at your wrist,' she once said to me, 'isn't it terrible?' 'Look at your own,' I said, 'mine's all right.'

"And one day she said to me, 'Where am I going to stay next week?' 'Here,' I told her.—'And the week after?' 'Here of course.'—'And the week after that?' 'This is your home,' I said, 'and you're going to be staying here as long as you want to.' "

For over a month she talked of taking a job, and of the kind of work she would like. She gave more time and care to her looks. And then, five months ago, she signed her name to her first pay check. She had begun to work half days in a box factory. At the factory she found a friend and now, says the friend, she is more sure of herself and quicker in her work. She was taken on full time. She decided on going to stay with another sister. Her work took the sister to another town, leaving Stephanie on her own; and she is thriving on it.

This could I think be described as accepted practice—though Ann has never opened a book on psychiatry. It's a compound of good manners and effective child-raising. Ann is a Christian Scientist. I am not, and I can't profess to do justice to her tenets, but she refuses to admit, I believe, the existence of imperfection, of which illness is an aspect. She keeps her attention on the good and healthy sides of a person, thus helping these to expression, for people often become what others consider them. And it's better treatment than some I've seen in hospitals. A patient's illness largely convicts the people—and all the people—he lives with.

In mental illness diagnoses are often referred to as impressions, and are rarely rigid. Paranoiac, schizophrenic, and manic-depressive reaction types are a spectrum with mingling margins. Life is elusive, protean, and categories are little use in coping with it. This is shown by such impressions as these: "schizophrenic with a paranoid thrust"; "manic-depressive psychosis, depressed phase, with a schizoid color." There are strictly as many diseases as there are sick men, for the absence of health has as many personal styles as health has, and their labels and their classes change as the generations. It may be we should look less for disease, for none are perfectly adjusted, and all are in a measure ill. What we desire, what we should seek, is health—label, class, diagnose it as we like, but ensure that everything we do waters and makes green the wellness that remains.

It's all very simple. The person who is "mentally" ill (more ill, that is to say, than ourselves) may show signs of brain hemorrhage, alcoholic or bromide poisoning, subluxion of the spine, goiter, low basal metabolism, or other gross and obvious physical concomitant. But in most cases physical signs are not with our present means detectable. In most cases the patient confronted the same types of situation as the rest of us. But he likely met more unkindness, more threats to his feeling of security, more thwartings than the rest of us; and he likely met them younger, when all his world was the doings of a few people, who were changeable, critical, neglectful, and he acted as if all men were like that few. So he became a little more withdrawn from the world we call real, or a little more excitable, or a little more suspicious, or a little more depressed than the rest of us.

The cure is to help him understand the growth and reasons for his illness; and the restoration of—call it peace, or security; and the acceptance of all that accrues from his own doings or decisions; breaking down his formulations about "all men," or "human nature," or "the police," or as the case may be; bringing him to search for the kind and the good in those he lives with; but these are words aplenty, for it is a common experience but expressed in as many ways as there are people. Insulin perhaps, or electro-shock, or metrazol can in a measure bring the world back to focus. But if we others act as we did before, or colder because he has come from a "crazy house," his vision will again blur.

And the things we do to help him hold the ground he has gained we shall find have made us the charming and understanding people we could be.

Sometimes I have a sense of being superior to those who are ill, and it's then I remind myself of my wife's grandmother. She was, I am told, a bitch of the darkest hide. She spoiled her boys and slandered their wives to their friends. When she grew old she was less careful and she began to treat her sons as she did their wives. The boys became concerned about her "going crazy." But one of the wives placed her arms akimbo and put them right: "She ain't no crazier 'n she ever was—she just can't hide it any more."

And there may be a day perhaps that neither can I.

Adrian Young is the pseudonym of a Canadian teacher who, among other things, has worked as an attendant in a mental hospital.

The Art of Psychoanalysis

JAY HALEY

ENOUGH research has been done by social scientists to corroborate many of Freud's ideas about unconscious processes. Yet there has been surprisingly little scientific investigation of what actually occurs during psychoanalytic treatment. Fortunately this situation has been remedied by a scholar on the faculty of Potter College in Yeovil, England. Assigned a field trip in America, this anonymous student spent several years here studying the art of psychoanalysis both as a patient and a practitioner. His investigation culminated in a three-volume work entitled *The Art of Psychoanalysis, or Some Aspects of a Structured Situation Consisting of Two-Group Interaction Which Embodies Certain of the Most Basic Principles of One-upmanship*. Like most studies written for Potter College the work was unpublished and accessible only to a few favored members of the clinical staff. However, a copy was briefly in this writer's hands and he offers here a summary of the research findings for those who wish to foster the dynamic growth of Freudian theory and sharpen the techniques of a difficult art.

Unfamiliar terms will be translated into psychoanalytic terminology throughout this summary, but a few general definitions are necessary at once. First of all, a complete definition of the technical term "one-upmanship" would fill, and in fact has filled, a rather large encyclopedia. It can be defined briefly here as the art of putting a person "one-down." The term "one-down" is technically defined as that psychological state which exists in an individual who is not "one-up" on another person. To be "one-up" is technically defined as that psychological state of an individual who is not "one-down." To phrase these terms in popular language, at the risk of losing scientific rigor, it can be said that in any human relationship (and indeed among other mammals) one person is constantly maneuvering to imply that he is in a "superior position" to the other person in the relationship. This "superior position" does not necessarily mean superior in social status or economic position; many servants are masters at putting their employers one-down. Nor does it imply intellectual superiority as any intellectual knows who has been put "one-down" by a muscular garbage collector in a bout of Indian wrestling. "Superior position" is a relative term which is continually being defined and redefined by the ongoing relationship. Maneuvers to achieve superior position may be crude or they may be infinitely subtle. For example, one is not usually in a superior position if he must ask another person for something. Yet he can ask for it in such a way that he is implying, "This is, of course, what I deserve." Since the number of ways of maneuvering oneself into a superior position are infinite, let us proceed at once to summarize the psychoanalytic techniques as described in the three-volume study.

Psychoanalysis, according to the Potter study, is a dynamic psychological process involving two people, a patient and a psychoanalyst, during which the patient insists that the analyst be one-up while desperately trying to put him one-down, and the analyst insists that the patient remain one-down in order to help him learn to become one-up. The goal of the relationship is the amicable separation of analyst and patient.

Carefully designed, the psychoanalytic setting makes the superior position of the analyst almost invincible. First of all, the patient must voluntarily come to the analyst for help, thus conceding his inferior position at the beginning of the relationship. In addition, the patient accentuates his one-down position by paying the analyst money. Occasionally analysts have recklessly broken this structured situation by treating patients free of charge. Their position was difficult because the patient was not regularly reminded (on payday) that he must make a sacrifice to support the analyst, thus acknowledging the analyst's superior position before a word was said. It is really a wonder that any patient starting from his weak position could ever become one-up on an analyst, but in private discussions analysts will admit, and in fact tear at their hair while admitting, that patients can be

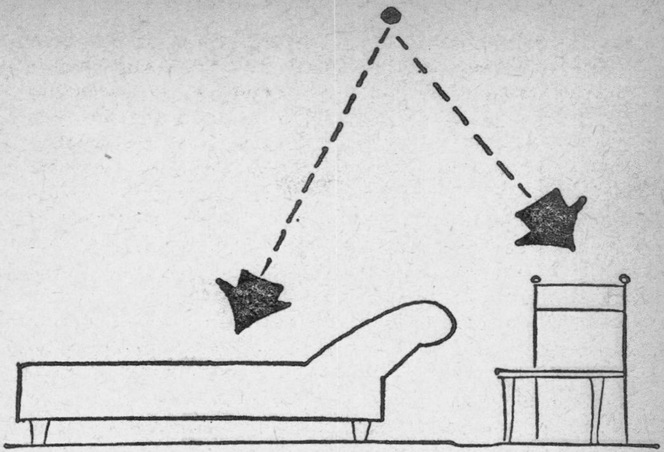

Freud's ploy ". . . was the use of a couch for the patient to lie down upon."

extremely adroit and use such a variety of clever ploys[1] that an analyst must be nimble to maintain his superior position.

Space does not permit a review of the history of psychoanalysis here, but it should be noted that early in its development it became obvious that the analyst needed reinforcement of the setting if he was to remain one-up on patients more clever than he. An early reinforcement was the use of couch for the patient to lie down upon. (This is often called "Freud's ploy," as are most ploys in psychoanalysis.) By placing the patient on a couch, the analyst gives the patient the feeling of having his feet up in the air and the knowledge that the analyst has both feet on the ground. Not only is the patient disconcerted by having to lie down while talking, but he finds himself literally below the analyst and so his one-down position is geographically emphasized. In addition, the analyst seats himself behind the couch where he can watch the patient but the patient cannot watch him. This gives the patient the sort of disconcerted feeling a person has when sparring with an opponent while blindfolded. Unable to see what response his ploys provoke, he is unsure when he is one-up and when one-down. Some patients try to solve this problem by saying something like, "I slept with my sister last night," and then whirling around to see how the analyst is responding. These

[1] A "ploy" is technically defined as a move or gambit which gives one an advantage in a relationship.

"shocker" ploys usually fail in their effect. The analyst may twitch, but he has time to recover before the patient can whirl fully around and see him. Most analysts have developed ways of handling the whirling patient. As the patient turns, they are staring off into space, or doodling with a pencil, or braiding belts, or staring at tropical fish. It is essential that the rare patient who gets an opportunity to observe the analyst see only an impassive demeanor.

Another purpose is served by the position behind the couch. Inevitably what the analyst says becomes exaggerated in importance since the patient lacks any other means of determining his effect on the analyst. The patient finds himself hanging on the analyst's every word, and by definition he who hangs on another's words is one-down.

Perhaps the most powerful weapon in the analyst's arsenal is the use of silence. This falls in the category of "helpless" or "refusal to battle" ploys. It is impossible to win a contest with a helpless opponent since if you win you have won nothing. Each blow you strike is unreturned so that all you can feel is guilt for having struck while at the same time experiencing the uneasy suspicion that the helplessness is calculated. The result is suppressed fury and desperation—two emotions characterizing the one-down position. The problem posed for the patient is this: how can I get one-up on a man who won't respond and compete with me for the superior position in fair and open encounter? Patients find solutions, of course, but it takes months, usually years, of intensive analysis before a patient finds ways to force a response from his analyst. Ordinarily the patient begins rather crudely by saying something like, "Sometimes I think you're an idiot." He waits for the analyst to react defensively, thus stepping one-down. Instead the analyst replies with the silence ploy. The patient goes further and says, "I'm *sure* you're an idiot." Still silence in reply. Desperately the patient says, "I said you were an idiot, damn you, and you are!" Again only silence. What can the patient do but apologize, thus stepping voluntarily into a one-down position? Often a patient discovers how effective the silence ploy is and attempts to use it himself. This ends in disaster when he realizes that he is paying twenty dollars an hour to lie silent on a couch. The psychoanalytic setting is calculatedly designed to prevent patients using the ploys of analysts to attain equal footing (although as an important part of the cure the patient learns to use them effectively with other people).

Few improvements have been made on Freud's original brilliant design. As the basic plan for the hammer could not be improved upon by carpenters, so the use of the voluntary patient, hourly pay, the position behind the couch, and silence are devices which have not been improved upon by the practitioners of psychoanalysis.

Although the many ways of handling patients learned by the analyst cannot be listed here, a few general principles can be mentioned. Inevitably a patient entering analysis begins to use ploys which have put him one-up in previous relationships (this is called a "neurotic pattern"). The analyst learns to devastate these maneuvers of the patient. A simple way, for example, is to respond inappropriately to what the patient says. This puts the patient in doubt about every-

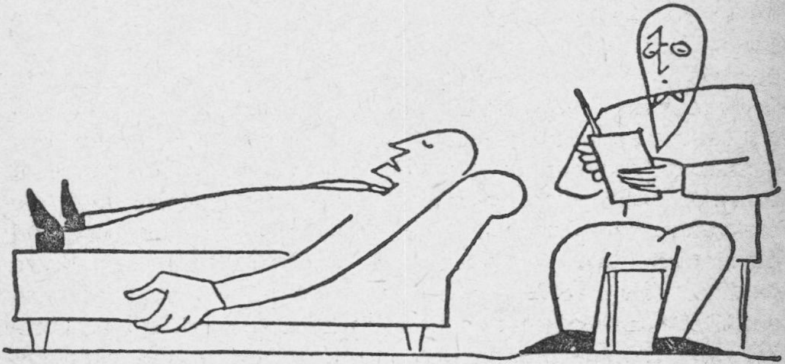

"The analyst gives the patient the feeling of having his feet up in the air and the knowledge that the analyst has both feet on the ground."

thing he has learned in relationships with other people. The patient may say, "Everyone should be truthful," hoping to get the analyst to agree with him and thereby follow his lead. He who follows another's lead is one-down. The analyst may reply with silence, a rather weak ploy in this circumstance, or he may say, "Oh?" The "Oh?" is given just the proper inflection to imply, "How on earth could you have ever conceived such an idea?" This not only puts the patient in doubt about his statement, but in doubt about what the analyst means by "Oh?" Doubt is, of course, the first step toward one-downness. When in doubt the patient tends to lean on the analyst to resolve the doubt, and we lean on those who are superior to us. Analytic maneuvers designed to arouse doubt in a patient are instituted early in analysis. For example, the analyst may say, "I wonder if that's *really* what you're feeling." The use of "really" is standard in analytic practice. It implies the patient has motivations of which he is not aware. Anyone feels shaken, and therefore one-down, when this suspicion is put in his mind.

Doubt is related to the "unconscious ploy," an early development is psychoanalysis. This ploy is often considered the heart of analysis since it is the most effective way of making the patient unsure of himself. Early in an analysis the skilled analyst points out to the patient that he (the patient) has unconscious processes operating and is deluding himself if he thinks he really knows what he is saying. When the patient accepts this idea he can only rely on the analyst to tell him (or, as it is phrased, "to help him discover") what he really means. Thus he burrows himself deeper into the one-down position, making it easy for the analyst to top almost any ploy he devises. For example, the patient may cheerfully describe what a fine time he had with his girl friend, hoping to arouse some jealousy (a one-down emotion) in the analyst. The appropriate reply for the analyst is, "I wonder what that girl *really* means to you." This raises a doubt in the patient whether he is having intercourse with a girl named Susy or an unconscious symbol. Inevitably he turns to the analyst to help him discover what the girl really means to him.

Occasionally in the course of an analysis, particularly if the patient becomes obstreperous (uses resistance ploys), the analyst makes an issue of free association and dreams. Now a person must feel he knows what he is talking about to feel in a superior position. No one can maneuver to become one-up while free associating or narrating his dreams. The most absurd statements inevitably will be uttered. At the same time the analyst hints that there are meaningful ideas in this absurdity. This not only makes the patient feel that he is saying ridiculous things, but that he is saying things which the analyst sees meaning in and he doesn't. Such an experience would shake anyone, and inevitably drives the patient into a one-down position. Of course if the patient refuses to free-associate or tell his dreams, the analyst reminds him that he is defeating himself by being resistant.

A resistance interpretation falls in the general class of "turning it back on the patient" ploys. All attempts, particularly successful ones, to put the analyst one-down can be interpreted as resistance to treatment. The patient is made to feel that it is *his* fault that therapy is going badly. Carefully preparing in advance, the skillful analyst informs the patient in the first interview that the path to happiness

"It is essential that the rare patient who gets an opportunity to observe the analyst see only an impassive demeanor."

is difficult and he will at times resist getting well and indeed may even resent the analyst for helping him. With this background even a refusal to pay the fee or a threat to end the analysis can be turned into apologies with an impersonal attitude by the analyst (the "not taking it personally" ploy) and an interpretation about resistance. At times the analyst may let the patient re-enter the one-down position gently by pointing out that his resistance is a sign of progress and change taking place in him.

The main difficulty with most patients is their insistence on dealing directly with the analyst once they begin to feel some confidence. When the patient begins to look critically at the analyst and threaten an open encounter, several "distraction" ploys are brought into play. The most common is the "concentrate on the past" ploy. Should the patient discuss the peculiar way the analyst refuses to respond to him, the analyst will inquire, "I wonder if you've had this feeling before. Perhaps your parents weren't very responsive." Soon they are busy discussing the patient's childhood without the patient ever discovering that the subject has been changed. Such a ploy is particularly effective when the patient begins to use what he has learned in analysis to make comments about the analyst.

In his training the young analyst learns the few rather simple rules that he must follow. The first is that it is essential to keep the patient feeling one-down while stirring him to struggle gamely in the hope that he can get one-up (this is called "transference"). Secondly the analyst must never feel one-down (this is called "countertransference"). The training analysis is designed to help the young analyst learn what it is like to experience a one-down position. By acting like a patient he learns what it feels like to conceive a clever ploy, deliver it expertly, and find himself thoroughly put one-down.

Even after two or three years in a training analysis seeing his weak ploys devastated, an analyst will occasionally use one with a patient and find himself forced into a one-down position. Despite the brilliant structure of the analytic fortress, and the arsenal of ploys learned in training, all men are human and to be human is to be occasionally one-down. The training emphasizes how to get out of the one-down position quickly when in it. The general ploy is to accept the one-down position "voluntarily" when it is inescapable. Finding the patient one-up, the analyst may say, "You have a point there," or "I must admit I made a mistake." The more daring analyst will say, "I wonder why I became a little anxious when you said that." Note that all these statements *seem* to show the analyst to be one-down and the patient one-up, but one-downness requires defensive behavior. By deliberately acknowledging his inferior position the analyst is actually maintaining his superior position, and the patient finds that once again a clever ploy has been topped by a helpless, or refusal to do battle, ploy. At times the "acceptance" technique cannot be used because the analyst is too sensitive in that area. Should a patient discover that this analyst gets embarrassed when homosexual ideas are discussed, he may rapidly exploit this. The analyst who takes such comments personally is lost. His only chance for survival is to anticipate in his diagnostic interviews those patients capable of discovering and exploiting this weakness and refer them to analysts with different weaknesses.

The most desperate ploys by patients are also anticipated in analytic training. A patient will at times be so determined to get one-up on his analyst that he will adopt the "suicide" ploy. Many analysts immediately suffer a one-down feeling when a patient threatens suicide. They hallucinate newspaper headlines and hear their colleagues chuckling as they whisper the total number of patients who got one-up on them by jumping off the bridge. The common way to prevent the use of this ploy is to take it impersonally. The analyst says something like, "Well, I'd be sorry if you blew your brains out, but I would carry on with my work." The patient abandons his plans as he realizes that even killing himself will not put him one-up on this man.

Orthodox psychoanalytic ploys can be highlighted by contrasting them with the more unorthodox maneuvers. There is, for example, the Rogerian system of ploys where the therapist merely repeats back what the patient says. This is an inevitably winning system. No one can top a person who merely repeats his ideas after him. When the patient accuses the therapist of being no use to him, the therapist replies, "You feel I'm no use to you." The patient says, "That's right, you're not worth a damn." The therapist says, "You feel I'm not worth a damn." This ploy, even more than the orthodox silence ploy, eliminates any triumphant feeling in the patient and makes him feel a little silly after a while (a one-down feeling). Most orthodox analysts look upon the Rogerian ploys as not only weak but not quite respectable. They don't give the patient a fair chance.

The ethics of psychoanalysis require the patient be given at least a reasonably fair chance. Ploys which simply devastate the patient are looked down on. Analysts who use them are thought to need more analysis themselves to give them a range of more legitimate ploys and confidence in using them. For instance, it isn't considered proper to encourage a patient to discuss a subject and then lose interest when he does. This puts the patient one-down, but it is a wasted ploy since he wasn't trying to become one-up. If the patient makes such an attempt then of course losing interest may be a necessary gambit.

Another variation on orthodox psychoanalytic ploys demonstrates a few of their limitations. The psychotic continually demonstrates that he is superior to orthodox ploys. He refuses to "volunteer" for analysis. He won't take a sensible interest in money. He won't lie quietly on the couch and talk while the analyst listens out of sight behind him. The structure of the analytic situation seems to irritate the psychotic. In fact when orthodox ploys are used against him, the psychotic is likely to tear up the office and kick the analyst in the genitals (this is called an inability to establish a transference). The average analyst is made uncomfortable by psychotic ploys and therefore avoids such patients. Recently some daring therapists have found they can get one-up on a psychotic patient if they work in pairs. This is now called the "it takes two to put one down" therapy, or "multiple therapy." For example, if a psychotic talks compulsively and won't even pause to listen, two therapists enter the room and begin to converse with each other. Unable to restrain his curiosity (a one-down emotion) the psychotic will stop talking and listen, thus leaving himself open to be put one-down.

The master one-upman with psychotics is a controversial psychiatrist known affectionately in the profession as "The

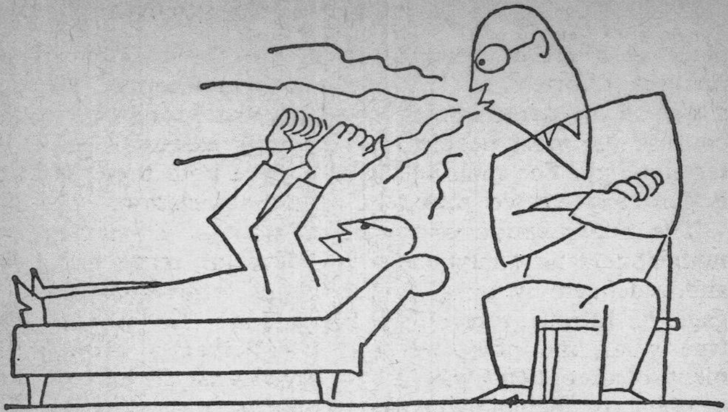

"The patient finds himself hanging on the analyst's every word."

Bull." When a compulsive talker won't listen to him, the Bull pulls a knife on the fellow and attracts his attention. No other therapist is so adroit at topping even the most determined patient. Other therapists require hospitals, attendants, shock treatments, lobotomies, drugs, restraints, and tubs to place the patient in a sufficiently one-down position. The Bull, with mere words and the occasional flash of a pocket knife, manages to make the most difficult psychotic feel one-down.

An interesting contrast to the Bull is a woman known in the Profession as "The Lovely Lady of the Lodge." Leading the league in subtle one-upmanship with psychotics, she avoids the Bull's ploys which are often considered rather crude and not always in the best of taste. If a patient insists he is God, the Bull will insist that *he* is God and force the patient to his knees, thus getting one-up in a rather straightforward way. To handle a similar claim by a patient, the Lady of the Lodge will smile and say, "All right, if you wish to be God, I'll let you." The patient is gently put one-down as he realizes that no one but God can *let* anyone else be God.

Although orthodox psychoanalytic ploys may be limited to work with neurotics no one can deny their success. The experienced analyst can put a patient one-down while planning where to have dinner at the same time. Of course this skill in one-upmanship has raised extraordinary problems when analysts compete with one another at meetings of the psychoanalytic associations. No other gathering of people exhibits so many complicated ways of gaining the upper hand. Most of the struggle at an analytic meeting takes place at a rather personal level, but the manifest content involves attempts to (1) demonstrate who was closest to Freud or can quote him most voluminously, and (2) who can confuse the most people by his daring extension of Freud's terminology. The man who can achieve both these goals best is generally elected president of the association.

The manipulation of language is the most startling phenomenon at an analytic meeting. Obscure terms are defined and redefined by even more obscure terms as analysts engage in furious theoretical discussions. This is particularly true when the point at issue is whether a certain treatment of a patient was *really* psychoanalysis or not. Such a point is inevitably raised when a particularly brilliant case history is presented.

What happens between analyst and patient, or the art of one-upmanship, is rarely discussed at the meetings (apparently the techniques are too secret for public discussion). This means the area for debate becomes the processes within the dark and dank interior of the patient. Attempting to outdo one another in explanations of the bizarre insides of patients, each speaker is constantly interrupted by shouts from the back of the hall such as, "Not at all! You're confusing an id impulse with a weak ego boundary!" or "Heaven help your patients if you call *that* cathexis!" Even the most alert analyst soon develops an oceanic feeling as he gets lost in flurries of energy theories, libidinal drives, instinctual forces, and superego barriers. The analyst who can most thoroughly confuse the group leaves his colleagues feeling frustrated and envious (one-down emotions). The losers return to their studies to search their minds, dictionaries, science fiction journals, and Freud for even more elaborate metaphorical flights in preparation for the next meeting.

The ploys of analyst and patient can be summarized briefly as they occur during a typical course of treatment. Individual cases will vary depending on what maneuvers the individual patient uses (called "symptoms" by the analyst when they are ploys no sensible person would use), but a general trend is easy to follow. The patient enters analysis in the one-down posture by asking for help and promptly tries to put the therapist one-down by building him up. This is called the honeymoon of the analysis. The patient begins to compliment the therapist on how wonderful he is and how quickly he (the patient) expects to get well. The skilled analyst is not taken in by these maneuvers (known as the "Reichian resistance" ploys). When the patient finds himself continually put one-down, he changes tactics. He becomes mean, insulting, threatens to quit analysis, and casts doubt upon the sanity of the analyst. These are the "attempts to get a human response" ploys. They meet an impassive, impersonal wall as the analyst remains silent or handles the insults with a simple statement like, "Have you noticed this is the second Tuesday afternoon you've made such a comment? I wonder what there is about Tuesday," or "You seem to be reacting to me as if I'm someone else." Frustrated in his aggressive behavior (resistance ploys), the patient capitulates and ostensibly hands control of the situation back to the anlyst. Again building the analyst up, he leans on him, hangs on his every word, insists how helpless he is and how strong the analyst, and waits for the moment when he will lead the analyst along far enough to devastate him with a clever ploy. The skilled analyst handles this nicely with a series of "condescending" ploys, pointing out that the patient must help himself and not expect anyone to solve everything for him. Furious, the patient again switches from subservient ploys to defiant ploys. By this time he has learned techniques from the analyst and is getting better. He uses what insight (ploys unknown to laymen) he has gained to try in every way to define the relationship as one in which the analyst is one-down. This is the difficult period of the analysis. However, having carefully prepared the ground by a thorough diagnosis (listing weak points) and having instilled a succession of doubts in the patient about himself, the analyst succeeds in topping the patient again and again as the years pass. Ultimately a remarkable thing happens. The patient rather casually tries to get one-up, the analyst puts him one-down, and the patient does not become disturbed by this. He has reached a point where he doesn't *really* care whether the analyst is in control of the relationship or whether he is in control. In other words, he is cured. The analyst then dismisses him, timing this maneuver just before the patient is ready to announce that he is leaving. Turning to his waiting list, the analyst invites in another patient who, by definition, is someone compelled to struggle to be one-up and disturbed if he is put one-down. And so goes the day's work in the difficult art of psychoanalysis.

Jay Haley, one of the co-authors with Gregory Bateson of the important theoretical paper, "Toward a Theory of Schizophrenia" (Behavioral Science, *October 1956), is communications analyst at the Veterans Administration Hospital, Palo Alto, California.*

Language and Truth

WELLER EMBLER

LEARNING to call things by the names that general agreement has bestowed upon them is an elementary exercise of the mind, one which we associate with the education of small children. The first step in teaching a child to talk usually consists of a fond parent's pointing to an object and repeating a word, such as "cow," or "horse," or "dog." The purpose of this exercise is, of course, to teach the child to connect the word with the thing. And when finally the little one himself points with his finger and says "cow," the happy parents applaud with pardonable pride. It is thus that the learning process proceeds—with the picture books that make cows so very cowlike, with trains, automobiles, and other readily available vehicles, with edible substances, with heat and cold, with the names of aunts and uncles, and so on. As we know from this experience with children, the mere accumulation of name words is but a beginning, a first faltering, unsure step toward knowledge.

There are some people who, intellectually at least, never seem to rise above or go beyond the mere naming of things, which for them constitutes knowledge, even truth. We all remember how when we were small boys and girls we had a playmate whose irritating business it was to learn by heart the names of certain objects, such as those which make up the equipment and parts of sailboats, the substance and manufacture of marbles, or the terminology used in dressmaking, or the names for tools in a carpenter's shop, and who turned the conversation whenever possible (which was most of the time) upon the subjects he knew so well, tense in argument over whether this was a this or that a that, and hilarious when he caught you in error, maddening because he was so often dead right.

Unhappily, this pride in so low an order of mental activity may be found in adults in varying degrees of intensity. That man is not hard to find who has studied up in advance of an occasion the names for things which are bound to become a considerable part of the conversation. Inevitably he will bring the talk around to what he has studied to remember—statistics, perhaps, the population of a certain city, some odd detail which *you* would have to ransack your memory for (providing you had time, which of course you never do); or he will engage you in conversation about the names of plants or animals or machines and their parts, or certain facts to be discovered from looking at maps, like distances between villages, or perchance dates (where he can be exasperatingly correct), like 1066 A.D., or even, indeed, the names of musical compositions or the titles of paintings, usually those of the old masters (Rembrandt particularly has been chosen for this sort of idle entertainment), and so on *ad nauseam.*

Now to be sure, a knowledge of names is indispensable in the struggle of the human race for survival. We all like to feel secure that when we ask the druggist for aspirin, we shall get aspirin and not bichloride of mercury tablets. We depend with a childlike faith on names, that they will go with that which we have been taught to expect them to go with. And in the higher reaches of thought, in the physical and biological sciences, a classification is a meaningful arrangement, and names become tools without which civilization, to say nothing of human thought itself, would be very nearly impossible. Yet even here one can be misled into thinking he knows something when he doesn't. Unless one has some kind of plan or purpose for the use of his knowledge, some imagination, in short, the memorization of names can be a waste of time.

When I was an undergraduate, I used to help my roommate, who was a forestry student, with his study of *Gray's Manual of Botany*. We had our taxonomic hours once a week when I would hear him recite from memory the divisions, the orders, the families, the genera, and the species of the flowering plants and ferns treated in the seventh edition of *Gray's Manual.* To this day I remember the names of some of the families, the rose family, for instance, which is called *Rosaceae;* the pulse family, *Leguminosae;* the beech family, *Fagaceae* (which I enjoyed hearing about more than many of the others as it had to do with trees I particularly admired—the beech, the chestnut, and the oak). But since at the time I speak of, these fearfully learned names (established by international congresses of botanists) meant nothing to me, and as I had no use to put them to, I knew the names only as prodigious to spell and for the most part ludicrous to hear. To a plant scientist, the name *Lentibulariaceae* (bladderwort family) is something he keeps to himself, seldom venturing it upon a lay company. With men of true learning—in the sciences, in the humanities, in the professions—the using of names with precision is a mark of skill and the result of long training.

If the using of names with precision within the context of an occupation is of a higher order of mind than mere information as to the names for things, the making up of names, the giving of names to things requires real creative ability. Naming a continent (Africa, Asia, America) would be a grave responsibility and would, I should think, call for a poet, or someone, at any rate, with an active, rich, and philosophic imagination. Consider the pain (though not perhaps depth of imagination) that often accompanies the naming of children and how in older times a contemplative working of the mind must have been required to suggest those Mercys and Charitys and Hepzibahs. Indeed, the giving of names summons up now a fine technique, now philosophic insight, now the folk wisdom of a people. It takes learning and understanding to give names to trees—for instance, the Judas tree, blushing as it does a pale pink in the spring, the Woman's Tongue tree of tropical climes with its clusters of dry pods that chatter in the slightest breeze. How were the names Hibiscus and Oleander arrived at as names for the shrubs they signify? Who decided upon Magnolia and Holly, and how did the Algonquins come to fancy Tamarack for the American Larch? The names of flowers, plants, and herbs are often richly suggestive and in time, after long association with what they stand for, become haunting and lovely: the Damask Rose (which Katherine Anne Porter says was the first recorded name of a rose), the Musk Rose, the yellow Eglantine, the Cup of Hebe—Tansy, Feverfew, Nightshade, Hyssop, Lavender, Monkshood, Foxglove, Rue.

Think at what a loss one would be to have to fancy names of places like Saranac, Capri, Madagascar, Paris, Soho, Damascus, or even Londonderry and Vermont. Tools have astonishing names, and one cannot but wonder who it was who told first how they should be called: awl, scythe, capstan, jackknife, colander. And what a brave world is it that hath in it such names as cashmere, velvet, cambric, canvas, silk, and chiffon. Naming the stars was no child's play, and now that we have them fixed who would venture to say whether they could be better named: Orion, Aldebaran, the Pleiades, the Hyades. And one would have to climb Parnassus more than halfway to fashion names for the gods—Tammuz, Osiris, Dionysus, Apollo. What a noble work of man, this making of names to stand for all the things of this various world, the things that can be seen and touched, and worked with, and names, too, for all the insubstantial pageants of the mind.

If the learning of names is an elementary exercise of the mind, the learning of facts is scarcely more, though as with naming, the learning of facts is another step in the direction of truth and can be made up of richly satisfying lessons. Most human beings have an instinct for facts, for those facts, at any rate, which it is profitable for them to have an instinct for. We often surprise an aura of truth shining through facts; and it is perhaps our own discovery of facts that means most to us educationally.

But one has to be wary. What are facts? Facts are not, it seems, always facts. Things are not always what they are *said* to be. Let us suppose that we are walking in a museum and that we stop before a painting which suddenly demands our attention. On the frame at the bottom is printed in black letters the name of a famous painter, Botticelli for instance. Let us suppose further that we are students of art appreciation and are so pleased with our discovery that we tell it to our teacher. Our teacher, being a knowledgeable person, replies that he is acquainted with the painting, that it is such and such a style, but that it is really "contemporary Botticelli." In other words, the painting was not done by Botticelli himself but by someone "of the school of Botticelli," one of the master's students perhaps. Our teacher informs us that many paintings whose artists are unknown but which are typical of a master are said to belong to a school and often carry the name of the painter whose style, etc., they so closely resemble. If one of us has the temerity to observe that since it is not a fact that Botticelli painted the picture, his name should not be attached to it, our teacher may well reply that if we like the picture and it says something to us, what difference does it make (except to professional art historians) who painted the picture.

In our hypothetical case, it has now become necessary to

dismiss from our minds the name of the painter of the picture as irrelevant. Instead, our interest lies in certain critical refinements and niceties of explanation as make a statement of fact not a statement of fact. Often, it seems, we are less interested in "facts" and more interested in what we say about them, and consequently, it is the talking about them that becomes important. We refine upon the so-called facts, modify and color them, put them on condition, and make them provisional.

Yet certain facts are so persistent that they will not knuckle under—the facts one works with, for instance. A poem by Robert Frost entitled "Mowing" comes spontaneously to my mind, especially the last six lines:

Anything more than the truth would have seemed too weak
To the earnest love that laid the swale in rows,
Not without feeble-pointed spikes of flowers
(Pale orchises), and scared a bright green snake.
The fact is the sweetest dream that labor knows.
My long scythe whispered and left the hay to make.[1]

It is a commonplace, of course, that Americans are a practical people (not caring enough, perhaps, for the imaginative and speculative), with a long heritage of faith in facts. That the early Puritans were a practical band of pilgrims is well known. Though they toiled in the wilderness to build a Holy Commonwealth, still they had a considerable regard for the practical affairs of everyday life. The church had its awe-inspiring words, but the woodpile was a fact of life. Not a few of our steeple-crowned forebears would have agreed quite readily with the Connecticut Yankee in Rose Terry Cooke's novel *Steadfast*, who says: "At heart every human being has the infidelity of the Apostle Thomas hidden in some shadowy recess, where it whispers to itself, 'I will not believe what I do not see and touch.'" Even Emerson the idealist paid his respects to the hard facts on many an occasion:

Bulkeley, Hunt, Willard, Hosmer, Meriam, Flint,
Possessed the land which rendered to their toil
Hay, corn, roots, hemp, flax, apples, wool and wood.

Though it is in the realm of the moral and spiritual that we expect to find the abiding *abstract* truths, there where the

[1] Excerpt from "Mowing" in *Complete Poems of Robert Frost.* Copyright, 1930, 1949, by Henry Holt and Company, Inc. By permission of the publishers.

masonry of accumulated facts has been transformed into the ideal design, nevertheless it is to the concrete everyday facts, objects of use and beauty and wonder—the inorganic earth substances, and air and fire and water, all the growing things of the earth and all the living creatures, all the people of the earth, and the works of their hands and minds, and the records of all their lives—it is to these that we turn for reassurance of the reality of the world and for support of our endeavors in it. One does well to hold fast to "facts" as firm friends to go by his side in the pursuit of the higher truths.

In the Ford Times Special Edition (Number 2) *New England Journeys*, there is a short piece by William Faulkner called "A Guest's Impression of New England." In this little appreciation Mr. Faulkner tells a revealing story.

> One afternoon (it was October, the matchless Indian summer of New England) Malcolm Cowley and I were driving through back roads in western Connecticut and Massachusetts. We got lost. . . . The road was not getting worse yet: just hillier and lonelier and apparently going nowhere save upward, toward a range of hills. At last, just as we were about to turn back, we found a house, a mailbox, two men, farmers or in the costume of farmers . . . standing beside the mailbox, and watching us quietly and with perfect courtesy as we drove up and stopped.
>
> "Good afternoon," Cowley said.
>
> "Good afternoon," one of the men said.
>
> "Does this road cross the mountain?" Cowley said.
>
> "Yes," the man said, still with that perfect courtesy.
>
> "Thank you," Cowley said and drove on, the two men still watching us quietly—for perhaps fifty yards, when Cowley braked suddenly and said, "Wait," and backed the car down to the mailbox again where the two men still watched us. "Can I get over it in this car?" Cowley said.
>
> "No," the same man said. "I don't think you can." So we turned around and went back the way we came.

Most of us spend most of our time getting and giving information. Certain pieces of information are basic to survival, the "where it is and how to get it" kind, and for the most part this simple information is readily available if we care to make use of it. Indeed, it is the purpose of the social order to make information available, and fortunately certain pieces (such as vital statistics) are required by law to be published. But in the socially less well-regulated affairs (or socially not regulated at all), information is by no means easy to come by or necessarily known or understood though it might stare one in the face. The location of an unknown oil deposit takes time and skill to find; if one really loses a twenty-dollar bill, information as to its whereabouts is impossible to get; if criminals wanted by the police are successful in hiding out against the law, information about them may be available, but it is not forthcoming; if one wants to know what the future movement of certain stocks is going to be, he has to have information which is apparently very difficult for the average man to find and, if achieved, is not always reliable anyway. Though actuarial tables will predict the probable length of your life, absolute information about your longevity is nowhere to be had. Information as to whether one has achieved salvation is, mostly, I believe, a jealously guarded secret; information about whether one is really loved is often singularly difficult to draw out; information about one's future prospects, though it *may* lie in the palm of one's hand, is by no means infallible even if offered; information about the plans of one's enemies can be got, but it is not always trustworthy and often requires such delicate interpretation that most of us lack the key required for decoding the messages. Then again, what passes for information today may turn out to be but opinion tomorrow—to emend Henry Thoreau. Dependable information about the nature of the physical world, about the universe and universes at large, is mighty hard to come by, though of course physicists and astronomers lay claim now and then to the receipt of valuable disclosures.

When we try to find out information about ourselves, we are altogether too often at a loss which way to turn. The doctor cannot always tell us what is wrong with us, nor can the psychiatrist. Information about oneself is very nearly the hardest information to get and may require the sufferings of Oedipus and a lifetime to achieve. Our "selves" lie buried deep, like hidden treasures, and the maps we have drawn up about ourselves are not so easy to follow as those we have made of the public highways.

Because we know so little about ourselves, or because the information we have got is so garbled, we have to ask ourselves over and over again what our conduct should be in this or that predicament. Where can we learn how to behave? There are books in abundance, there is the law, there are other people who will suggest the rules for our conduct. For want of dependable information, we often resort to what the Existentialists call "role-playing." We learn the kind of conduct expected of a person who engages in our kind of activity, and we try to behave according to the stereotype established for that activity. Information about how to play a role is helpful in a complicated society, but following it to the letter is, after all, denying one's own uniqueness and cutting one's self to the common pattern.

Except for downright dangerous indifference to accurate information (say the information on labels in a druggist's shop), we tend to believe what we want to believe. So deeply embedded in us is the will to believe what it suits us at the moment to believe that we stand in need of constant correction, of being corrected by others around us who do not cherish the same illusions as we do. Curiously, it is easy to believe what one wants to believe. Facts are not so stubborn and brutal as we have been led to think, and one can get

How Do I Know What They Are Unless I Label Them?

information which will support his wishful thinking without much trouble. Misinterpreting information is a common enough practice, but willful perversion or misconstruction of information is a daily strategy. Deep inner desires will cause outward facts to suffer rare changes; wanting things desperately enough will change the face of reality altogether, so that what seems and what is become two different realities. Sophistical or false interpretation of factual information colors ethics, judgment, taste. As our desires become more intense, we tend willfully to alter, in our minds, the nature of the world around us.

When Prospero in *The Tempest* tells Miranda how his brother, the false Antonio, usurped his dukedom, it was because, Prospero says, he had given Antonio too much trust, and too much power, so that being thus lorded

Not only with what my revenue yielded,
But what my power might else exact, like one
Who having into truth, by telling of it,
Made such a sinner of his memory,
To credit his own lie, he did believe
He was indeed the duke.

Because information about anything beyond the time of day or one's neighbor's telephone number often requires such toil to secure, is often unreliable, and often, also, so set with thorns, true information is one of the most precious of man's acquisitions and the purpose of all his searching. Is it any wonder that information is power? We make a great effort to share certain kinds of information, the discoveries and findings of medicine, for example; unshared information, military secrets for instance, can be used as a weapon, giving the owner unimaginable power and profit. There are times when we have some but not all the necessary information; there are times when we are not willing to give up the information we have; now and then we are unwilling to receive information, if it is of a kind painful to us; and there are many instances where we do not know how to go about getting information. This explains why education today is devoted almost exclusively to the principles for procuring information, is devoted to skills and training in the use of instruments designed to extract information from intractable and obstinate sources.

The most accurate and dependable information we have for practical daily use is achieved through the techniques and principles of research developed by modern science in all its branches. And modern science has built up an enormous body of information which it is constantly measuring, sifting, and interpreting, so that it may be made applicable in human affairs. Since the seventeenth century, the people of the Western world have looked to science for information about the world; and science, as a method of investigation, has proved miraculously successful and effective.

If knowledge of naming and of facts, if the accumulation of information and the testing and weighing of it are the materials of learning, creative use of the materials, as in the making of judgments and the finding of truths is the final goal of learning—that is, of an education. It is of judgment and truth that I should like to speak in the remainder of this essay.

The formation of value judgments takes time—more time,

usually, than we feel we can give, in this workaday world. As a matter of fact, centuries may be required to sift the best from all the many contenders in all the fields of human experience—in social institutions, in political thought, in literature and the arts, as well as French cooking. Time, we say, is the judge, but time has always needed allies, generations of human beings whose wish is to be civilized. Perhaps the most important part of all higher education is the learning to discriminate, to distinguish among all things to find that which is best and most worthy to be preserved. The monuments of a civilization survive because, after long acquaintance with them, a people have valued them worthiest of survival, have found them lasting in value and worthy of preservation. There is a difference between a crab apple and an orchard apple (as I believe John Burroughs, the naturalist, once pointed out), between a just government and a tyrannical one, between the *Iliad* and hundreds of forgotten war novels since the time of Homer. And the difference between these examples is not quite a matter of personal taste, despite the theory of cultural relativity. It is very real, as most people know.

As with the gathering of information, the making of judgments is often conditioned by prejudice toward those judgments which it will benefit us personally to make. Objectivity is a rare talent and always has been. Wishful thinking often dictates what we shall like and hold good. If our interests are at stake (and in matters of taste our *feelings* are certainly involved), we *can* prefer the monstrous to the beautiful and good. All the subtle demands of vanity and self-interest, of the ego studying to be heard in the world tend to make our judgments deeply subjective. But who can say absolutely what is good and what is beautiful?

How shall we learn to judge? How shall we judge, for instance, the value of a work of art? What standards shall we employ? At this point I shall certainly disappoint some of my readers. I cannot give the answer ready-made; for if I could, there would have been little purpose in the thoughts I have thus far labored to bring forth. Fashions change, fads come and go, but somehow through that drop-by-drop process known as education, the superior things remain and serve as touchstones for the future. To emend the Spanish philosopher José Ortega y Gasset, it is the daily plebiscite of civilized people carrying the vote for the best that makes the best survive. The formation of taste is not alone a matter of learning the rules. It is rather more a matter of immersing oneself in that which has been tried and found good, in the accumulated body of judgments of the people of a culture. It is the purpose of higher education, and the purpose of the humane studies especially, to help all students to learn to distinguish between that which is good and that which is not so good, so that they may participate in the universal judging of the best. It is the price of civilization that people must evaluate and re-evaluate, else a culture will fall into a state of maximum mediocrity. And if we tremble and grow faint before the task of making the great judgment, of judging, that is, between good and evil, it is no wonder, since this task has plagued mankind from the beginning of time. But we know only too well that we cannot surrender, nor even despair.

"You are too fond of your liberty," said Mrs. Touchett to her niece, Isabel, in Henry James's *Portrait of a Lady*. "Yes, I think I am very fond of it," Isabel replied. "But I always want to know the things one shouldn't do." "So as to do them?" asked her aunt. "So as to choose," said Isabel.

So as to choose—not only between right and wrong among the strictly moral issues, but among all the multitudes of ideas of our time. And that is where, in our time especially, the agitation lies—in determining what to choose, surrounded as we are by such abundance, such unimaginable plenty, not only in material goods and things, but in ideas, theories, possible beliefs. We enjoy a feast of notions, that is, more probably than we need. Our world of ideas is like an enormous department store where we move idly from counter to counter, trying to decide what we should like to have and whether we can afford the intellectual purchases we might make—for there are entanglements in the big purchases. For one thing we may have to keep up the payments; and in any event we have to protect our prizes from thieves and destroyers. Moths creep into ideas, too. Shall we put all our intellectual and emotional savings into something that will rust when exposed to a little damp air? Sometimes we toy with gewgaws or with the trinkets laid out in an inviting display. We wander through the bargain basement among the cheaper thoughts, those that may serve for a time. Some notions take our fancy, the work of far romantic places and peoples, ideals which have grown up in other cultures than our own. Toward some ideas we are curious, are not sure, and we entertain mingled feelings about them. Toward some we are detached and critical. For some notions we have no use at all, and we hardly see them. Toward some we are attentive; some, in the light, spacious higher galleries, we behold with rapture.

And what shall we wish to save and to keep permanently after we have brought our purchases home and viewed them in a more sober moment; for we shall have to decide sooner or later what to keep and what to throw away. I venture to say that if ever we bring ourselves to make the final choices, we shall discover that they are very simple ones —the image of a landscape that speaks of all the possibilities of freedom; the possession of a love that is all-consuming; the ripening knowledge of what a great poem is saying; the daily revelations of a work of art; the full possession of a disciplined mind; the words of a philosopher that never diminish in their power to help us; the music that does not diminish in its power to move us; the infinite satisfactions of a great religious belief; a noble friendship; a wholly unselfish way of life. But it must be remembered that all these are choices which when we have made them have ruled out the many other possibilities; and it is therefore incumbent upon us to select with the greatest care, lest through ignorance we let the prizes slip through our fingers, remembering also (as Mr. E. M. Forster says in his essay "What I Believe") that "there lies at the back of every creed something terrible and hard for which the worshipper may one day be required to suffer."

Anyone who has the temerity to speak of "truth" usually finds that he is performing verbal dances around the *word* truth, rather than letting truth perform for itself. The truth is as hard to talk about as it is to tell, though it is not, I think, so hard to find as people say, nor so ready with a dusty answer. If there is one thing certain, the truth will not be caught *once and for all* in a net of words alone, nor does it like to be imprisoned in a theory; it is much too fond of its liberty. At the outset of any inquiry into the nature of truth, one has, in my opinion, to begin with "facts," that is, with things themselves.

The gross material facts of the world are ready at hand for use in giving mode to the truths drawn from the well of being; and literature and art and history and philosophy and science are the crafts that shape the disembodied truth and make it concrete. Observe how music gives measure to *time*, how painting and architecture and sculpture inform *space*, how history gives a scheme to *past* and *present*, how science makes arrangement of *cause* and *effect*, how philosophy builds the structure of *thought* and literature makes epiphanies of vague *justice*, *beauty*, and *love*. And do not mistake that the toil exacted to tell the truth is more prodigious than the labors of Hercules, more passing strange, more abundant of enemies and frustration, more unlikely of adjournment. But it is to literature and particularly to the art of poetry that in closing I would turn now, well aware that the same justice might be done the sciences and all the humane studies.

Sun, gold, light, queens, flame, dawn, heart, moon, tears, fields, time, mountains, darkness, wind, the sea, gardens, lions, trees, home, dreams, night, roses, the grave, stars, nightingales—these veritables have been the substance of poetry for a very long time, sense experiences used to express by proxy the thoughts and feelings that are imaginative life. Every now and then someone cries out against them as overworked and worn out. It is not so much that they are overworked, for they are indefatigable; it is rather that they backslide and refuse to work for some masters. Though the rose, for instance, may have become commonplace in our gardens (as well as in poetry), it is still a flower whose charms are inexhaustible. The rose by no means appeals to all poets in the same way. Each poet will request it to carry *his* message. But like the dawn, and fire, and darkness, and the sea, the rose is always accommodating, if the poet is well-intentioned toward it.

Oh, my luve is like a red, red rose,
That's newly sprung in June . . .

sang Robert Burns. Roses are lovely and so are young Highland girls. The poet was moved by the analogy that spoke unhesitatingly to him as appropriate and true. With A. E. Housman, roses mostly fade—in fields where "rose-lipt girls are sleeping." With T. S. Eliot the rose is self-conscious, at least the roses of "Burnt Norton" have "the look of flowers that are looked at." And Gertrude Stein, bored, perhaps, with antique similitudes, or indignant with the age-long using of the rose as servant to help any poet on with his singing robes, will have it that "the rose is a rose," only itself with its own life.

The common object is known in its immanence, but not until it is touched by the hand of poetic metaphor is it informed and made vivid with the rich garments of thought and feeling. The metaphor of poetry redeems the thing itself, saves it from being the clod and lump mere use and wont have made of it. Finally, however, it is in the design which the chosen objects make that the truth is realized and becomes a firm and permanent truth of the world, a truth not made but rather "discovered" by the poet, a truth perpetually verified by the experience of mankind.

> Fame *is the spur that the clear spirit doth raise*
> *(That last infirmity of Noble mind)*
> *To scorn delights, and live laborious days;*
> *But the fair Guerdon when we hope to find,*
> *And think to burst out into sudden blaze,*
> *Comes the blind* Fury *with th' abhorred shears,*
> *And slits the thin spun life. But* not the praise,
> Phoebus *repli'd, and touch'd my trembling ears;*
> Fame *is no plant that grows on mortal soil,*
> *Nor in the glistering foil*
> *Set off to th' world, nor in broad rumour lies,*
> *But lives and spreads aloft by those pure eyes,*
> *And perfect witness of all-judging* Jove;
> *As he pronounces lastly on each deed,*
> *Of so much fame in Heav'n expect thy meed.*

An abstract *Fame* has here in the hands of Milton become a poetic fact and a massive truth.

But eventually even the poet has to confess that

> *Words strain,*
> *Crack and sometimes break, under the burden,*
> *Under the tension, slip, slide, perish,*
> *Decay with imprecision will not stay in place,*
> *Will not stay still.*
> (T. S. Eliot, "Burnt Norton," *Collected Poems, 1909-1935*)

From the last and highest promontory of time, we may see that the truth is not made up of words at all, only that we have had to use words to lure it from its hiding places. And after all is said, it may be (if we can *know* what this means) that the truth is not more than being itself, innocent, eternal being.

But here and now we are obliged to use language and human thought with which to draw up our agreement with reality. Truth is the name we give to the highest and deepest insights, the fruit of long experience, to those ideas and phenomena which have stood the test of our straining at them, which we have judged most likely to endure, which are universally human, and about which disagreement is only inconsequential quibbling.

Unfortunately, the wish for power is sometimes greater than the wish for truth. People sometimes invent the "truth" where it suits them to do so. And sometimes the "truth" seems to be whatever strong and powerful men say it is, and we are stampeded into thinking something is true that deep within us we know is not. The work of our time which deals most commandingly with the willful perversion of truth is George Orwell's *1984*. "You believe that reality is something objective," says the novel's Party leader, O'Brien, something "external, existing in its own right." O'Brien is talking to Winston Smith, the unregenerate believer in the ultimate victory of truth and humanity over power and the Party. O'Brien refers to Winston Smith sarcastically as "the last man." He says to him:

> When you delude yourself into thinking that you see something, you assume that everyone else sees the same thing as you. But I tell you, Winston, that reality is not external. Reality exists in the human mind, nowhere else. Not in the individual mind, which can make mistakes, and in any case soon perishes; only in the mind of the Party, which is collective and immortal. Whatever the Party holds to be truth *is* truth. It is impossible to see reality except by looking through the eyes of the Party. That is the fact that you have got to relearn, Winston. It needs an act of self-destruction, an effort of the will.

Winston Smith withstands as long as he can the torture and the degradation. He insists heroically that reality is not a matter of power and propaganda. Men are not "infinitely malleable." "There is something in the universe . . . some spirit, some principle . . . that the power-mad will never overcome."

That spirit, that principle, is the indifferent, innocent truth, indifferent, that is, to parties and politics, by nature incapable of self-corruption. It is that which we are a part of and is a part of us, that which is ours as well as everyone else's; it is individualistic as well as communal, the possession of all people, like life and hunger and time, self-evident like fire and air and one's personality, inhabiting space, yet individually experienced as wholly and legitimately one's own, which cannot be gainsaid, short of bitter divorce between the nature of the world and human thought. For human thought searches out the closest possible correspondence between things in the outside world and our inner understanding of them, it seeks (with a hopefulness which if it were naïve would be intolerable mockery) the near-perfect adaptation of a sane intellect to a sane world. And that is why the human perversion of even the smallest truths strikes us as so perilous, and why the perversion of the massive truths becomes so unforgivable. One may well shake one's head with George Eliot's puzzled Mr. Tulliver over the thought that a perfectly sane intellect is hardly at home in an insane world—is hardly at home, that is, in a world made insane by those who, power hungry, prefer darkness to light.

Weller Embler is chairman of the Department of Humanities, Cooper Union for the Advancement of Science and Art, New York City.

Index